V&R

Research in Contemporary Religion

Edited by
Hans-Günter Heimbrock, Daria Pezzoli-Olgiati, Bryan P. Stone,
Heinz Streib, Claire Wolfteich, Trygve Wyller

In Co-operation with
Sunhee Ahn (Seoul, Korea), Bärbel Beinhauer-Köhler (Frankfurt/Main, Germany), Wanda Deifelt (São Paolo, Brazil), Jaco S. Dreyer (Pretoria, S. Africa), Mehmet Emin Köktas (Izmir, Turkey), Bonnie J. Miller-McLemore (Nashville, USA), Siebren Miedema (Amsterdam, The Netherlands), Bradd Shore (Atlanta, USA), David M. Wulff (Norton, USA), Margaret Yee (Oxford, UK), Dale P. Andrews (Boston, USA), Hanan Alexander (Haifa, Israel), William Storrar (Princeton, USA), Carla Danani (Macerata, Italy)

Volume 2

Vandenhoeck & Ruprecht

Trygve Wyller
Usha S. Nayar (ed.)

The Given Child

The Religions' Contribution to Children's Citizenship

Vandenhoeck & Ruprecht

Mit 4 Abbildungen

Bibliografische Information der Deutschen Nationalbibliothek

Die Deutsche Nationalbibliothek verzeichnet diese Publikation in der Deutschen Nationalbibliografie; detaillierte bibliografische Daten sind im Internet über http://dnb.d-nb.de abrufbar.

ISBN 978-3-525-60436-6

Druck- und Bindung: ⊕ Hubert & Co., Göttingen.

Gedruckt auf alterungsbeständigem Papier.

Contents

1 Introduction

The Other Child as Gift?

A Historical Challenge for Religions in Late Modernity

TRYGVE WYLLER/USHA S. NAYAR
Oslo/Mumbai

1. A Paradigmatic Challenge for Religions

From a moral point of view global society owes full cultural and social citizenship to all its children. We think this is evident and obvious, but at the same time: Empirically we know it is not. Many children still lack cultural and social citizenship, they are not included in the basic standards of universal human rights. This is both a moral and political scandal. Still, the question is: How to improve the situation?

The global struggle for universal human rights is often a struggle with religions. Even if world religions recognize universal human rights and give important contributions to the development of citizenship for the less included, religions also have their problems: Human rights are universal and secular, religions often argue from a particularistic and explicit religious point of view.

Still, universalism is no longer the dominating paradigm in late modernity, similarly in the field of children's rights and citizenship (among many titles, see: Kymlicka: 1995, Aleinikoff/Klusmeyer: 2001, Castles/Davidson: 2000, Korsgaard: 2004). No one doubts the political and moral importance of universal human rights. But the question today is: How to achieve such rights for everyone, including children?

This is one important discussion in the international citizenship dialogue. There is a growing interest in the contributions to including citizenship and human rights from particularistic traditions and practices. But this is not a very simple and easy road to follow. It is true that late modernity has seen a growing critique of the abstract, Kantian rights of high modernity. Whatever the authors are, communitarians, phenomenologists, deconstructivists, religious or any kind of combination of them all, they do not look at traditional religion with much enthusiasm. So there is no easy way to follow for world religions.

It is true that the universal and secular human rights movement are experiencing a theoretical and empirical challenge in these years. But this does not mean that there is once again space for traditional religions. They are also challenged with the rising of new paradigms. If religions are to be able to contribute and take different kinds of fruitful initiatives in the struggle for excluded children worldwide, they also have to change and adapt to the new discussions.

We think religions should be a place to take care of the otherness and difference of children. The human rights movement today is under heavy critique, due to this movement's lack of awareness of otherness and difference. But there is also often the impression that much of the same critique could be raised towards parts of the traditional religious discourses and practices as well. The challenge could be summarized in one word: gift. Some religions tend to talk about children as gifts of God. Due to influences from Marcel Mauss (2002), Jacques Derrida (1992) and Jean-Luc Marion (2002), the gift discussion has also entered the more general discussion.

However, in the context of children's rights and citizenship we still think the gift discourse should be developed a little further. Religious tendencies to talk about the child as gift are both wise and beautiful. But it is neither critical nor focused enough to address the most evident challenge: Many children lack human rights and are not fully recognized as citizens, both in Western and in non-Western societies. So the question is: Can religions make any contribution to this current complicated situation? We think there is a need for a paradigm shift, which can be expressed in one sentence. Religions should change from talking about the child as gift to a new discourse on the other child as gift. The challenge for everyone, both religions and human rights movements, is to develop both an awareness and a practice for the otherness of children. It is part of a global obligation to do this, but this book addresses first of all the responsibilities of religions.

This is the important context, which has to be designed, for the initiation of a new and late modern discussion regarding the religious contributions to children's citizenship.

The question is, then, can we expect contributions from religions to an improvement of children's rights and citizenship worldwide? The tendency in this book is interesting: All the authors agree. The answer is yes, religions still have important contributions to make. This is the first, unanimous tendency in this book. But there is one more, parallel answer, which is as important. Religions can contribute only if they focus on situated, social practice and take special notice of the intersubjective relations in their own practice. Religions do not contribute positively to children's rights if they continue to claim abstract principles regarding children.

2. Perspectives from Four Continents

The book is divided into four sections, addressing the question of religion's possible contribution to children's otherness and possible citizenship in late modern societies from different perspectives.

The introductory part of the book draws the general picture and connects it to the global struggle for children rights. *Irene Rizzini* (Rio de Janeiro, Brazil), the president of the global organization Childwatch International and her colleague, *Udi Mandel Butler*, take us into the shift from legal rights to participation. Being both an internationally acknowledged scholar and the leader of an important organization for children rights, Rizzini grapples with the paradigmatic shift mentioned above. The importance of children's rights is not reduced, but the shift has to do with how one realizes such rights. Legal rights have had their day, now the time has come to understand what children's participation and social practice mean. Social practice and involvement have innate values and must be analyzed in more detail. What kinds of social practice developing in religions have the potential to contribute to an increase in children's citizenship?

In the second section of the book, *Reports from the world religions,* three researchers comment on the situation in three world religions, Christianity, Islam and Hinduism. Even if these are different and competing religions, the authors have a surprisingly common interpretation when it comes to the challenges these religions meet in the context of children's right and dignity.

Marcia J. Bunge (Indiana, US) looks into some of the important narratives on children in Christianity. This is a tradition dominating the discourse regarding children and young people in the Western world, even today. But these narratives have to be read critically. It is false to stick to the one-sided interpretation of children as either victims, gifts, autonomous or whatever. Bunge opens up for a new Christian narrative on children, a narrative where one both learns from children and teaches them at the same time. Developing an interesting reflection on the Lutheran discussion of vocation, Marcia J. Bunge challenges Christianity to understand that the children who call us are diverse, complex and intersubjective living persons.

Alfons H. Teipen (Furman, US) opens an important discussion on children in Islam. Traditionally the Islamic approach to children tends to be thought of as a rather patriarchical attitude. Children have to obey their parents and are not expected to develop any kind of independent position in either family or society. Teipen admits that this more "conservative" interpretation of Islam undoubtedly exists and plays an important role in current Islamic thought and practice as well. Even more interesting, then, is the existence of the more liberal and "modern" Islamic interpretation of children.

Usha S. Nayar (Mumbai, India) introduces an Indian-Hindu discussion of the impact of spirituality on childhood. Being a social psychologist, Nayar also goes into the impact of modernity on traditional Indian-Hindu traditions and values. So not even Hindu traditions can ignore the influence of late modern discourses. Therefore Hindu-Indian traditions will also have to take the context of late modernity into consideration when it interprets and practices what it means to stimulate children's participation. Participation is also a key concept in the Indian-Hindu context.

All in all, there are interesting common tendencies in all the three reports from the world religions. A book like this is not intended to give detailed and lengthy presentations of different aspects of the world religions. The important perspective in this book is that all three authors seem to find parallel approaches to the development of citizenship. All three presentations point to tendencies within their own religions, which re-introduce religions as contributors to the development of children's citizenship. The condition is, however, that religions develop potentialities within their own traditions. Religions are ambiguous and it is no longer religion in itself, which contributes to the recognition of children. To contribute religions have to focus on the potential within their own tradition, that is, potential aiming at the increase of participation, complexity and intersubjectivity. The ways these traditions care will be very different in the specific religions. But the important tendency is obvious. The new discussion of citizenship seems to come close to ongoing discussions in the world religions. Spirituality and religions can contribute to children's citizenship, but this requires the development of certain traditions and certain practices on the one hand and the decrease of other traditions and practices on the other hand.

The third section of the book discusses this tendency in more detail with cases from different traditions within Christianity. The four authors come from three continents and evidently belong to different confessions within Christianity. Still, they all share the same passion for situated participation as a key factor in the development of children's citizenship. The important contribution of religions is to create life worlds, situations, practices where the experience of participation, belonging and relationality is substantially present.

Annemie Dillen (Leuven, Belgium) recognizes the development towards the increase and expansion of children's rights. In this way children are given positions as citizens in a society even if they do not have the right to vote. The problem, however, is that the concrete child and the specific relations they live in, fall out of this general perspective. For Dillen this lack of concrete relationality in childhood studies remains a critical question. Coming from an explicitly Catholic position, she therefore suggests that religion should take the responsibility to develop practices of concrete relationalities. In this way the Catholic religion still has a contribution to make to children's rights and citizenship.

John Wall (New Jersey, US) opens a discussion parallel to Dillen's, but this time more from the point of view of ethics and philosophy. The children rights movement took the Kantian and Enlightenment position as its point of departure. By this it opened the way to modernity and its strong impact on the position of children in contemporary society. But the challenge still remains: There are millions of children who do not participate in the rights which they morally deserve. Wall's way out of this dilemma is to turn to postmodern ethics and philosophy. Here there is a more generous recognition of otherness and difference. It is no longer such, that a child has to be one of us to receive full citizenship and the moral demand to be a subject in society. For Wall postmodernity addresses otherness in a fruitful and promising way. It is this discourse he hopes to introduce in the language of Christian religion. In Christianity the demand coming from the other child must be met by a theology of incarnation and love.

The Mexican researchers *Yolanda Corona* and *Carlos Perez* (Mexico City, Mexico) bring us into an ethnographic case of how religions contribute to children's participation and belonging as "citizens". Indigenous people in certain parts of Mexico have struggled for years to receive their legal rights. Important traits in this struggle are the close interrelationship between cultural and social belonging on the one hand, and the social impact of religious ceremonies on the other hand. Corona/Perez leave no doubt that children's participation in religious rituals makes a substantial contribution to a stronger child belonging in society. Religion is in no way only a private matter in this material. The ethnography of Corona/Perez shows a religion with impact for the construction of society. Participation is a key to the increase of "belonging" for young people.

Marta Maria Espeseth (Oslo, Norway) presents an analysis of her experience as a teacher with responsibility for multi-handicapped, autistic children. Taking her point of departure in some moving narratives where specific children relate to their way of expressing emotions and relationality to the external world, Espeseth then uses these narratives to develop a phenomenological interpretation. Using especially the phenomenological discourse of Maurice Merleau-Ponty, Espeseth shows that an interpretation based on embodied intersubjectivity opens up for an alternative, far more "positive" understanding of the subjectivity of the autistic child. If one only approaches the child's seemingly lack of language and communication, one tends to look at the child as an object. Taking notice of the sense-based intersubjectivity already between the child and her teacher gives a totally other picture. On this background, Espeseth advices religions to take analysis like her own more into consideration. The introduction of phenomenology into religion will contribute to the recognition of children who often lack any kind of recognition or sense of belonging.

In the fourth and concluding section of the book three researchers discuss the impact of Christianity in a more explicitly theological way. Within the context of this book, the intention behind this part is to get a little further into the theologies required for the development of citizenship. The analysis so far has shown a potential (section two) for world religions to contribute to citizenship and a potential within the new ethical wave of intersubjectivity and participation to be introduced in the discourses of religion. In the last section of the book theologians discuss different theological perspectives to be taken into consideration if religions, and especially the Christian religion, are to be able to contribute to children's citizenship.

Jone Salomonsen (Oslo, Norway) presents an analysis of the Norwegian Lutheran ritual of confirmation. In the pietistic tradition of Norway, both theologians and lay people often give a very negative account of the family parties connected to the religious confirmation rite. Salomonsen, however, gives an alternative interpretation. The social side of confirmation is not something outside the religious; it is an important part of religion. The dualistic interpretation, the "real" inner experience on the one hand, and the external family party on the other hand must be reconnected. It is in this interrelatedness of inside and outside that the experience of belonging is born. Religions that contribute to this anti-dualistic interpretation of life develop spirituality. This is an interpretation which leads to a reflection where religion convincingly contributes to the belonging part of citizenship.

Trygve Wyller (Oslo, Norway) comments the position of the French theologian Jean Vanier and his explicitly religious discourse on the child as gift. Vanier has developed a practice with a global response. In many parts of the world there are L'Arche communities where multi-handicapped children and grown-ups live together with persons with no visual handicaps. In this context Vanier talk about the child as a gift. In his article Wyller refers to the current philosophical discussion on gift and givenness. Taking phenomenology as the basis he concludes that a better way of developing the gift discourse would be to say that children do not owe us anything at all. This lack of indebtedness might be a better way to express the otherness of the child. It is this otherness that religions have to address if they really want to contribute to children's citizenship and rights.

John M. Hull (Birmingham, England) takes up a final discussion of what it could mean, positively, to name the child as gift. From a Christian, theological point of view, this has to be connected to Creation. A gift participates in the created world. So the only way to talk convincingly about the gift in the context of Christian religion is to use the language of creation. Everyone participates in creation. So therefore everyone is given. The final question of Hull is, therefore: How are we to give if the child is given? We think this is the question where the other child remains our common demand. We have to give in such a way that the other child is seen as given, comes into the religious focus. Then, we think, religions impact on children's citizenship can be reflected and approved.

3. Acknowledgments

Besides the different perspectives and efforts trying to address a new relationship between religions and the movements for children's citizenship, participation and rights, there is one more interesting tendency in this book: The contributors come from four continents. This is an interesting tendency showing that the discussion about otherness, participation and children is no longer a local one or a discussion restricted to some parts of the world. The paradigmatic discussion in this field is global and must be so. The cases, narratives and empirical studies must, of course, be local and concrete. But the option for the other child is more than local.

The authors of this book all participated in a session focusing on spirituality and children in a huge Childhood conference, which took place in the summer of 2005 at the University of Oslo, Norway. 2005 was the centennial for the Norwegian nation's independence from Sweden. To celebrate and to reflect an organizing committee at the University of Oslo and the NGO Childwatch International hosted the Childhoods 2005 conference. Thousands of people gathered in Oslo for a few nice summer days.

One of the sessions concentrated on spirituality and religions in the context of children's rights. It seemed to have been a stimulating experience for most of the session's participants, to have been in a context where researchers from all different countries and traditions seemed to concentrate on one thing: How to develop a religious language where the otherness of the child is respected and given dignity? So the idea came up to make a book out of the session. But there is always a long road to walk from the session to the book.

Many persons have to be thanked, first of all the authors. You have all taken up the different tasks and deadlines in a loyal and disciplined manner and in this way given your individual contribution to this important discussion. The Vandenhoeck & Ruprecht publishing house is to be thanked for its offensive and positive strategy to establish a new book series and the editors for taking this volume into the new RCR series. But the final thanks go the group of assistants in The Faculty of Theology in Oslo, Kaia Dorothea Schultz, Margit Lappegard and Andrew Thomas. You all worked so hard to develop the manuscripts to the technically demanding printable text and into good English, which is not the native language of many of the present authors. We thank you all and hope for an interesting reading.

References

ALEINIKOFF, A. T./KLUSMEYER, D. (ed.) (2001), From Migrants to Citizens: Membership in a Changing World, Washington D.C.

CASTLES, S./DAVIDSON, A. (2000), Citizenship and Migration: Globalization and the Politics of Belonging, Basingstoke.

DERRIDA, J. (1992), Given Time: I Counterfeit Money, Chicago.

KORSGAARD, O. (ed.) (2004), Medborgerskab, Identitet og Demokratisk Dannelse, Copenhagen.

KYMLICKA, W. (1995), Multicultural Citizenship: a Liberal Theory of Minority Rights, Oxford.

MAUSS, M. (2002), The Gift: the Form and Reason for Exchange in Archaic Societies, London.

MARION, J.-L. (2002), Being Given: Toward a Phenomenology of Givenness, Stanford.

The Affective Citizen

Childhood and Belonging in the Contemporary Era

IRENE RIZZINI/UDI MANDEL BUTLER[1]
University of Rio de Janeiro/Goldsmiths College, University of London

1. Introduction

During the last decades, international and national laws about the rights of children have expanded in a dramatic fashion.[2] These laws, moreover, go beyond the traditional definitions of rights centered around legal rights, to rights that encompass the range of phenomena related to children fully developing all their capacities. They also include the rights for them to participate in the processes of decision-making on issues that affect their lives. While the spread of such laws is remarkable, many children in many countries still live in conditions of absolute poverty without shoes on their feet or clothes on their back, and where finding the next meal or clean drinking water is a major challenge.

The contradictions between the ideal and the actual do not undermine the importance of the spread of legal rights. But they raise questions about how to think about abstract rights in the face of dire need. This paper adds another layer of complexity to this disjunction between legal rights and children's situations. In addition to rights, there are deep-seated quests that children have which are at a different level of human experience than implementable legal rights, but which have to do with a search for belonging, respect and meaning. Where do these quests fit into a discussion about rights and needs? This paper explores these issues as they connect with contemporary thinking on 'participation' and 'citizenship'. One element which the paper draws out, concerns a dimension of participation that relates to its affective and symbolic domains and that contribute to a sense of belonging, solidarity, purpose or meaning. The authors' real world context for the conceptual paper is their

---

1 The authors are grateful to Malcolm Bush, President of the Woodstock Institute, Chicago, for his encouragement and thoughtful remarks to the text.

2 In this text, we will be referring to young people from childhood to young adulthood. Different countries have different definitions of youth, but here we follow the Brazilian usage and that of the International Labour Organization both of which define youth as young people up to the age of 24. There remains the linguistic challenge of referring to children and youth in an abbreviated form. Sometimes we use the term children to refer to both, a designation which youth dislike, and sometimes we use the term young people. The problem is further complicated in translation but the most we can do here is explain the terms in English.

current work on the theme of young people, citizenship and participation in the public sphere in contemporary, urban Brazil.

This paper appears in a book about children and spiritual quests. The concept of meaning in relation to the purpose of life and to the individual's place in the world will be different depending on the worldview. For those who hold formal religious beliefs, meaning is prescribed by the mandates of sacred texts and teachings which set out the parameters of a divinely created world and the instructions as to how one should conduct oneself in that world. For those without formal religious beliefs, meaning may include the search for less clearly defined spiritual goals with spiritual meaning as something apart from and more fundamental than the material or worldly. For those who reject the supernatural, there may still be a purpose that transcends the everyday and persists despite living in an uncaring universe. Existentialism, for example, tends to view human beings as subjects in an indifferent, objective, often ambiguous, and "absurd" universe, in which meaning is not provided by the natural order, but rather can be created, however provisionally and unstably, by human beings' actions and interpretations.

2. Children's Rights – Reality of Rhetoric?

The notion of children as active participants in society and as young citizens, with rights, obligations and a role in society, appear widespread in the contemporary world. These ideas started to take shape in the last two decades of the 20th century, becoming embodied as a set of rights that children are entitled to in the United Nations Convention on the Rights of the Child (1989). Following the ratification of the Convention, many countries adopted children's rights laws based on the Convention. This critical shift in paradigm to the acceptance of children having full human rights was developing throughout the twentieth century.

The rejection of the notion that children lack human rights has been developing throughout the century most notably since the Declaration of the Rights of the Child in 1924. The Convention on the Rights of the Child lays aside any lingering idea that children are not entitled to human rights.[3] The Convention covers the largest scope of any single human rights treaty and states take on extensive obligations for the survival, development, protection, and participation of children. The language includes all children and is in the form of binding obligations. 'States shall respect and ensure the rights set forth in the present Convention to each child within their jurisdiction without discrimination of any

3 The Convention was preceded by the non-binding United Nations Declaration on the Rights of the Child, 1959.

kind, irrespective of the child's or his or her parent's or legal guardian's race, color, sex, language, religion, political or other opinion, national, ethnic or social origin, property, disability, birth or other status' (Article 2, paragraph 1). (Kaufman/Rizzini: 2007, 3).

It is important to point out that these notions of children as 'young citizens' and entitled to rights, vary in different cultures according to their political and social histories. It is also true that, in practice, people experience their roles as citizens in different ways. For instance, in a country like Brazil, with a high level of social and economic inequality,[4] despite all the rhetoric about children's rights and citizenship, it is not only children and youth growing up in poverty who may not see themselves as citizens, but also their parents and family members. Denied their basic rights to access to a range of state resources (such as health, social benefits, and so forth), legal protection, and often actively discriminated against by virtue of their ethnicity or socio-economic status, many people in the country are deprived of critical components of full civic rights. This in turn is reproduced in the next generation, amongst their children.

The harsh reality of many children and their families lacking basic elements of citizenship does not undermine the fact that the international movement around children's rights is an amazing phenomenon. It has had an impact in most countries in one way or another. The United Nations Convention on the Rights of the Child was ratified by the vast majority of the world, with the exception of the U.S. and Somalia.[5]

There are, however, disagreements as to the extent to which the Convention can be considered a practical universal standard. One key question is whether the Convention can be applied in countries that experience such different realities without being disrespectful of people's cultures and beliefs. Nonetheless, the Convention, followed by many national laws, has challenged a number of ideas and practices in the treatment of children and youth.

Under the Convention, children and youth become citizens who have a voice and the right to express their wishes in ways that were not permitted just a generation ago. However, the gap between theories that talk about the *defense and guarantee of children's rights*[6] and their implementation is enormous. The most basic rights of children are violated on a daily basis. Equally problematic is the premise of equality enshrined in the idea of rights; that all children have equal rights and rights should be the same for all. Instead, massive discrimination, hostility and injustice against certain groups continue to exist today and in some places seem to be getting worse. The gap between the

4 There is a massively unequal income distribution in the country and a relatively small middle class population. Brazil's income distribution is one of the most unequal in the world as exemplified in the fact that it has the fourth highest Gini coefficient of income inequality.

5 Somalia is unable to ratify the treaty because currently it has no recognized government.

6 Quote from the Brazilian Children's Rights Act, the Statute of the Child and the Adolescent, 1990.

privileged and the under-privileged is not diminishing. Old and new forms of controlling undesirable children, the *dangerous classes* continue to appear. While different indicators may give different answers to the question of whether gaps between *have* and *have-not* children have increased, the fact is that new levels of global communication beam the visual facts of the differences into the home of rich, middle-income and poor children throughout the world. The differences that exist are, therefore, more salient to the dispossessed.

These issues lead us to raise several vital questions. Have we just changed the rhetoric? Why does the gap between theory and practice continue to be so large and so resistant to change? It is important to add that, when we speak of less privileged or marginalized children, we are not only speaking in economic terms, but also of discrimination based on such characteristics as skin color, ethnicity, religion or gender.

The term globalization is often used carelessly to account for some key contextual changes in the conditions of children. But, while aspects of global interaction have a history as long as human history, the contemporary experience of globalization seems qualitatively and quantitatively different from changing relationships between communities and countries in the past. Our economic lives, for example, are increasingly interdependent as more markets become world markets. One result is that children who live in villages or even countries which are not major players in the growth industries of that globalized economy are denied many economic opportunities from birth. But globalization has also brought improvements in the lives of children. We should celebrate the fact that more children have risen above poverty and that India and China are experiencing an explosion of economic growth. At the same time, income inequality between and within many countries is increasing and the capacity of the have-nots to make it to the global economy diminishes as the price of entry gets higher in terms of education, skill levels and levels of capital investment. As we pointed out elsewhere,

> The age-old tragedies of war, famine, and disease continue to wreck the lives of vast numbers of children. And poverty is not just about income. It is also, as one world religious leader said recently, about the stability of a domestic or an education environment, about access to unpolluted natural space, and, in a wonderful expression, familiarity with the practices and languages that offer access to human meaning (Rizzini: 2005, 3).[7]

The last phrase from a speech given by Dr. Rowan Williams, the Archbishop of Canterbury, provides at the same time a poetic and a substantive gloss to the concept of the search for meaning.

---

7 Rt. Rev. Dr. Rowan Williams, Archbishop of Canterbury, "Christianity, Islam and the Challenge of Poverty", speech to the Bosniak Institute, Sarajevo, May, 2005, www.archbishopofcanterbury.org/sermons_speeches last accessed June 19, 2005.

There is a complex interplay between theories of rights, the implementation of rights, the needs of children in different circumstances, and children's own inner quests for meaning and connection. We discuss some of these questions separately, aware of their interconnection, and conclude with some comments about the interplay between them.

3. Current Notions of Children as Citizens and Active Participants in Society

The idea of children's participation has been gaining a broader international acceptance. Several authors have highlighted the importance of cultural constructs of the notion of childhood in historically situated ways (Flekkøy/Kaufman: 1997; James: 2004; Limber/Kaufman: 2002; Morrow: 1999; Reddy: 1997; Smith: 2005; Weis/Fine: 2000). In order to increase opportunities for truly meaningful participation in culturally responsive ways, it is important to know more about how particular cultures and societies and the children who live in them understand and exercise these rights of participation (Rizzini/Thapliyal: 2006).

One aspect that is under-researched refers to what we may term the affective and symbolic dimensions of participation. Juan Dias Bordenave (1995) defines participation as the way through which humans fulfill and affirm themselves, make things and dominate nature and the world. For the author the practice of participation also involves:

> Other necessities that are no less important such as the interaction with others, self-expression, the development of reflexive thought, the pleasure in creating and re-creating things, and, further, to value oneself and be valued by others. In conclusion, participation has two complementary bases: an affective one, we participate because we feel pleasure in doing things with others – and an instrumental base – we participate because doing things with others is more effective and efficient than doing them by ourselves (Bordenave: 1995, 16).[8]

According to the author then, there are two key aspects of participation: its instrumental side and its affective (and we would add symbolic) side, themes that were very evident in our research with young people in Brazil. As such, the affective aspect of participation though crucial, is a much neglected theme in writings and research on the topic.

Corroborating Bordenave's statement, one of the most important aspects young people spoke of as regards their participation in projects and organizations in Rio de Janeiro's public sphere, related to affective and symbolic

8 Translation by Udi Mandel Butler.

themes: the possibility of meeting, exchanging with, and getting to know other young people, of feeling a sense of solidarity, feeling valued and that one belongs some place.

This distinction of the utilitarian and affective/symbolic aspects of participation is important, but should not be taken as a clear-cut distinction, as a participation initially conceived as utilitarian can develop affective processes. Similarly, the creation of feelings of solidarity and belonging, of 'empowerment' are also commonly connected to struggles for rights and the creation of collective forms of cultural expression.

The affective and symbolic aspects of participation appear to link with current rethinking of the notions of citizenship as entailing not only a set of rights and obligations under a State, but as a continuous practice and process of struggle. Summing up these re-considerations of the notion of citizenship Isin and Turner write in the introduction to their edited volume *Handbook of Citizenship Rights*, that,

> The modern conception of citizenship as merely a status held under the authority of a state has been contested and broadened to include various political and social struggles of recognition and redistribution as instances of claim-making, and hence, by extension, of citizenship. As a result, various struggles based upon identity and difference (whether sexual, 'racial', 'ethnic', diasporic, ecological, technological, or cosmopolitan) have found new ways of articulating their claims as claims to citizenship understood not simply as a legal status but as political and social recognition and economic redistribution (Isin/Turner: 2002, 2).

As Turner writes elsewhere, this new understanding of the necessarily incomplete nature of citizenship provides us with a new conception of citizenship,

> Citizenship may be defined as a set of practices (juridical, political, economic and cultural) which define a person as a competent member of society, and which as a consequence shape the flow of resources to persons and social groups (Turner: 1994, 2).

Citizenship understood as a set of practices, means that the definition is broader than merely a collection of rights and obligations. As a set of practices, citizenship is then in a process of constant construction and reconstruction, changing historically as a consequence of political struggles. This definition also places the concept within the field of debates on inequality, power differences and social class, as the concept is inevitably bound to the problems of the unequal distribution of resources in society.

New descriptions of citizenship as a way of life mean that the subject is constantly engaged in political struggle at various sites, including that of one's own identity. But citizenship is not considered as an identity possessed by subjects but an activity that constructs identity. As Rasmussen and Brown point out, addressing the post-structuralist influence in radical democracy's conception of identity:

> Identity could not be understood as pre-political, either an authentic essence or the private construction of the subject – the liberal subject, but nor could it be fully determined by the essence of the social structure – the Marxist version. Rather, identity must become the ultimate site of politics, determined neither by the agent nor by the process but in a process of struggle (Rasmussen/Brown: 2002, 182).

This process of struggle is particularly acute within groups that have been excluded or which continue to be marginalized and to whom the guarantee of basic rights is still a far off promise. The struggle here, as Turner writes, is for the flow of resources and social recognition of particular groups. But we would also add that, experienced from the inside, such struggle is also one for belonging, for being accepted and respected.

4. Participation, Belonging and the Bearch for Meaning

In order to shed more light on how participation contains the dimensions of affectivity and an aspiration for belonging and meaning, (which can encompass the domain of the 'spiritual'), we need to trace the history of the concept in the West. Such an exercise has been carried out by Heiko Henkel, and Roderick Stirrat, (2004), who trace the term 'participation' not to the bourgeois emancipation of Europe in the eighteenth and nineteenth centuries, through their increasing claims to the economic and political sphere, but further back to the Protestant Reformation.

In this early modern use, Henkel and Stirrat argue, participation meant the participation of man in the infinite grace of God. As such, participation was replete with spiritual connotation, though this notion was not restricted to an abstract theological concept. It became one of the central concerns of the Reformation. Here 'participation' was relevant in liturgical practice and as an administrative principle as well as a theological question. The translation of the bible into vernacular languages making the scriptures more accessible to the people, the participation of the whole congregation in the sacrament, as well as the radical remaking of the bureaucratic structure of the church with its decentralized administrative structure, all can be seen as fashioning new forms of participation from spiritual as well as political motivations. The key point here though is how participation comes to acquire a moral imperative, as the authors argue;

> The Protestant Reformation not only made the direct participation of the believer possible, but placed a moral imperative on participation. To be a good Christian required participation: in reading the scriptures, in participating in the liturgy, in governing the Church. Salvation was to be attained through individuals actively participating in the duties of the community (Henkel/Stirrat: 2004, 174).

Henkel and Stirrat go on to trace this moral imperative through the history of British nineteenth-century working class non-conformity, pointing out how a number of trade unions, the cooperative movement, the Labour Party and others all to an extent grew out of non-conformist religious backgrounds. The authors then conclude that the concept of participation is rooted in a specific tradition with particular religious overtones. Regardless of whether one supports Henkel and Stirrat's conclusion that the concept of participation is therefore culturally specific rather than a universal value, very interesting questions have been raised about how participation as understood in contemporary discourse is implicitly bound to religious, spiritual and moral undertones.

The relationship between participation and religion is important to consider. The anthropologist Victor Turner has written extensively on the subject using the idea of *communitas* to refer to the feelings of brotherhood and sisterhood, equality and joint purpose that appear in a whole range of social organizations (both religious and secular) which oppose or find themselves temporarily removed from the established social structure (Turner: 1969).

5. Children and Youth's Perceptions of Citizenship and Participation in Society in Brazil

In the case of Brazil three points are of significance. First is the fact that one of the most important popular participatory mobilizations in Brazilian civil society originated through the actions of Liberation Theology, a non-conformist grass-roots movement on the part of members of the Catholic church, who sought to re-interpret the scriptures through Marxism and other philosophical and sociological writings. Liberation Theology had a lasting impact on Brazilian society and catalyzed social movements (such as the MST – the landless movement),[9] political parties like the PT (the workers party), and through its actions and the ideas of its proponents such as Paulo Freire, generated forms of popular participatory education and notions of 'conscientization' that are still used by a number of non-governmental organizations.

The second important fact is that recent quantitative research with young people has found that one of the most popular forms of participation for young

9 The Landless Movement is a large grass-roots movement present throughout Brazil, fighting for the rights of landless rural dwellers. As well as their more visible direct-action occupation of unused lands, they are involved in a whole range of initiatives especially those around education and awareness raising in cities and rural areas. The Movement is said to have around 300,000 families, and as such a considerable number of young people. Many of these young people come to take leadership positions in local groups, and increasingly also on a national level.

people is in church organizations.[10] Of a large sample of 8,000 18–24 year olds from across the social spectrum interviewed all over Brazil, 28% stated that they participated in some kind of group or organization. Of these 28%, just under half stated that this organization was of a religious nature (42%), as compared to four per cent who said that they participated in a party-political organization (IBASE 2005). Similar research carried out in Rio de Janeiro, with a sample of about 1,000 young people, asking the question of which of the following do you participate or have participated in, obtained results that showed that 69% of the respondents were or had participated in groups or movements connected to a church. This compares to the 48% of youngsters who had or were participating in the student movement, and 9.8% in a political party (ISER 2002). That religion provides a catalyst for actively participating in the life of the community is uncontroversial, yet the kinds of participation that religious organizations offer, and how young people experience this needs to be further investigated.

The third important point refers back to Turner's notion of the feelings of *communitas* generated through participating in particular groups and initiatives and to what we referred to, expanding on Bordenave, as the affective and symbolic dimensions of participation. It is this last point that we will address here using examples from our research in Brazil.

In the last few years, the authors have carried out several studies focusing on children's perceptions about important aspects of their own lives as well as their understanding about the concepts of citizenship, rights, obligations and their participation in society.[11] Here we will focus on issues related to their inner quests, particularly their search for a sense of belonging, affectivity, solidarity and humanity.

In our projects, we were able to listen to approximately 150 children and youth, age eight to 24, from 2004 to 2007, in the city of Rio de Janeiro.

One of the questions asked during this research was what changed in young people's lives as a consequence of their participation in a range of organizations and initiatives concerned with issues of citizenship and social justice. This is what a young woman in her early twenties, who was taking part in a youth media project had to say:[12]

---

10 Just to give the reader a rough idea of what kind of churches we are talking about, according to Census Data (2000), 83.7% of the population in 1991 and 73.7% in 2000 declared themselves as Catholics. The second largest group was that from the evangelical churches: nine per cent in 1991 and 15.4 in 2000.

11 For a description of these projects, see www.ciespi.org.br. Rio de Janeiro: CIESPI (The Centre for Research and Policy on Childhood) and Childwatch International. See also Rizzini et al.: 2005; Rizzini/Butler/Thapliyal: 2007. The projects include: *Children's perspectives on citizenship and nation building*, *Cultures of participation* and *Engaged youths in the Americas*.

12 Interview held in 2006, in Rio de Janeiro (Butler/Princeswal/Abreu: 2007).

> Before I was reluctant to say I live in a favela [urban shanty]. The person jolts, the person retreats, it is horrible. But you have to own up, I always own up now, about the place where I live. And it doesn't matter, the place doesn't make you up, it is you who makes up the place. Many people who live in the community [favela] are ashamed of saying that they live in a community. Afterwards I started having this other perspective, I gave more emphasis to the fact of the place where I live, to my origins, to the fact of being black too.

The statement is emblematic of a common response given by many young people, who were part of a number of initiatives we came to know. This shift in consciousness can be described as one of *identification* with the individual's own 'community', 'race' or 'ethnicity', sexual orientation, and even class. The consequences of this are variously described as having to do with a sense of 'self-esteem', of not feeling ashamed to be considered as belonging to a particular group or category, but rather, a renewed sense of pride at being part of a constituency with a particular history and culture. In a society marked by inequality, social segregation and racism, this is no mean feat. Yet, though a large step, and one which perhaps only a relatively few take, this initial micro-revolution is a crucial one for many young people, and an important consequence of their engagement in public action.

A further element that we found in a number of the interviews is a concern with solidarity. Solidarity, or the aspiration to it in a society seen as increasingly individualistic, was a key element in many of the narratives of young people who participated in different initiatives in the public sphere in Brazil. The sense of solidarity was often cited as one of the most valued qualities in their participation in these initiatives, and as something described as a potential antidote to this increasing individualism in our consumer society.

A very important aspect of solidarity was the potential of certain initiatives or groups, to transform the individual's identity from a more restrictive sphere (concerned with immediate personal gains) to a more expansive sense of self that encompassed a notion of the common good, whether of the local community, neighborhood, city, nation, or some conception of society or humanity as a whole. These transformations through participation, over time, bring about profound changes in how the individual thinks, and relates with others and with the world.

An example can be seen in how some young people answer the question of what participation means to them:

> It is a collective exercise, for the good of others. Every progress if it is not for the good of the community, if it does not have a perspective of solidarity, and carries on in an individualistic way … soon there will be no more planet. (Young woman, 20 years old, from a community news initiative).

Another young man, 23 years old, involved in an adolescent worker's rights union had this to say about the same question:

It has to do with belonging. I think that what has moved me the most, because I felt I was really participating in Brazil's history, was when I got my voting title for the first time and I voted for the first time, in 2002 for president. I was very emotional, there I felt "I am really participating in society."

6. Conclusion

Participation always occurs within particular historical contexts that offer different opportunities, forms and themes that provoke it and make it possible. As we have outlined in this article, over the last couple of decades the theme of young people's participation in society and the enshrining of children's rights in law has offered novel opportunities for young people to participate in a whole range of processes that affect their lives. At the same time each historical moment offers challenges to participation, and we have noted the continuing discrepancy between the 'rhetoric' of rights and participation and their actual implementation and realization, particularly amongst those groups that continue to be marginalized and discriminated against. A further challenge, sensitively perceived by a number of young people we talked to, relates to the growing individualism of a consumer society where projects of solidarity and of building collective futures have a tendency of being drowned out by the mainstream. We refer back to Archbishop Williams' point about the need for societies to provide *familiarity with the practices and languages that offer access to human meaning*. As a number of young people who participate in a range of different groups and initiatives related to the themes of social justice and citizenship in Rio de Janeiro's public sphere demonstrate, there is a real aspiration for understanding what it is to be human not just as an individual but as part of a collectivity of humans.

It might be thought that the disjunctions we described at the beginning of the paper between practical wants and other human aspirations would not be salient to children struggling to survive in urban slums. But the values of solidarity and the possibility of building a collective future inspired by ideals of equality and social justice appear alive and well for many young people from disadvantaged as well as comfortable backgrounds. The question becomes how best to support such aspirations.

References

Bordenave, J. (2002 [1983]), O que é Participação? São Paulo.

Butler, U. M./Princeswal, M./Abreu, R. (2007), Cultures of Participation: Young People and Their Perceptions and Practices of Citizenship, Rio de Janeiro.

Flekkøy, M. G./Kaufman, N. H. (1997), The Participation Rights of the Child: Rights and Responsibilities in Family and Society, London.

Henkel, H./Stirrat, R. (2004), Participation as Spiritual Duty; Empowerment as Secular Subjection, in B. Cooke/U. Kothari (ed.), Participation: The New Tyranny? London.

Isin, E./Turner, B. (ed.) (2002), Handbook of Citizenship Rights. London.

Ibase (2005), Juventude Brasileira e Democracia: Participação, Esferas e Políticas Públicas. Rio de Janeiro.

James, A. (2004), Understanding Childhood from an International Interdisciplinary Perspective: Problems and Potentials, in P. R. Pufall/R. P. Unsworth (ed.), Rethinking Childhood, New Brunswick.

Kaufman, N. H./Rizzini, I. (2007), Closing the Gap Between Rights and Realities of Children's Lives, Rio de Janeiro.

Limber, S./Kaufman, N. H. (2002), Civic Participation by Children and Youth. In N. H. Kaufman/ I. Rizzini (ed.), Globalization and children's lives. New York.

Morrow, V. (1999), We are People too. Children and Young Peoples's Perspectives on Children's Rights and Decision-Making in England, in The International Journal of Children's Rights, vol. VII, no. 2, pp. 149–170, London.

Novaes, R./Mello, C. C. (2002), Jovens do Rio: Circuitos, Crenças e Acessos. Comunicações do ISER, no.57, Rio de Janeiro.

Rasmussen, C./Brown, M. (2002), Radical Democratic Citizenship: Amidst Political theory and Geography. In E. Isin/B. Turner, (ed.) Handbook of Citizenship Rightsm, London.

Reddy, N. (1997), Have we Asked the Children? Different Approaches to the Question of Child Work, Bangalore, India.

Rizzini, I. et al. (2005), Children's Perspectives on Citizenship and Nation Building. Rio de Janeiro.

Rizzini, I. (2005), The Futures of Children: the Challenges and Opportunities of Diversity. Childhoods Conference opening remarks. Oslo: Childwatch International Research Network, University of Oslo, June 29.

Rizzini, I./Thapliyal, N. (2006), Perceptions and Experiences of Participation of Children and Adolescents in Rio de Janeiro, Brazil. Rio de Janeiro: CIESPI. Colorado: University of Colorado Press (forthcoming).

Rizzini, I./Butler, U. M./Thapliyal, N. (2007), What Does Citizenship Mean for Children and Adolescents in Brazil? Rio de Janeiro: CIESPI; Oslo: Childwatch International; Research Report publication (forthcoming).

Smith, A. (2005), Research Forum on Children's Views of Citizenship: Cross Cultural Perspectives: An Introduction and Overview of Results (Symposium on Children and Young People's Views on Citizenship and Nation Building). Childhoods 2005, Oslo, Norway.

Turner, V. (1969), The Ritual Process: Structure and Anti-Structure: A Demonstration of the Use of Ritual and Symbol as a Key to Understanding Social Structure and Processes, London.

Turner, V. (2002), Liminality and Comunitas. In M. Lambek (ed.), A Reader in the Anthropology of Religion, London.

Turner, B. (ed.) (1994), Citizenship and Social Theory, London.

Weis, L./Fine, M. (2000), Construction Sites: Excavating Race, Class and Gender Among Urban Youth, New York.

2 Reports from the World Religions

Beyond Children as Agents or Victims

Reexamining Children's Paradoxical Strengths and Vulnerabilities with Resources from Christian Theologies of Childhood and Child Theologies

Marcia J. Bunge
Valparaiso University, Valparaiso, IN

In both religious communities and countries around the world, we see many examples of concern for and care of children. National and international initiatives and programs offer food, housing, and medical assistant to poor children and orphans. Governmental and non-governmental organizations and agencies support social and political policies that aim to protect children and to provide them with the resources they need to thrive. All countries except the United States and Somalia have signed the United Nations' "Convention on the Rights of the Child" (UNCRC). Religious communities also attend to the spiritual and moral development of children and seek ways to nurture it in the home and through religious education programs.

Despite such efforts to address child well-being, we nevertheless often treat children as truly the "least of these." For example, in the United States, every person over sixty five years of age has health care, but nine million children do not. Most affluent children have access to a good education, but many poor children must often attend inadequate or even dangerous schools. Furthermore, many children, regardless of their economic situation, suffer neglect and abuse and struggle with drug and alcohol abuse, suicide and depression, and lack of sexual boundaries.[1]

Around the world, one child every three seconds dies of hunger or a preventable disease, and many poor children are being used as cheap laborers or soldiers. According to the International Justice Mission in Washington D.C., more than a million children a year are forced into child prostitution (Haugen:

---

1 For more information about the situation of children see the following web-sites: www.census.gov; www.childrensdefense.org; www.unicef.org and www.nccp.org.

1999, 42).[2] In a global economy, scholars also wonder about the effects of technology, the media, and market pressures on rich and poor children alike.

Within Christian communities, perhaps the most alarming example of injustice to children is that they have been sexually abused, and reputations of priests, pastors, and bishops have taken priority over the safety and needs of children. However, children are neglected or treated unjustly in many far more subtle ways in their congregations and homes. For example, although sound religious education programs do exist, many congregations offer weak religious education programs and fail to emphasize the importance of parents in faith development. The curricula of many programs are theologically weak and uninteresting to children, and they assume children themselves have no questions, ideas, or spiritual experiences. Programs for children and youth are often under funded, and leaders for them are difficult to recruit and retain. Furthermore, there is little coordinated effort between the church and the home in terms of a child's spiritual formation. Many parents don't even know what their children are learning in their congregation's educational programs, and parents are also not given the sense that they are primarily responsible for the faith formation for children.

Furthermore, the Church in general has not effectively used its wisdom to become a strong and reliable advocate for children in contemporary public and political debates on children's rights and child well being. For example, in the United States, mainline Protestant churches support legislation to protect children's health and safety, yet they hesitate to contribute significantly to public debates about strengthening families. Protestant evangelical and conservative churches, on the other hand, are more vocal in nationwide debates about the family, yet these churches sometimes focus so narrowly on parents' rights that they inadequately address children's rights and the responsibilities of parents, church, and state to protect, educate, and support all children. Although the Roman Catholic Church has supported the UNCRC and taken a constructive role in international debates on children's rights, many Protestant churches in the United States have not. Some outright oppose the UNCRC and UN itself. Many others are sympathetic with the UNCRC's goals but are not yet certain if its rights-based framework is compatible with Christian values and beliefs.

Lurking behind this lack of commitment to children are simplistic views of children found in the Church and the wider culture. In the Church today and in the past, theological discourse has been dominated by narrow and often ambivalent views of children that diminish their complexity and integrity, fostering narrow understandings of adult-child relationships. For example, some Christians today and in the past have perceived children mainly as blessings,

2 For more about the situation of sexually exploited children, e. g. Haugen/Hunter: 2005.

innocent creatures, or spiritually wise, and they have thereby often underestimated adult responsibilities of teaching and guiding children and helping them develop morally and spiritually. However, other Christians have tended to view children primarily as sinful, in need of instruction, or even "not yet fully human," thereby narrowly restricting their view of adult-child relationships to instruction, discipline, and punishment and neglecting the lessons that children can teach adults.

These kinds of simplistic conceptions of children in the Church inform and reflect other widely held perceptions about children also found in contemporary culture. Popular magazines and newspapers tend to depict infants and young children as pure and innocent beings whom we adore and teenagers as hidden and dark creatures whom we must fear. In debates about reproductive technology children are discussed as gifts and blessings yet also commodities and products. Children are also the objects of intense marketing campaigns and viewed as consumers who buy products themselves and highly influence the economic choices of their parents.

Even within national and international debates about children's rights and responsibilities, the nature of children and their roles in communities are often narrowly defined or conceived, resulting in narrow conceptions of children and child-adult relationships. For example, some people emphasize children's rights without a corresponding discussion of their responsibilities, narrowly perceiving children as victims or vulnerable beings alone. Others do focus on children as responsible citizens and social agents who can positively influence communities yet neglect to emphasize the corresponding roles of adult citizens to support parents and children and to ensure that all children have the resources they need to thrive. Still others in the debate speak of children and young people more as rebellious, even deviant, beings who, armed with "rights language," would to undermine the authority of their parents and religious traditions.

These and others kinds of simplistic views diminish children's complexity and intrinsic value and thereby undermine our appreciation of children and sense of obligation to them in religious communities around the world and in civic life both nationally and internationally.

Christian theologians today are beginning to help overcome such simplistic views of children and thereby strengthen the church's commitment to them by developing both robust "theologies of childhood" and "child theologies."[3] This distinction is just beginning to be used among some Christian theologians and

3 Recent studies in the areas of ethics and systematic and practical theology on children and childhood include, e. g.: Anderson/Johnson: 1994; Couture: 2000; Dawn: 1997; DeVries: 2001a; Herzog: 2005; Jackson: 2005; Jensen: 2005; Marshall/Parvis: 2004; Mercer: 2005; Miller-McLemore: 2003; Moltmann: 2000, 592–603; Nkurunziza: 2004, 121–138; Yust: 2004. For a fuller discussion of current trends, Bunge: 2006; Wall: 2006.

practitioners in the United States and around the world. "Theologies of childhood" primarily provide sophisticated understandings of children and childhood and our obligations to children themselves. "Child theologies" not only reexamine conceptions of children and obligations to them but also rethink fundamental doctrines and practices of the Church as a whole.[4] Drawing on analogies to feminist, black, and liberation theologies, child theologies have as their task not only to strengthen the commitment to and understanding of a group that has often been voiceless, marginalized, or oppressed – children – but also to reinterpret Christian theology and practice as a whole. Just as feminist theologians, for example, focused not simply on women's history or constructions of gender but made significant strides in theology, church practice, and social justice by using gender as a category of analysis to re-examine Christian theology as a whole, some theologians and ethicists are now beginning to use "the child" as a lens to reevaluate the Christian tradition and to critically retrieve elements of it that can strengthen the Church's overall theology and practice today.

Understood in these ways, the aims of theologies of children and child theology are distinctive from but related to other areas of theology and practice that are often blurred together under one large yet vague category of "children." Such distinctive areas include but are not limited to children's spirituality; children's theology; religious education; spiritual formation; children and family ministry; and child advocacy. By distinguishing these and other areas, and by taking all of them seriously, Christian communities can begin to build up stronger theological reflection on children in all areas of faith and practice and strengthen its overall commitment to children themselves.

The aim of this particular paper is to explore a few of the resources that Christian theologies of childhood and child theologies might offer for developing robust Christian understandings of children that acknowledge both their vulnerabilities and strengths and that can strengthen the Church's commitment to and appreciation of children themselves.

Through this exploration the paper finds that although theologians within the Christian tradition have often expressed narrow and even destructive conceptions of children and childhood, there are several diverse and even paradoxical ways of speaking about the nature of children and their duties and responsibilities within the Christian tradition that, when critically retrieved and held in tension, can broaden our understanding of children and our obligations to them. The paper briefly outlines six central perspectives on the nature of children found within the Bible and the Christian tradition (chapter 1); and

4 The term, "Child Theology," has been coined by Keith J. White, Haddon Willmer, and John Collier, leaders of the "Child Theology Movement" (a not-for-profit limited company registered in London, England). For more information, see www.childtheology.org.

it then critically retrieves six particular duties and responsibilities of children articulated within Christian understandings of vocation and calling (chapter 2). Each Part concludes with some specific implications for strengthening spiritual formation and religious education programs; deepening theological and ethical reflection on children, including Christian understandings of children's rights and responsibilities; and renewing the Church's commitment to serving and protecting children around the world. The chapter concludes with overall implications of both sections of the paper for a deeper understanding not only of the needs of children and our responsibilities to them but also a richer appreciation of the gifts they offer to communities (chapter 3).

By mining just a few of these diverse and seemingly paradoxical resources from the Christian tradition for today and holding them together, the paper challenges many contemporary understandings of children and childhood. It highlights the limitations of reducing the vulnerabilities and strengths of children to any one category – whether speaking in more secular terms of children as "victims of injustice," "social agents," or "citizens"; or in more religious terms of children as "gifts of God," "sinful and defiant creatures," or "models of faith." Furthermore, the paper challenges all of us – regardless of our religious or philosophical backgrounds and commitments – to honor the complexity and dignity of children and to renew our commitment to both protecting them and learning from them.

1. Resources from Theologies of Childhood[5]

As research on children and childhood emerges in all areas of theology and religious studies, and as biblical scholars and historians mine resources from the Christian tradition, many misconceptions about Christian understandings of children and childhood have been challenged and at least six important and almost paradoxical perspectives on children have emerged. Although these six perspectives and others are found within the Christian tradition, Christian theologians today and in the past have often viewed them in isolation from one another, resulting in narrow and destructive understandings of children and our obligations to them. Theologians have often focused on one or two such perspectives alone, failing to appreciate the range of Christian perspectives on children and critically retrieving them into a serious and full-blown theology of childhood. Thus, even though the six perspectives outlined below are not exhaustive, they do remind theologians of the complexity and dignity

5 This part of the paper is taken from sections of previously published articles by M.J. Bunge: 2006; 2003a, 11–19; 2003b, 72–87.

of children and can help combat simplistic and distorted views of children in the Church and the wider culture.

1.1. Gifts of God and Sources of Joy

First, the Bible and the Christian tradition often depict children as gifts of God and sources of joy who ultimately come from God and belong to God.[6] Whether biological or adopted, children are gifts not only to parents but also to the Church and the community. They are members of a community from the start, and they play various and complex roles within it. In addition, they will grow up to be not only sons and daughters but also husbands, wives, friends, neighbors, and citizens. Viewing children as gifts of God to the whole community radically challenges common assumptions of them as "property" of parents, as consumers, or as "economic burdens" to the community.

Related to this notion that children are gifts and signs of God's blessing, the tradition speaks of them as sources of joy and pleasure. Here, too, there are many examples. Sarah rejoiced at the birth of her son, Isaac (Gen 21:6–7). Even in his terror and anguish, Jeremiah recalls the story that news of his own birth once made his father, Hilkiah, "very glad" (Jer 20:15). An angel promises Zechariah and Elizabeth that their child will bring them "joy and gladness" (Luke 1:14). In the gospel of John, Jesus says, "When a woman is in labor, she has pain, because her hour has come. But when her child is born, she no longer remembers the anguish because of the joy of having brought a human being into the world" (John 16:20–21).

1.2. Sinful Creatures and Moral Agents

Second, the Christian tradition often describes children as sinful creatures and moral agents. "The whole nature" of children, John Calvin says, is a "seed of sin; thus it cannot be but hateful and abominable to God." (Pitkin: 2001, 167). Johann Arndt claims that within children lies hidden "an evil root" of a poisonous tree and "an evil seed of the serpent." (1979, 34–35). Jonathan Edwards writes that as innocent as even infants appear to be, "if they are out of Christ, they are not so in God's sight, but are young vipers, and are infinitely more hateful than vipers." (Brekus: 2001, 303). The view of children as sinful is based on interpretations of several biblical texts. For example, Genesis states that every inclination of the human heart is "evil from youth" (Gen 8:21), and Proverbs claim that folly is "bound up in the heart" of chil-

6 Many passages in the Bible speak of children as gifts of God or signs of God's blessing. E.g., Leah, Jacob's first wife, speaks of her sixth son as a dowry, or wedding gift, presented by God (Gen 30:20). Several biblical passages indicate that parents who receive these precious gifts are being "remembered" by God (Gen 30:22; 1 Sam 1:11, 19) and given "good fortune" (Gen 30:11). To be "fruitful" – have many children – is to receive God's blessing. The Psalmist says children are a "heritage" from the Lord and a "reward" (Ps 127:3).

dren (Prov 22:15). The Psalms declare that "the wicked go astray from the womb; they err from their birth" (Ps 58:3; cf. 51:5). Paul writes that all people are "under the power of sin," and "there is no one who is righteous, not even one" (Rom 3: 9–10; cf. 5:12).

On the surface, this way of thinking about children can seem negative and destructive, and as some historical studies have shown, viewing children exclusively as sinful has often warped Christian approaches to children and led in some cases to child abuse and even death. However, the notion that children are sinful is worth revisiting and critically retrieving. It can correct an equally simplistic and dangerous view of children as primarily pure and innocent beings who automatically love God and their neighbors. Such a view leaves no room for appreciating a child's own growing autonomy and accountability, and thereby the "innocent child" easily becomes a passive cipher for the hopes and fears of adults. Viewing children as sinful underscores two important points in Christian theology. On the one hand, it recognizes that they are "born in a state of sin"; they live in a world that is not what it ought to be. Their parents are not perfectly loving and just; social institutions that support them, such as schools and governments, are not free from corruption; and the communities in which they live, no matter how safe, have elements of injustice and violence. On the other hand, viewing children as sinful recognizes that, as they develop, they carry out "actual sins" and are moral agents who bear some degree of responsibility for their actions. They can act in ways that are self-centered, unjust, and harmful to themselves and others. This view of "actual sins" of children becomes distorted if theologians mistakenly equate a child's physical and emotional needs or early developmental stages with sin. However, when used cautiously and with attention to psychological insights into child development, it can also strengthen the awareness of a child's growing moral capacities and levels of accountability.

It is also important to note that theologians who spoke of children as sinful have often emphasized that infants and young children are not as sinful as adults; they should be treated tenderly. Furthermore, some who viewed children as sinful also radically viewed them as equals and thereby shattered barriers of gender, race, and class. The 18th century German Lutheran pietist, August Hermann Francke, for example, attended to poor children in his community by building hospitals, schools, and orphanages to serve them and their families. He emphasized the breaking of a child's will and religious conversion, yet these notions, set within the context of his broader theological framework, fostered his humane and compassionate treatment of children. Although he lived in a highly class-conscious period, his theology led him to possess a deeper concern for the education and well being of poor children than many of his "enlightened" contemporaries, including John Locke (Bunge: 2001, 247–278).

1.3. Developing Beings Who Need Instruction and Guidance

A third helpful and central perspective within the tradition is that children are developing beings who need instruction and guidance. Adults are to nurture, teach, and guide children, helping them to develop intellectually, morally, emotionally, and spiritually. Several biblical passages speak about these responsibilities. Adults are to "train children in the right way" (Prov 22:6) and bring up children "in the discipline and instruction of the Lord" (Eph 6:4). Parents and caring adults are to tell children about God's faithfulness (Isa 38:19) and "the glorious deeds of the Lord" (Ps 78:4b). They are to teach children the words of the law (Deut 11:18–19; 31:12–13), the love of God with the whole heart (Deut 6:5), and doing what is right, just, and fair (Gen 18:19; Prov 2:9).

There are also many examples in the tradition of theologians who took seriously the spiritual formation and education of children. They encouraged adults to pass on the faith to the next generation and to help children develop particular skills, virtues, and habits that would enable them to cultivate friendships and to contribute to the common good. For example, John Chrysostom, in the fourth century, wrote sermons on parenting and the duties of parents to nurture the faith of their children. He viewed the home itself as "a little church" and ranked parental neglect of children's needs and their spiritual formation among the gravest injustices (Guroian: 2001, 64, 73). Martin Luther and John Calvin also wrote catechisms and religious education materials for parents to use in the home, and they emphasized the responsibility of parents to guide and to instruct their children in the faith.[7] In his popular book, *Christian Nurture,* Horace Bushnell, a Nineteenth Century Congregational pastor and scholar, emphasized that parents are the primary agents of a child's spiritual formation, claiming, "Religion never penetrates life until it becomes domestic." (Bushnell: 1994, 63).[8]

1.4. Fully Human and Made in the Image of God

Fourth, although children are developing, they are, at the same time, whole and complete human beings made in the image of God. Thus, they are worthy of human dignity and respect from the start. The basis of this claim is Gen 1:27, which states that God made humankind, male and female, in God's image. It follows that children, like adults, possess the fullness of humanity. Regardless of race, gender, or class, they have intrinsic value. Although parents nurture them, they are not made in the image of their parents but in the greater image of God. The sense of the integrity of each person, including children, is also grounded in a view of God who intimately knows the number

7 For discussions of Luther and Calvin, see Strohl: 2001, 134–159; Pitkin: 2001, 160–193.

8 For a full discussion of Bushnell, see Bendroth: 2001, 350–364.

of "even the hairs of your head" (Matt 10:30), forms your "inward parts," and "knit" you together in the womb (Ps 139:13).

The notion that children are fully human and made in the image of God has often been neglected in Christianity, and some parts of the tradition describe children as "animals," "beasts," "pre-rational," "pre-adults," "almost human," "not quite human," or "on their way to becoming human." However, there are some theologians who have emphasized the full humanity of children, including infants. For example, Cyprian in the third century, depicts infants as complete human beings. All people, regardless of age or character, are "alike and equal since they have been made once by God." All share a "divine and spiritual equality" and are able to receive God's grace and gifts. "For what is lacking," he wonders, to one who "has once been formed in the womb by the hands of God?"(Cyprian: 1964, 217–218, Letter 64.3).[9] The twentieth century Catholic theologian, Karl Rahner, also asserts that children have the value and dignity in their own right and are fully human from the beginning. Thus, he believes that we are to respect children from the beginning of life. We need to see them as a "sacred trust" to be nurtured and protected at every stage of their existence.[10]

1.5. Models of Faith and Sources of Revelation

Fifth, the New Testament depicts children in striking and even radical ways as moral witnesses, models of faith for adults, sources or vehicles of revelation, and representatives of Jesus. The gospel passages turn upside down common assumptions held in Jesus' time and our own: that children are to be seen but not heard and that the primary role of children is to learn from and obey adults. In contrast, these New Testament passages remind us that children can teach and challenge adults. They can prophesy and praise God. They can be vehicles of revelation, models of faith, and even paradigms for entering the reign of God. "Unless you change and become like children, you will never enter the kingdom of heaven," Jesus warns. "Whoever becomes humble like this child is the greatest in the kingdom of heaven. Whoever welcomes one such child in my name welcomes me" (Matt 18:2–5). Viewing children as models for adults or vehicles of revelation does not mean that they are creatures who are "near angels," "closer to God," or "more spiritual" than adults. However, these passages and others do challenge adults to be receptive to the lessons and wisdom that children offer them, to honor children's questions

---

9 Although Cyprian is making strong claims for the spiritual and divine equality of children, he does not draw implications for their social equality.

10 Cf. Rahner: 1971, 33–50. For an excellent discussion of Rahner's views on children and childhood see Hinsdale: 2001, 406–445.

and insights, and to recognize that children can positively influence the community and the moral and spiritual lives of adults.

Like the notion that children are fully human and made in the image of God, the idea that children can be teachers, bearers of revelation, or models of faith has not been emphasized and has often been completely neglected in the Christian tradition and among Christians today. However, throughout the tradition and today, we do find theologians who have grappled seriously with these New Testament passages, forcing them to rethink their assumptions about children and exploring what adults learn from them. For example, Friederich Schleiermacher, the nineteenth-century Protestant theologian, emphasized that adults who want to enter the kingdom of God need to recover a childlike spirit. For him, this childlike spirit has many components that we can learn from children, such as "living fully in the present moment," being able to forgive others, or being flexible.[11]

1.6. Orphans, Neighbors, and Strangers in Need of Justice and Compassion

Finally, in the sixth place, there are many biblical passages and examples in the tradition that remind us that children are also orphans, neighbors, and strangers who need to be treated with justice and compassion. The Bible depicts many ways that children suffer and are the victims of war, disease, or injustice. In addition, numerous biblical passages explicitly command us to help widows and orphans – among the most vulnerable people in society (e. g. Exod 22:22–24; Deut 10:17–18; 14: 28–29). In the New Testament, Jesus also healed, embraced, and blessed children. These and other passages clearly show us that caring for children is part of seeking justice and loving the neighbor.

Although we cannot ignore the Church's neglect and harm of children, Christians have also at times protected children and helped them to achieve wholeness, and there are many examples within the past and today of those who have taken seriously the situation of orphans and poor children. For example, Luther and Phillip Melancthon influenced positive policies and reforms in Germany for universal education that included girls and the poor. Like Luther and Melancthon, Francke also influenced positive educational policies and reforms in Germany so that all children could receive a good education. John Wesley, the founder of Methodism, is another strong example of a theologian who attended to the poor in concrete ways, and he inspired Methodists from his time to today to care for the poor and to establish a number of institutions and initiatives to serve them. Today, congregations and denominations around the world support numerous national and international

11 For an excellent discussion of Schleiermacher, see DeVries: 2001a, 300–328; DeVries: 2001b, 165f.

relief agencies for the poor and for children at risk, and a few seminaries in various countries are beginning to develop graduate programs for those who wish to serve in such agencies.[12]

1.7. Implications of these Six Perspectives on the Nature of Children

When incorporated into theologies of childhood, and when held in tension instead of in isolation from one another, these six perspectives have tremendous implications for combating simplistic and destructive conceptions of children and strengthening the Church's commitment to them.

For example, when held in tension, these six ways of speaking about children could strengthen spiritual formation, religious education, and children's ministry programs. If Christians saw children as gifts of God and sources of joy, then they would include them in worship services as true participants and welcome them as full members of the church, and they would incorporate more joy and laughter into religious education at home and at church. Furthermore, if Christians saw children as sinful and in need of instruction, then they would develop more substantial religious educational materials and programs for children in the church and create Christian education programs that emphasize the importance of the family in spiritual formation and faith development. They would also more readily cultivate the growing moral capacities and responsibilities of children in many other ways, such as by introducing them to good examples, mentors, and stories of service and compassion; including children in service projects and teaching them financial responsibility; and helping them discern their vocations and explore how they can best use their gifts and talents to contribute to the common good. Finally, if they believed, as Jesus did, that children can teach adults and be moral witnesses, models of faith, and sources of revelation, then they would listen more attentively to children and learn from them; structure their religious education programs in ways that honor their questions and insights; and recognize the importance of children in the faith journey and spiritual maturation of parents and other adults.

The six ways of speaking about children could also deepen theological and ethical reflection on children and generate strong Christian theologies of childhood. For example, if Christians saw children as gifts of God and developing beings in need of instruction, then they would no longer see children as "belonging" to their parents, but rather as gifts to them and the whole community. They would also take more seriously their obligations to all children and strengthen theological and ethical reflection on the role of church and state in protecting children and on the responsibilities of parents. They would also begin to understand spiritual formation as a serious area of inquiry in all

12 See, e. g., the programs that are being developed at Fuller Theological Seminary (United States), Malaysia Baptist Theological Seminary, and SEMISUD Seminary (Ecuador).

areas of theological and biblical studies – not just pastoral care or religious education.

The six ways of speaking about children could help renew the church's commitment to serving and protecting all children. If the Church viewed children as made in the image of God, as fully human, and as orphans, neighbors, and strangers in need of compassion and justice, then it would treat all children, regardless of age, race, class, country, or gender, with more dignity and respect. Christians would no longer tolerate the abuse or harsh treatment of children, and they would warn against equating "discipline" with physical punishment. Furthermore, they would support local and federal legislation that addresses the needs of all children and families, such as fighting for a truly working wage, parental leave policies, and strong educational programs for all children. The church would also promote governmental support of proper nutrition and adequate health care for children. Christians would attend to the needs of poor children in local communities and around the world, work more diligently to protect and serve all children in need, and become stronger and more creative advocates for children in their own countries and around the world.

2. Resources from Christian Understandings of Calling and Vocation[13]

The Christian tradition articulates additional perspectives on children not only in biblical and theological sources that directly address the themes of children and childhood but also from doctrines and practices that initially appear to have little to do with children. Central themes of Christian faith and practice, when critically reexamined with the "lens" of the child and concern for children and childhood, not only challenge our assumptions about children but also deepen our understanding of Christian faith and practice as a whole.

This particular section of the paper outlines six additional perspectives about children, especially their duties and responsibilities, by reexamining Christian understandings of "vocation" or "calling." These two terms are not generally associated with children. They are used commonly today to refer either to one's profession (such as the calling to be a teacher or medical doctor) or to full time service in the Church (such as a calling to ordained ministry, the priesthood, or the monastic life). However, within the Christian tradition, "vocation" or "calling" is a rich concept that embraces far more than the adult world of paid work or ordained ministry. Most Christian theologians

13 For a fuller discussion of the vocation of children on which this Part of the paper builds, see Bunge: forthcoming.

and ethicists, regardless of their particular denominations, claim that the concept of vocation, rightly understood, addresses our deepest human longings for purpose and meaning in life and encompasses the totality of our lives. Although Christians have certainly interpreted "vocation" and "calling" in various ways, central to many of these interpretations is the notion God is calling us to a life centered in Christ and to ways in which we meaningfully participate in and contribute to God's work in the world. Thus, vocation is a term that applies to everyone – regardless of gender, race, class, or age.

The understanding of vocation as a religious term that applies to everyone was emphasized during the Reformation. Since that time, Protestants have often stated in various ways that all people have a have a "vocation" or "calling" in two senses (Placher: 2005, 206).[14] On the one hand, they are all called to follow Christ and to love God and to love and serve the neighbor, especially those in need.[15] This is their common vocation or calling: it is, as some Protestants have said, a "general" or "spiritual" vocation that all Christians share. It is the call to discipleship and to unity with Christ. On the other hand, people are also called by God to particular "vocations": to specific "offices", "stations," or "places of responsibility" in which they use their gifts and talents serve the well-being of others, whether at home, at work, at church, or in civic life. They serve others in particular ways, for example, as spouses and parents; doctors and lawyers; pastors and deacons; or politicians and soldiers. This is sometimes called their "particular" or "external" vocation.

Even though vocation understood in this twofold way refers to how all people, in various ways, are called to unity with Christ and to contribute in specific ways to the welfare of the community, most Christians, and even most Christian theologians and ethicists, do not discuss the particular vocation of children. This is the case, in part, because very few theologians and ethicists speak about children at all. Nevertheless, some theologians in the past and today have reflected deeply on the central tasks and responsibilities of children, and they have incorporated the child into their views of vocation or calling as a whole. For example, in his writings on vocation, Martin Luther emphasizes that all believers, including children and young people, are to love God and serve the neighbor in specific callings and places of responsibility – whether at home, at work, at church, or in civic life.[16] For Luther, everyone has these "roles" or "offices" – whether given or chosen, for in addition to our

14 Placher's book is an excellent introduction to various understandings of vocation in the history of Christianity.

15 This sense of calling is built on Jesus' command to his followers to "love the Lord your God with all your heart, and with all your soul, and with all your mind, and with all your strength" and to "love your neighbor as yourself." Cf. Mark 12:28–24; Matt 22:34–40; Luke 10:25–28.

16 For an excellent discussion of Luther's view of vocation in general, see Schuurman: 2004. For primary texts by Luther on vocation, see e. g.: Luther: 1989; 1959).

professional roles and duties, even our social and familial relationships are places into which God calls us to serve God and the neighbor. Thus, whatever an individual's age, class, or status, he or she has a specific vocation – certain duties, roles, and responsibilities that benefit the family and the community.

This part of the paper builds on the insights of Luther and other Protestant theologians, affirming that a sound theological understanding of vocation can and should include children, and addresses the questions: If children, too, have a specific calling, then what does it look like? What are their specific duties, roles, and responsibilities that contribute to the life of the community? What is their "work" or "office"? What is their relationship to familial and social structures? The paper finds the Bible and the tradition emphasize that the specific vocation of the child contains at least six almost paradoxical elements. Each of these elements is built on a complex theological understanding of the nature of children, and each one is coupled with corresponding duties and responsibilities of parents and other caring adults. Although this chapter paper builds primarily on Lutheran views of vocation, it illustrates the possibility of critically retrieving the concept of vocation from various strands of the Christian tradition in ways that honor the dignity and complexity of children and their roles and responsibilities in the community.

2.1. Honor and Respect Your Parents

Throughout the Christian tradition, one of the most commonly cited duties of children is to honor and respect their parents. The fourth commandment is "Honor your father and mother so that your days may be long in the land that the *Lord* your God is giving you" (Exod 20:12; Deut 5:16), and several other biblical passages command children to honor and respect their parents (Lev 19:3; Eph 6:2–3; Heb 12:9). The term for honor in Heb literally means "to make heavy," and the fourth commandment calls children to regard their parents as worthy of this weighty respect and dignity.

Corresponding to this first duty of children are also particular assumptions about the nature of children and the duties of parents. It assumes that children are dependent and vulnerable beings, and parents, in turn, are to love, serve, and protect them by providing them with food, clothing, and other basic needs. Children should honor their parents, in part, because parents must do so much for them to nourish them, protect them, and keep them alive.

Luther states, for example, that God commands children to honor their parents because parents have "nourished and nurtured them," and they owe their parents "body and life" and "every good." Without parents a child would have, as Luther says so delicately, "perished a hundred times in his own filth" (Luther: 1959, 383). He believes that even young children can honor their parents by being grateful for the love and protection of their parents or guardians. For him, children have a duty "to show gratitude for the kindness and for all the good things we have received from our parents." (Luther: 1959, 382). He believes that children should not grumble, and they should remember the many blessings they have already received.

However, the commandment to honor and respect parents does not stop with childhood, and the particular vocation of the "child" includes some duties that are life-long. This particular duty of the "child" continues into adulthood, since as long as one's parents are alive, one still has an obligation to honor and respect them. Indeed, the Jewish scholar, Elliot Dorff, has stated that the Rabbis understood the commandment to honor and respect parents as "primarily governing the interactions of adult children of elderly parents." (Dorff: 2003, 123). Thus, adult children of elderly parents have an obligation to provide food and clothing for them, and they honor their parents by caring for them as they grow older.

2.2. Obey Your Parents

Another duty of children often cited in the Christian tradition is that children are to obey their parents. They are commanded: "Children, obey your parents in everything, for this is your acceptable duty in the Lord" (Col 3:20). They are to obey their parents "in the Lord, for this is right" (Eph 6:1). Several biblical passages call children to obey their parents, and their prosperity is often seen to be dependent on their obedience to parents (Deut 4:40; 12:24, 28; Ps 128:1–3). Obedience also includes recognizing the authority of parents over their children. The "younger must accept the authority of the elders" and "clothe" themselves with humility (1 Pet 5:5–6). The New Testament also lists disobedience to parents as a particular vice (Rom 1:30; 2 Tim 3:2).

The duty to obey assumes that children are not yet able to discern fully right from wrong, and they need to learn from and follow the example of their parents and other adults in authority. They need to be told what is right and wrong and what God requires of them (Mic 6:6). Parents, in turn, have an obligation to be good examples to their children and to be their moral and spiritual teachers. Given their authority and significance in a child's life, they should also understand that their example and actions can influence not only a child's relationship to other human beings but also his or her understanding of God.

Many Christian theologians have emphasized that children should honor and obey their parents to such a degree that they regard them as God's representatives. Luther, for example, states children should honor and revere their parents "as God's representatives" and hold them in distinction and esteem above all things "as the most precious treasure on earth."(Luther: 1959, 379f). For Luther, "Honor includes not only love but also deference, humility, and modesty, directed (so to speak) toward a majesty hidden within them. It requires us not only to address them affectionately and reverently, but above all to show by our actions, both of heart and of body, that we respect them very highly and that next to God we give them the very highest place." (Luther: 1959, 379). Luther claims that the greatest and noblest work of children is "obedience to father and mother, which God has appointed and commanded next to obedience to his own majesty."(Luther: 1959, 381).

In the 20th century, the Protestant theologian Karl Barth also spoke of parents as "God's representatives." "From the standpoint of children parents have a Godward aspect, and are for them God's primary and natural representatives." (Barth: 1961, 243). For Barth, parents are really the "elders" in relation to their children, and they represent not only their own knowledge and experience to children "but that conveyed to them by their own predecessors." Thus, children are to heed and obey them. This does not mean, Barth clarifies, that children are the parents' "property, subjects, servants or even pupils." Rather, children are their parents' "apprentices, who are entrusted and subordinated to them in order that they might lead them into the way of life. The children must be content to accept this leading from their parents. In general outline, this is what the command of God requires of them." (Barth: 1961, 243).

2.3. Disobey Your Parents and Other Adult Authorities

Although almost all theologians today and in the past would emphasize that children should honor and obey their parents, they often neglect a third and corresponding responsibility of children that is also part of the tradition: children have a responsibility and duty *not* to obey their parents, if their parents or other adult authorities cause them to sin or to carry out acts of injustice. Although children should honor and obey their parents, their ultimate loyalty is to God.

Several examples in the Bible illustrate that parents are sometimes unjust and unfaithful or that children must follow God's law above the commands of parents when the two conflict. Ezekiel, for example, commands children, "Do not follow the statues of your parents, nor observe their ordinances, nor defile yourselves with their idols. I the *Lord* am your God; follow my statues, and be careful to observe my ordinances, and hallow my sabbaths (Ezek 20:18–19). In the New Testament, Jesus also points out potential conflicts between parents and children, when one is called to follow him.[17] Speaking to his disciples, he says "You will be betrayed even by parents and brothers, by relatives and friends; and they will put some of you to death. You will be hated by all because of my name" (Luke 21:16–17).

Related to this responsibility is an understanding that children (whether young children or adults) are not subject to their parents absolutely. Rather, as noted above, all children are made in the image of God (not primarily in

17 For a fuller discussion of the tension between obedience to parents and following Jesus, see Carroll: forthcoming.

the image of their parents), they are worthy of respect from the start, and even as young children, they are active moral agents with growing moral capacities and responsibilities of their own. Since children are fully human moral agents who are made in God's image, and since their ultimate loyalty is to God and not to any adult authority, parents and other caring adults have a duty to recognize that they are certainly not gods on earth and that their authority over children is always limited. It is never absolute. Although the Bible emphasizes that children should obey their parents, it also warns parents not to provoke their children to anger (Col 3:21; Eph 6:4). Parents have a responsibility to examine critically their own actions and behaviors, to admit their mistakes, and to ask God and their children for forgiveness.

Although theologians esteem parents, they generally qualify absolute parental authority because they recognize parents are sometimes sinful, unjust, or just plain inept. They also recognize that as children grow and develop, their moral capacities and responsibilities also grow and develop, and children must be prepared to challenge the authority of their parents and even political and ecclesiastical authorities if they lead to injustices. Thus, parents are given authority over their children, but this authority is limited, and it is never an excuse for treating children unjustly or unkindly or for failing to recognize that children are moral agents, too, who already as children can challenge and benefit the community (Bushnell: 1994, 63).

Although Luther, for example, compared the authority of parents to God's own authority, he gave examples of the abuse of parental authority. Building on Scripture, he believed that even though children should generally tolerate the injustices of their parents and obey them, they could under certain circumstances and in good conscience act contrary to the will of tyrannical or unjust parents (Luther: 1962, nr 45, 385–393). He believed, for example, that parents should neither force nor hinder the marriage of their children and asserted:

> Parental authority is strictly limited; it does not extend to the point where it can wreak damage and destruction to the child, especially to its soul. If then a father forces his children into a marriage without love, he oversteps and exceed his authority. He ceases to be a father and becomes a tyrant who uses his authority not for building up – which is why God gave it to him – but for destroying. He is taking authority into his own hands without God, indeed, against God. The same principle holds good when a father hinders his child's marriage, or lets the child go ahead on his own, without any intention of helping him in the matter. (Luther: 1962, nr 45, 386).

Barth, too, qualified absolute obedience to parents when he stated that "no human father, but God alone, is properly, truly and primarily Father. No human father is the creator of his child, the controller of its destiny, or its savior from sin, guilt and death." (Barth:1961, 245).

Another 20th century Lutheran theology, Dietrich Bonhoeffer, helps explain the tension between a child's call to obedience and disobedience in his discussion of the intimate connection between obedience and responsibility. He recognizes that although not all human beings lead highly public professional lives with a range of duties and responsibilities, the lives of all human beings, even those who are most dependent and vulnerable, demand responsibility. This is because "even where free responsibility is more or less excluded from one's vocational and public life, one's relation to other human beings, from the family to one's co-worker, will always demand responsibility. As he states,

> There will always be relationships based on obedience and dependence. The only thing that is important, though, is that they not eliminate responsibilities[…] By no means does a relationship of dependence as such preclude free responsibility[…] Obedience without freedom is slavery, freedom without obedience is arbitrariness. (Bonhoeffer: 2005, 286f).

Theologians have offered other ways of articulating the growing responsibility of children in connection with their understanding of child obedience, and we can all think of examples in our own day of the courage and competence of even very young children to face injustices and to challenge authority. Ruby Bridges, the first African American child in the United States to attend an all-white elementary school, for example, was just six years old when, escorted by federal marshals, she marched through an angry and jeering crowd of adults who demanded segregated schools. Even though the protests continued for months at the Frantz Elementary School in New Orleans, Ruby attended year after year and graduated from that school and went on to high school. She not only faced the protesters daily but also prayed twice a day, before and after school, asking God to forgive them. She had the love and support of her parents, and the courage to challenge unjust authorities in her community.

Recognizing the limits of parents and other adult authorities challenges a simplistic view of children as well as many popular Christian conceptions of discipline. Disciplining children, from a Christian perspective, should never be equated physically punishing them. Parents are commanded to bring up their children "in the discipline and instruction of the Lord" (Eph 6:4). True discipline is therefore Christ-centered and aims not to punish children but rather to help them become followers and disciples of Christ.

2.4. Fear and Love God

Consonant with children's responsibility to evaluate adult demands and to disobey unjust authority is the call to fear the Lord.[18] Although parents are to be honored and obeyed, God alone is to be feared and held in reverence. Again and again, the biblical texts emphasize that everyone, including chil-

18 For rich discussions of the "fear of the Lord," see Miller: forthcoming at Eerdmans; Brown, forthcoming.

dren, is called to "fear the Lord" (Deut 4:10; 6:1–2; 14:23; 17:19, 31:12–13). "The fear of the LORD is the beginning of knowledge; fools scorn wisdom and instruction" (Prov 1:7; cf. 9:10). As the biblical scholar, William Brown notes, in Proverbs the "fear of God is eminently edifying and life-enhancing" (10:27; 14:27; 19:23).

The duty of children to fear God is connected to the notion that both parents and children are to fear God. Here is where true security for both children and parents has its root: "In the fear of the *Lord* there is strong confidence, and one's children will have a refuge" (Prov 14:26).

2.5. Go to School and Study Diligently for the Future

The tradition often emphasizes a fifth duty or responsibility of children: to go to school, to study diligently, and to cultivate their unique skills, gifts, and talents so that they can love and serve others and contribute to the common good in the future.

This duty is tied to the idea of vocation and built on the notion that children are uniquely created with diverse gifts and talents that enable to them to serve others, thereby offering families and communities hope for the future. Indeed, many people today and in the past speak about children as our future or as our hope. As Jürgen Moltmann and others have recognized, the child and childhood are powerful metaphors for hope, and children themselves give us hope and open up new possibilities for the future (Moltmann: 2000, 592–603).

Thus, a major responsibility of parents is to help children discern and name their gifts and to provide them with good schools and a solid education. By doing so, they prepare children to use their gifts in service to others, thereby strengthening the community and building for the future. In the Jewish tradition, too, one of the major responsibilities of parents is to provide their children with an education that prepares them for a trade or a profession. Thus, many theologians and religious leaders in both the Jewish and Christian traditions have started or supported schools and colleges, fought for educational reform, and demanded that all children, including girls and the poor, be given an excellent education. What Luther stated in the 16th century can be affirmed still today, "We must spare no diligence, time, or cost in teaching and educating our children" to serve God and the world (Luther: 1959, 388).

2.6. Play and Be in the Present

Finally, although children are to cultivate their gifts and talents to serve others in the future, at the same time, they have a role of strengthening and enlivening families and communities here and now simply through their openness, playfulness, and ability to be laugh and be in the present. This aspect of their vocation or calling is another positive social role they serve as children right here and now.

This dimension of their specific calling is informed by the biblical conviction, noted above, that children are gifts of God and sources of joy and that parents should cherish, enjoy, and be grateful for their children as they are now--not for what they will become in the future. Furthermore, the notion of children at play is tied to visions of restoration and peace and to the notion of divine wisdom itself. For example, the prophet, Zechariah, included the image of children at play in his vision of a restored Zion. At a future time, when Jerusalem is restored as a faithful city, "the streets of the city shall be full of boys and girls playing in its streets" (Zec 8:5). In Proverbs, divine wisdom, often portrayed solely as a woman, is also depicted as a child who is playing, delighting, and growing (Brown: forthcoming):

> When [God] established the heavens, I [Wisdom] was there,
> When he circumscribed the surface of the deep,
> When he secured the skies above,
> When he stabilized the spring of the deep,
> When he assigned the sea its limit,
> Lest the waters transgress his command,
> When he cared out the foundations of the earth,
> I was beside him growing up.
> And I was his delight day by day,
> Playing before him always,
> Playing in his inhabited world,
> And delighting in the human race. (Prov 8:27–31).

As Brow notes, such imagery highlights the "primacy of play when it comes to the sapiential way of life. The authority that wisdom embodies is not 'grave' but creative, and playfully so." (Brown: forthcoming).

We all recognize that children often have a sense of awe and wonder that delights and refreshes us. They are also often far more forgiving than adults and can often bring humor to difficult situations and help adults move forward. As some contemporary philosophers have recognized, children are also gifts in the sense that they offer us fresh and open perspectives. They often ask fundamental questions about life that open our eyes to new possibilities in our thinking. They are like the new employees in a company who can ask, "Why do you do things like this?" Their questions force us to reevaluate our priorities and to reexamine "business as usual." The biblical texts go further to suggest that play, too, is an aspect of true wisdom.

2.7. Implications of These Six Perspectives on the Vocation of Children

By examining these six elements, we discover that a robust understanding of the vocation of the child must be built on a vibrant theological understanding of children themselves. Furthermore, a sound theological understanding of vocation that incorporates these six elements and others and thereby offers a complex view of the child and adult responsibilities to children has several positive implications for the church and our understanding of children.

For example, a strong theological understanding of the vocation of the child can encourage the church to be a stronger national and international advocate for child well-being in areas such as health care and education. It stresses the need for parents and the community to provide for the needs of children. It also emphasizes that the common good of society requires educated citizens, that all children should receive a good education, and that the education of young people is a shared responsibility.

At the same time, reflecting on the concept of the vocation of children also deepens our understanding of children as social agents and citizens themselves. Based on a Christian understanding of vocation, children clearly have a responsibility to serve others now – not just in the future when they are "grown up." Furthermore, they are also called to name and to reject injustices in their own families and communities. Although they are to honor and respect their parents, they also have a responsibility to disobey them and any other adults who ask them to cause or to perpetuate injustices.

Even as a Christian understanding of vocation heightens the child's role as social agent and citizen, it also leaves room for some of the other important qualities of children that heal and help families and communities. Part of their vocation and their genuine gifts to communities is their sense of play, their ability to be in the present, and their awe and wonder at what adults sometimes regard as mundane and ordinary.

A strong concept of the child's vocation also prompts both parents and children to recognize that they are on a mutual journey of faith, striving together to fear God and to love the neighbor. With this as their common focus, both children and parents might speak more intentionally and frequently about their beliefs and values, carry out central religious practices that nurture faith in their homes, and listen to and learn from one another. In general, when we also consider that in our current consumer culture adults and now even very young children are the targets of intense and highly sophisticated marketing campaigns, vying for their money and brand loyalty and shaping their values and assumptions, adults and children both all have an important role to play in helping one another continually examine and assess values and priorities in their families and communities.

This part of the paper has provided only a brief sketch of one theological view of the vocation of children, yet even this short sketch reminds all of us – regardless of our philosophical or religious backgrounds or convictions – that children, too, have vocations. Like people of all ages, races, gender, and social classes, children are meant to and already do participate in and contribute to the life of their families and communities. Furthermore, any strong view of the vocation of the child can be built only by cultivating, at the same time, a vibrant and complex understanding of children themselves that includes attention not only to their vulnerabilities and weaknesses but also their gifts and strengths. Finally, reflection on the vocation of the child certainly challenges all of us to think more seriously about our own duties and responsibilities to children – whether or not we have children of our own.

3. Conclusion

This paper has highlighted implications of a more complex, biblically-informed, and theologically sound understanding of the nature of children and their specific calling, duties, and responsibilities. Taken together, these rich and often paradoxical perspectives provide a wider and more complex vision of both children's vulnerabilities and strengths than is often the case in either religious or secular contexts. On the one hand, as we have seen above, the Christian tradition certainly does speak of children as agents and citizens and acknowledges their positive roles in families and communities. At the same time, resources within the tradition "heighten" this already positive language of children's strengths to also claim that they are models of faith for adults and even vehicles of revelation. They are also called to name injustice and, at times, to challenge adult authorities. They are not only citizens and social agents but also prophets, teachers, and models. They are spiritual and moral beings who also have much to contribute to the spiritual formation of adults. On the other hand, the tradition also speaks of children's needs and vulnerabilities and the obligations of adults to protect, nurture, teach, and guide them. Here, too, the tradition "heightens" this already strong statement of adults' obligation to all children by emphasizing that all children – every child on earth regardless of country, race, gender, or class – is made in the image of God and is a gift to the community. Thus, attention to children and their vulnerabilities and needs extends not merely to our "own" children – whether in our immediate families, churches, or communities – but rather to all children.

By appropriating and holding together such perspectives on children found in the Bible, the tradition, and Christian understandings of vocation, all those in the Church can strengthen their commitment to children in a number of areas, such as religious education and faith formation; theologies of childhood and child theologies; and child advocacy. They can reject any theologies of childhood that narrowly define children, and they can criticize any treatment of children that ignores their dignity and integrity, Furthermore, by attending to and holding in tension these rich, often paradoxical perspectives on the nature of children and their roles and responsibilities, the Church will also be able to contribute more fully to interfaith and public policy debates about children,

children's rights, and child wellbeing both nationally and internationally. The Church can build on and engage in a whole range of secular and religious debates regarding children, whether starting from concerns about children's rights and responsibilities; children's social agency and citizenship; or children's vulnerabilities and needs. At the same time, the Church can also enrich and enhance these discussions by challenging narrow conceptions of children and by articulating more fully and with fresh language the dignity and integrity of all children, and the strengths and gifts they offer both Church and society.

References

ANDERSON, H./JOHNSON, S.W. (1994), Regarding Children, Louisville.

ARNDT, J. (1979), True Christianity, trans. Peter Erb, New York.

BARTH, K. (1961), Church Dogmatics, II/4, ed. G.W. Bormiley/T.F. Torrance, Edinburgh.

BENDROTH, M. (2001), 'Horace Bushnell's Christian Nurture', in M.J. Bunge (ed.), The Child in Christian Thought, Grand Rapids, 350–364.

BONHOEFFER, D. (2005), Ethics, English edition, Clifford Green (ed.), Minneapolis.

BREKUS, K. (2001), 'Children of Wrath, Children of Grace: Jonathan Edwards and the Puritan Culture of Child Rearing', in M.J. Bunge (ed.), The Child in Christian Thought, Grand Rapids, 300–328.

BROWN, W. (forthcoming), 'To Discipline without Destruction: The Multifaceted Profile of the Child in Proverbs' in M.J. Bunger/T. Fretheim/B. Gaventa (ed.), Children and Childhood: Biblical Perspectives, Grand Rapids.

BUNGE, M.J. (2001), 'Education and the Child in Eighteenth-Century German Pietism: Perspectives from the Work of A.H. Francke,' in M.J. Bunge (ed.), The Child in Christian Thought, Grand Rapids, 247–278.

BUNGE, M.J. (2003a), 'A More Vibrant Theology of Children', in R.B. Kruschwitz (ed.), Christian Reflection: A Series in Faith and Ethics, vol. 6, 11–19.

BUNGE, M.J. (2003b), 'Retrieving a Biblically Informed View of Children: Implications for Religious Education, a Theology of Childhood, and Social Justice', Lutheran Education 139, no. 2, 72–87.

BUNGE, M.J. (2006), The Child, Religion, and the Academy: Developing Robust Theological and Religious Understandings of Children and Childhood, Journal of Religion 86.4.

BUNGE, M.J. (forthcoming), 'The Vocation of the Child: Theological Perspectives on the Particular and Paradoxical Roles and Responsibilities of Children', in P. Brennan (ed.), The Vocation of the Child, Grand Rapids.

BUSHNELL, H. (1994), Christian Nurture, first printed 1861, Cleveland.

CARROLL, J.T. (forthcoming), "'What, then will this Child Become?': Perspectives on Children in the Gospel of John," in M.J. Bunger/T. Fretheim/B. Gaventa (ed.), Children and Childhood: Biblical Perspectives, Grand Rapids.

COUTURE, P. (2000), Seeing Children, Seeing God: A Practical Theology of Children and Poverty, Nashville.

CYPRIAN (1964), Letters, trans. Sister Rose Bernard Donna, Washington, D.C.

DAWN, M. (1997), Is it a Lost Cause? Having the Heart of God for the Church's Children, Grand Rapids.

DEVRIES, D. (2001a), Toward a Theology of Childhood, Interpretation 55, no. 2.

DEVRIES, D. (2001b), "'Be Converted and Become as Little Children': Friedrich Schleiermacher on the Religious Significance of Childhood," in M.J. Bunge (ed.), The Child in Christian Thought, Grand Rapids, 300–328.

Dorff, E.N. (2003), Love Your Neighbor and Yourself: A Jewish Approach to Modern Personal Ethics, Philadelphia.

Guroian, V. (2001), 'The Ecclesial Family: John Chrysostom on Parenthood and Children', in M.J. Bunge (ed.), The Child in Christian Thought, Grand Rapids, 61–77.

Haugen, G.A. (1999), Good New about Injustice: A Witness of Courage in a Hurting World, Downers Grove.

Haugen, G.A./Hunter, G. (2005), Terrify No More, Nashville.

Herzog, K. (2005), Children and Our Global Future: Theological and Social Challenges, Cleveland.

Hinsdale, M.A. (2001), "'Infinite Openness to the Infinite': Karl Rahner's Contribution to Modern Catholic Thought on the Child," in M.J. Bunge (ed.), The Child in Christian Thought, Grand Rapids, 406–445.

Jackson, T.P. (ed.) (2005), The Morality of Adoption: Social-psychological, Theological, And Legal Perspectives, Grand Rapids.

Jensen, D.H. (2005), Graced Vulnerability: A Theology of Childhood, Cleveland.

Luther, M. (1959), 'The Large Catechism', in T.G. Tappert (trans., ed.), The Book of Concord, Philadelphia.

Luther, M. (1962), 'That Parents Should Neither Compel nor Hinder the Marriage of Their Children, and that Children Should Not Become Engaged Without Their Parents' Consent', in W.I. Brandt (ed.), Luther's Works (LW), Philadelphia, 385–393.

Luther, M. (1989), 'The Freedom of a Christian', in T. Lull (ed.), Martin Luther's Basic Theological Writings, Minneapolis.

Marshall, K./Parvis, P. (2004), Honouring Children: The Human Rights of the Child in Christian Perspective, Edinburgh.

Mercer, J.A. (2005), Welcoming Children: A Practical Theology of Childhood, St. Louis.

Miller, P. (forthcoming), 'That the Children May Know', in M.J. Bunger/T. Fretheim/B. Gaventa (ed.), Children and Childhood: Biblical Perspectives, Grand Rapids.

Miller-McLemore, B. (2003), Let the Children Come: Reimagining Childhood From a Christian Perspective, San Francisco.

Moltmann, J. (2000), Child and Childhood as Metaphors of Hope, in Theology Today 56/4, 592–603.

Nkurunziza, D. (2004), African Theology of Childhood in Relation to Child Labour, African Ecclesial Review 46, no. 2, 121–138.

Pitkin, B. (2001), "'The Heritage of the Lord': Children In the Theology of John Calvin," in M.J. Bunge (ed.), The Child in Christian Thought, Grand Rapids, 160–193.

Placher, W. (ed.), (2005), Callings: Twenty Centuries of Christian Wisdom on Vocation, Grand Rapids.

Rahner, K. (1971), 'Ideas for a Theology of Childhood', trans. by David Bourke, in Theological Investigations 8, 33–50.

Schuurman, D. (2004), Vocation: Discerning Our Callings in Life, Grand Rapids.

Strohl, J.(2001), "The Child in Luther's Theology: 'For What Purpose Do We Older Folks Exist, Other Than to Care for…The Young?'", in M.J. Bunge (ed.), The Child in Christian Thought, Grand Rapids, 134–159.

Wall, J. (2006), 'Childhood Studies, Hermeneutics, and Theological Ethics', Journal of Religion 86.4.

Yust, K.M. (2004), Real Kids, Real Faith: Practices for Nurturing Children's Spiritual Lives, San Francisco.

www.census.gov
www.childrensdefense.org
www.unicef.org
www.nccp.org
www.childtheology.org

Submission and Dissent: Some Observations on Children's Rights within the Islamic Edifice[1]

ALFONS H. TEIPEN
Furman University, Greenville, SC

Just as any other religious tradition, Islam contains multiple and variegated concepts, attitudes, and practices concerning children and childhood issues. Many Muslim children in different parts of the world enjoy similar love and tenderness, care, education, and wellbeing as their friends, be they Hindu, Buddhist, Jewish, Christian or of other religious backgrounds; yet many Muslim children also face the challenges of verbal, mental, physical, and sexual abuse, again like their friends of other religious traditions (cf. Bhandari/Karki: 2005). Some of these abuses of children are defended by Muslim practitioners on religious grounds,[2] yet many Muslims also claim that such abusive practices are incompatible with Islam.

In the following I will discuss Muslim sacred texts and religiously informed practice in an attempt to elucidate the question of Muslim understandings of and attitudes toward childhood, as well as the question of compatibility between Islamic normative texts and practices and the rights of children as outlined in the U.N. Convention on the Rights of the Child (Office of the United Nations High Commissioner for Human Rights).[3] My observations will be very preliminary: Islam, just like other religions, is a highly variegated religious tradition, and thus any observation about a religious tradition's stance toward a particular issue will be partial, incomplete, and simplified. Yet, in my observations of various Muslim perspectives about, and practices concerning children, I also want to suggest how Muslim traditional thinking can move beyond traditionalists' paradigms to more fully explore theological possibilities for the rights of children. I argue that the Qur'an does provide a basis for anchoring the rights of children in Muslim traditional sacred texts. I will argue that the tension between the universalizable and particular voices of Qur'an and Sunna call for a re-interpretation, and that the particularist texts have to

---

1 It might be appropriate to say a few words about myself in the interest of self-disclosure. I identify myself as a person raised Roman-Catholic, currently leaning toward Unitarian Universalist theology, with a strong appreciation of other religious traditions.

2 See, for example, Imam Ahmed Raza Khan Barlevi, Parents [sic] Obligation to Children. Muhammad Khetab, tr. Stockport, England: Raza Academy Publication, 1994. Barlevi endorses beating a child with whip and stick (13) and encourages a girl's marriage at the age of twelve (15).

3 For discussions of Human Rights and Islam, see Hassan, 1992.

be understood through the lense of the universalizable. Additionally, I will suggest that Muslim tradition does hold keys to opening up the concept of Sunna, and thus in a modest way allows children and youths themselves to become empowered to actively participate in a struggle against the commodification of children, and violences and injustices committed against them.

1. Theological Pre-Considerations

Before delving into the various aspects of children's rights within the Muslim theological framework, a few broad considerations on Muslim theology in comparative perspective may be appropriate. As the youngest of the three major Abrahamic religious traditions, Islam both inherits and challenges aspects of Judaism and Christianity. While Christianity's central narrative involves a divine child, whose life both as child and as adult are central to Christian theology, Islam's textual edifice at first glance seems to be empty of such child-focused narratives; instead, the Qur'an repeatedly emphasizes that God does not have children (cf. O'Shaughnessy: 1991, 44), most famously in Surah 112:

> Say: He is Allah, the One and Only;
> Allah, the Eternal, Absolute;
> He begetteth not, nor is He begotten;
> And there is none like unto Him.[4]

Yet, such absence of children does not negatively impact the Qur'an's perspective on children (Pruett: 1994, 35–46);[5] but rather the repeated insistence on a childless God serves to differentiate the God of the Qur'an from both pre-Islamic notions of God, as well as from a Christian understanding of God.

Among the various figures mentioned in the Qur'an and in later Muslim narrative tradition, the most central figure is the prophet Abraham. The Qur'an insists that Abraham originally was a "hanif," (cf. Qur'an 2:135) that is: a radical monotheist, as well as a prototypical Muslim, that is "submitter" to the will of God. The most prominent story of Muslim tradition in this regard is Abraham's willingness to sacrifice his son (cf, Qur'an 37:102ff), whom tradition later identifies as Ishmael; Abraham's willingness to submit to God's will is regarded by Muslim tradition as a most significant paradigm of what it means to submit to the will of God. The centrality of Abraham's

4 All quotations from the Qur'an are taken from Yusuf Ali: 1983, unless otherwise noted.

5 Pruett correctly points out that Qur'anic verses insisting that God has no offspring do not abnegate the Qur'anic God's characteristics of mercy, forgiveness, and nurture. Pruett emphasizes that the verse needs to be understood as a vehement negation of any attempt to see God as a sexual or procreative being in need of offspring.

act of submission is relived annually by millions of Muslims, who reenact Abraham's utter submission to God on their pilgrimage to Mecca (the Hajj), or at home during the concurrent celebration of the Eid al-Adha, the feast of sacrifice which commemorates Abraham's sacrifice.

A one-sided overemphasis of submission and sacrifice, to the utter exclusion of subjectivity and autonomy, may have negative repercussions on the development of a child, as it may foster passivity and blind acceptance.[6] The centrality of these notions of sacrifice and submission in Islamic tradition, however, oftentimes overshadows another aspect of the life of Abraham, namely that of autonomy. The same Abraham who as a father willingly and unquestioningly submitted to God's command to sacrifice his son, earlier in his life as a child exhibited a strong degree of autonomy. Violating his father's own religious tradition of idol-worship, Abraham the youth went on an autonomous quest, highly critical of the religion and authority of his elders, to discover the true religion of monotheism. I will argue that a proper appreciation of childhood in Islam needs to rediscover this oft-forgotten, other side of the central figure of Islam, Abraham.

2. Definition of "Child"

Muslim ritual practice toward children and Muslim theological understanding of childhood are usually impacted by various factors. The textual edifice of Qur'an, Hadith (for Sunni Islam, to which is added, in the case of Shi'a Islam, the teachings of the Imams), and shari'a / fiqh, is shared by Muslims in all parts of the world, and provides a certain degree of unity upon a religious tradition with widely disparate linguistic, cultural, political, and historical backgrounds (cf. Arkoun: 2002, 266f). Yet, the textual edifice is somewhat vague on the precise definition of childhood, and no clear, textually defined ritual demarcation exists which would signify the transition from childhood into adult life.[7]

---

6 To a certain extent, this was the central point of criticism that Theo van Gogh's film *Submission* attempted to portray. Of course, the director's choice of imagery, the selective, very biased, highly Orientalist portrayal of a supposed utter misogyny of Muslim culture in sensationalist and eroticist fashion was little more than propagandist in nature.

7 Where Jewish religious practice traditionally marks the onset of adolescence with the ritual of Bar Mitzvah / Bat Mitzvah, and declares a bar mitzva'd person to be an autonomous being, no equivalent rite exists in the traditional, scriptural Islamic tradition. Some regional parallel practices, such as celebrations upon a boy's (and occasionally girls') successful completion of the Qur'an school in parts of the Muslim world, would be somewhat similar (cf. Warnock Fernea, 1995:9).

Medieval Muslim texts contain a rich vocabulary of designations for infant and child during different stages of development from embryo to adolescent; correspondingly, Muslim tradition is rich in rites that signify the child's development from one stage to the next (Giladi: 1995, q. v.). Within these stages of development, three are particularly significant. The first stage of childhood is demarcated from the second stage by the assumed ability of the child to differentiate between good and evil. This ability of discernment is assumed to be reached usually by age seven, at which point the second stage of childhood begins, during which the child is assumed to begin formal education (cf. Gil'adi: 1992, 23,52ff; ibn al-Naqib al-Misri: 1991, 109).

This second phase is understood to be delimited in turn by the onset of puberty. Childhood is thus understood to come to a close at the point of physical maturity (bāligh). Yet the transition from minority to majority is understood to be a gradual process: in addition to physical maturity, other criteria such as soundness of mind and discretion or responsibility are necessary before a person is recognized to be capable of contracts and disposition of property. Different schools of law stipulate that majority can be assumed at either age fifteen or eighteen years in case that physical maturity does not become apparent in the person (Baligh: 1960). Since the Muslim traditional textual corpus does not contain clear stipulations regarding a minimum age for marriage, the border between childhood and full adulthood remains somewhat unfixed. According to O'Shaughnessy, Sura 46:15[8] suggests that the "extreme limit of maturity" can be regarded to be as late as forty years of age; whereas the beginning of maturity in various lexica is given at "seventeen, eighteen or thirty years of age." (O'Shaughnessy: 1991, 43).

3. Childhood Rituals[9]

Muslim scriptural tradition knows of a variety of religious rituals that signify developmental stages of children. Some of these rituals appear to be practiced almost universally among Muslim communities in various parts of the world. A first ritual, usually performed by the father on the day of the birth, consists of reciting the call to prayer into the right ear of the newborn baby. This ritual is interpreted to be a symbolic invitation of the newborn to become a Muslim, or

8 We have enjoined on man kindness to his parents: In pain did his mother bear him, and in pain did she give him birth. The carrying of the (child) to his weaning is (a period of) thirty months. At length, when he reaches the age of full strength and attains forty years, he says, „O my Lord! Grant me that I may be grateful for Thy favour which Thou has bestowed upon me." (46:15)

9 For Muslim Childhood rituals, see: Giladi: 1992, 35ff, Erbay: 2001, 11–21; Warnock Fernea: 1995, 3–16; Giladi: 1995, q. v.

a first teaching of the central tenets of Islam (Motzki: 1986, 412f). Possibly of pre-Islamic origin, the ritual of *tahnīk* consists of the rubbing of the newborn's gums with a date or some sweet fluids (Motzki: 1986, 413; cf. Gil'adi: 1992, 35ff). The naming of the newborn is usually considered a right of both parents; making the name public is considered a prerogative of the father; according to many sources, the child is entitled to a beautiful name (Motzki: 1986, 413, cf. Al-Minawi: 1993, 27ff). The seventh day after a child's birth is associated with a number of rituals, including the child's first haircut and the slaughter of an animal (*'aqīqa*). Both the sacrifice of the animal and the accompanying tradition to weigh the newborn's hair against precious metal (gold or silver) which then is donated to the poor appear to be of pre-Islamic origin, but are practiced in many areas of the Muslim world (Motzki: 1986, 415ff).

One other almost universally accepted childhood ritual among Muslims is male circumcision, yet no uniformity of practice exists as to the precise prescribed age for circumcision. The age at which the rite is undertaken varies from as early as seven days after birth to as late as the age of fifteen (cf. Adamek: 1968, 133; cf. Wensinck: 1986 q. v.).[10]

Yet other local, sometimes "Islamized" childhood rituals exist in various parts of the Muslim world. Among the Mandinga from Guinea-Bissau, for example, one finds the "writing-on-the-hand" ritual which introduces Mandinga children to the study of the Qur'an (cf. Johnson: 2006, 50–77). Similarly, among girls in North Africa, an ear-piercing ceremony around age four or five is common (Warnock Fernea: 1995, 9). Various local – geographical rites of passage for adolescence do however exists; oftentimes such rituals are a continuance of pre-Islamic rites, or are heavily indebted to such rites.

In the absence of a clear taxonomy of rites of childhood which would be universally accepted among various Muslim communities, the larger question of definition of the limits of childhood within an Islamic framework is thus also dependent on local, geographical interpretations. Yet in the absence of a clearly defined, universal criterion establishing the delimiter between childhood and adulthood, the definition of child of the UN Convention on the Rights of the Child is not in conflict with traditional Muslim understanding.

4. The Qur'an

As the Qur'an is understood by Muslims to be the central, sacrosanct revelation given to the Muslim community by God, any theological discussion must start here. Children are frequently referenced in the Qur'an, in a variety

10 For a personal memory of experiencing circumcision at age five, see Almassian, 2002:20ff.

of contexts. Very frequently, the Qur'an pairs children together with wealth (amwaluhum wa - awladuhum), and occasionally calls these "a temptation." (cf. Qur'an 3:10; 3:116; 8:28; 9:55; 9:69; 9:84; 18:39; 23:55; 34:35; 57:20; 58:17; 63:9).[11] This Qur'anic pairing is parallel to, and seems to be influenced by its Semitic biblical precursor: the strong concern for offspring, combined with a concern for agricultural success in produce and livestock is also a frequently recurring theme in the Hebrew scriptures. Similarly, children are occasionally paired with cattle (cf. Qur'an 26:133), slaves and women (cf. Qur'an 24:58). Yet, what might appear at first sight to be a strong endorsement of a commodification of children in the Qur'an, upon closer inspection turns out to be a voice highly critical of such commodification. The pairing of wealth and children is in many instances attributed to the addressees of the Qur'an, whose infatuation with worldly concerns is criticized.[12] The Qur'anic voice reminds the reader that children are a gift from God, the sovereign of the universe: "He bestoweth female (offspring) upon whom He will, and bestoweth male (offspring) upon whom He will, and he leaveth barren whom he will." (42:49).[13] Additionally, a number of verses in Qur'an evoke to the reader the divine dignity inherent in each individual person, young and old. While the Qur'an, unlike the Bible, does not talk about the "imago dei" of humankind, God has breathed something of his spirit into humankind (Qur'an 32:9; cf. 15:29; 38:72). Additionally, Muslim theologians read Qur'an 7:172 as a reference to a primordial covenant, in which all potential future humankind was asked whether God be indeed their Lord, and all humankind universally assented to a covenant with God (Rahman: 1989, 17ff).

According to this reading, all of humankind, Muslims and non-Muslims, male and female, from the baby to the aged, is included in God's covenant, and is valued, sustained and protected, and recipient of divinely granted rights under this covenant (cf. Fitouri: 1998, 204). The Qur'an thus clearly rejects any type of commodification of children, such as seems to have been practiced in pre-Islamic Arabia. More specifically, the Qur'an strongly rejects the notion that children might be "property of their fathers," an attitude that appears to have been somewhat prevalent in pre-Islamic Arabia (Giladi: 1995 q.v.). Instead, children are endowed by divine decree of the Qur'an with inalienable rights. Specifically, the (alleged) pre-Islamic practice of infanticide of both

11 Also: 17:6 "amwal wa-banina;" 18:46 "al-malu wal-banun;" for other variations, please see 19:77; 68:14; 71:21.

12 Those who reject Faith, "neither their possessions nor their (numerous) progeny will avail them aught against Allah: They are themselves but fuel for the Fire." (3:10; cf. 3:116). Cf. O'Shaughnessy:1991, 38ff.

13 In this context, it helps to remind ourselves that the Qur'an insists that God has not begotten any children. Cf.: 37: 152.

male or female children is utterly rejected in the Qur'an (cf. 6:137; 6:140; 17:31).[14] Additionally, the Qur'an is critical of those who prefer male to female offspring (16:58f; cf. Fitouri: 1998, 208). Children, among the weakest members of society, are to be protected by society at large. Any type of oppression is severely criticized in the Qur'an; indeed, according to the Qur'an, fighting against those who oppress the weak is incumbent on all those who are able to combat such oppression;

And why should ye not fight in the cause of Allah and of those who, being weak, are ill-treated (and oppressed)? Men, women, and children, whose cry is: "Our Lord! Rescue us from this town, whose people are oppressors; and raise for us from thee one who will protect; and raise for us from thee one who will help!" (4:75; cf. 4:98)

The Qur'an also encourages children's kindness toward their parents:

> We have enjoined upon man
> Kindness toward his parents:
> In pain did his mother
> Bear him, and in pain
> Did she give him birth.
> The carrying of the (child)
> To his weaning is
> (A period of) thirty months.
> At length, when he reaches
> The age of full strength
> And attains forty years,
> He says, 'My Lord!
> Grant me that I may be
> Grateful for Thy favour (46:15)

Among the major religious sacred scriptures, the Qur'an is probably somewhat unique in its insistence on breast-feeding: "Mothers shall suckle their children for two whole years; (that is) for those who wish to complete the suckling. The duty of feeding and clothing nursing mothers in a seemly manner is upon the father of the child." (Qur'an 2:223).[15]

The verse continues:

No-one should be charged beyond his capacity. A mother should not be made to suffer because of her child, nor should he to whom the child is born (be made to suffer) because of his child. And on the (father's) heir is incumbent the like of that (which was incumbent on the father). If they desire to wean the child by mutual consent and (after) consultation, it is no sin for them; and if ye wish to give your children out to nurse, it

14 The Qur'anic reference to the Pharaoh's slaughter of the firstborn (7:127; 7:141) reinforces the condemnation of the slaying of any children. See also Fitouri: 1998, 207ff.

15 Islamic teachings on various family relationships that are established through breastfeeding from the same mother are complex and intriguing. See also Abu Dawud, 1984, 549.

is no sin for you, provide that ye pay what is due from you in kindness. Observe your duty to Allah, and know that Allah is Seer of what ye do. (2:223)

Amina Wadud points out that this verse does not put the obligation of rearing the young solely on the mother's shoulder; rather, "the basic nurturing of even the very young child is optional" upon the mother, as the Qur'an provides for the option of hiring a wet-nurse (Wadud: 1999, 90).

Yet, the Qur'an also features a fair amount of particular verses regarding children that seem to betray a socio-historical milieu of strong patriarchal structures. In this discussion, I will emphasize three areas of concern,[16] in which the Qur'an appears to be ambivalent, namely possible gender discriminatory inheritance practices, stipulations on marriage, sexual intercourse, and the issue of full marital consent, particularly vis-à-vis the question of guardianship through a male guardian (*wali*),[17] and lastly the larger theological – ethical question of the possibility of child autonomy.

5. Inheritance

The Qur'an contains highly detailed verses that deal with the question of inheritance, and exhibit preferential treatment for male offspring (cf. Qur'an 4:11ff).[18] Among a wide variety of the relatives of a deceased person who are entitled to inheritance shares, a female's share is ordinarily only half a male's share:

> God (thus) directs you
> As regards your children's
> (Inheritance): to the male,
> A portion equal to that

16 Also, a specific regulation regarding the naming of "adopted" or foster children is mentioned in the Qur'an: "Allah hath not assigned unto any man two hearts within his body, [...] nor hath He made those whom ye claim (to be your sons) your sons. This is but a saying of your mouths. But Allah saith the truth and He showeth the way." (33:4) According to later Muslim tradition, this verse was revealed in connection with Muhammad's marriage to a former wife of his adopted son, Zayd b. Haritha; it criticizes the pre-Islamic practice of naming children not by their original patronym, but rather by "fictional" filiation, calling the adopted son after the adopting father. For a discussion of adoption in traditional Islam and the UN Convention on the Rights of the Child, please see: Lababidy: 1996, 11–30.

17 While a minimal marriage age is not specified in the Qur'an, mention should be made of Qur'anic verses that potentially allow for the sexual exploitation of "those whom your right hand possesses," i. e.: female slaves who have reached puberty (cf. Qur'an 4:3;33:50). On this topic, please see: Ali: 2006. Yet, according to Thomas J. O'Shaughnessy, some verses concerning female slaves in the Qur'an seem to betray a genuine concern for the sexual rights of young female slaves (cf. O'Shaughnessy: 1991, 45).

18 On the practical effects of Qur'anic legislation regarding inheritance in practice, see: Keddie/Baron: 1992.

Of two females: if only
Daughters, two or more,
Their share is two-thirds
Of the inheritance;
If only one, her share
Is a half. (Qur'an 4:11)

This verse stands in strong tension with many other verses in the Qur'an which appear to be much more egalitarian in tone. Thus, the Qur'an often explicitly addresses males and females, implying an "importance of women's issues and their equality with men before God" (Karmi, 1996:73). Yet on the other hand, the Qur'an contains verses such as the one just quoted which would be "hard to reconcile with the concept of equality" (Karmi: 1996, 73).

6. The Spiritual-Egalitarian Voice of the Qur'an

Verses in the Qur'an which appear to suggest that women are inferior to men in abilities and rights stand in contrast with other verses which suggest a more egalitarian Qur'anic attitude toward women. Muslim feminist discourse has struggled with tensions between such inequitable verses and their egalitarian counterparts. While traditionalist scholarship has leaned toward interpreting these verses as a Qur'anic basis for differential treatment between men and women, and has seen the non-egalitarian verses as supportive of patriarchal structures, many modern interpreters have argued that the inconsistencies between these verses need to be understood as a function of the historical situatedness of the Qur'an.

Some Muslim scholars point out that this Qur'anic injunction on inheritance presupposes males to be the sole responsible providers for the family unit, and that in absence of such male support, the Qur'anic injunction should not apply (Ma'ruf al-Dawalibi: 1998, 196). Raga' el-Nimr likewise argues that the division of inheritance as indicated in these Qur'anic verses is reflective of a societal reality where males carried the greater share of economic responsibility; as modern day responsibility for the maintenance of the household has shifted, these particular verses have lost their applicability (El-Nimr: 1996, 100).

Amina Wadud argues that while the overall Qur'anic formula for inheritance indeed would appear to grant twice a share to a male relative, a closer look at the same verse "enumerates a variety of proportional divisons between males and females." (Wadud: 1999, 87). As a matter of fact, Ghada Karmi points out that the Qur'an also contains a more egalitarian voice on the question of inheritance, as Sura 4:7 reads: "to men a share of what parents and kinsmen leave and to women a share of what parents and kinsmen leave." (Karmi: 1996,73).

Karmi thus sees the particular verses of inheritance as reflective of the context of seventh century Arabia, and not applicable to modern circumstances.

Leila Ahmed argues that these specific, gender differentiating verses of the Qur'an have to be seen within the wider historical context within which the message of Islam came into being.

> The affirmation of women's right to inherit and control property and income without male guardians [...] constitutes a recognition of women's right to economic independence [...] [and] fundamentally qualifies the institution of male control as an all-encompassing system. (Ahmed: 1992, 63).

Ahmed argues that with the coming of Islam a "new ethical and spiritual field of meaning" had come into existence; yet the "spiritual egalitarian voice" of this system as articulated in the Qur'an became subdued by "the interests and perspectives of those (males) in power during the age that transposed and interpreted the Islamic message into the textual edifice of Islam." (Ahmed: 1992, 67).[19] Ahmed thus sees both the particular socio-historical circumstances of the Arabian Peninsula during Muhammad's lifetime, as well as later influences brought to bear on the developing Islamic textual edifice by converts who privileged their own "assumptions about women and gender" (Ahmed: 1992, 82) as primary culprits that subdued the "egalitarian voice" of the Qur'an. A responsible reading of the Qur'anic text thus will uncover and advance that egalitarian voice.

Amina Wadud develops a similar understanding of the "Qur'anic scheme of justice and equity." (Wadud: 1999, 12). Wadud argues that the text of the Qur'an is universal; calling the narrow, literal application of particular Qur'anic injunctions situated in a 7th century Arabian milieu "an injustice to the text," (Wadud: 1999, 95). Wadud argues that "the goal has been to emulate certain key principles of human development: justice, equity, harmony, moral responsibility, spiritual awareness, and development." (Wadud: 1999, 95).

7. Marriage, Sexual Intercourse and Consent

The Qur'an contains a vast number of verses about marriage, many of which reverberate well with the overall egalitarian spirit of the Qur'an. Thus, Sura 30:21 reads:

> And among His Signs
> Is this, that He created

---

19 Similarly, Amina Wadud's path-breaking Qur'an and Woman. Reading the Sacred text from a Woman's Perspective (1999), has allowed Muslim women to differentiate the universal from the particular in the Qur'an.

For you mates from among
Yourselves, that ye may
Dwell in tranquility with them,
And He has put love
And mercy between your (hearts):
Verily in that are Signs
For those who reflect. (Qur'an 30:21)

Unlike the Biblical creation account, where woman is said to have been created out of man's rib, and furthermore the first woman is portrayed as significantly responsible for the "fall," the Qur'anic creation account and account of the first human couple's violation of God's command is arguably less misogynist in outlook (cf. Smith/Haddad: 1982). Consequently, Sura 4, titled "Women," begins with an egalitarian tone:

O mankind! reverence
Your Guardian-Lord,
Who created you
From a single person,
Created, of like nature,
His mate, and from them twain
Scattered (like seeds)
Countless men and women;-
Reverence God, through Whom
Ye demand your mutual (rights),
And (reverence) the wombs
(That bore you): for God
Ever watches over you. (Qur'an 4:1)

Likewise, the Qur'an stipulates that marriage partners be mutually compatible in various respects, including their religious dedication:

Women impure are for men impure,
And men impure for women impure
And women of purity
Are for men of purity,
And men of purity
Are for women of purity (Qur'an 24:26).

Yet, many Qur'anic verses dealing with women and marriage violate this egalitarian ethos, such as verses permitting polygony, specific injunctions for women's dress code, verses that later Muslim tradition has interpreted to grant unilateral divorce rights to men, and many other non-egalitarian materials.[20] For our present concern, we shall focus on Qur'anic verses pertaining

20 For an overview of issues pertaining to women in the Qur'an, see: Ahmed: 1992 and Wadud: 1999.

to children and marriage. The Qur'an does not stipulate a minimum age for marriage, and does not outrightly prohibit child marriage. Avner Giladi points out that whereas in general jurisprudic considerations children are regarded as occupying a "special legal status," and thus incapable of undertaking legally binding contracts, the allowance of child marriages in classical Islamic law seems to contradict this overall maxim of incapability. (Giladi: 1995 q.v.).

Traditionally the Islamic marriage consists of two steps, namely the initial contract (for which no minimum age is stipulated), and the actual consummation. According to most authorities, the consummation of marriage can only take place after puberty, which is interpreted to mean that the person has reached maturity (El Jerrari: 2002, 211).[21] While legal reforms in different parts of the Muslim world that have raised the minimum age for marriage (cf. Esposito: 2001), child marriages are still occurring, particularly in South Asia (El Jerrari: 2002, 209–224; cf. Ali: 2006, 191n43).[22] Such child marriages are often arranged by the family of the affected children, more specifically by the *wali*, or guardian, of the child, who often is the nearest male relative, often a father or grandfather of the child. In classical Islamic law, the *wali* occupies a central position in contracting a marriage. While the *wali* acts as a representative of a male child only until the latter has reached maturity, a female, according to most classical schools of Islamic Law cannot contract a marriage without her *wali*. More importantly, a *wali* may contract a marriage for the child, or even for a not previously married woman, without the child's or woman's express consent (El Jerrari: 2002, 211f). Ghada Karmi rightly observes that this and other injunctions in the Qur'an "infantilize" women (Karmi: 1996, 79). While most traditional schools of Islamic law reserve the right of annulment for the spouse upon reaching puberty, but before consummation of the marriage, in practical terms such annulment is difficult as it leads to frictions with the child's family of origin (El Jerrari: 2002, 211). The practice of child marriage, as still it is experienced in a number of countries, together with the role of the *wali*, thus stand in stark contrast to the egalitarian spirit of the Qur'an which emphasizes the dignity and freedom of each individual human.

Various verses in the Qur'an also stipulate a dowry as necessary part of a valid marriage (cf. Qur'an 2.236; 2.237; 4.4; 4.19; 4.20; 4.24; 60.10; 60.11). Such an insistence on dowry stands in tension with verses which imbue women with dignity, arguing against a commodification; as Kecia Ali and others have convincingly shown, the Qur'anic institution of the dowry / *mahr* renders a woman and her sexuality, that is her sexual and reproductive capabilities, into

21 See, however, Ali: 2006, 144, who argues that medieval Fiqh manuals do not presuppose a person's reaching puberty as a necessary condition for consummation of marriage.

22 Ali: 2006, references anecdotal evidence for parts of the Middle East.

a commodity (Siddiqui: 1996, 49–68). In view of the larger, egalitarian voice of the Qur'an that imbues all humans with dignity and sternly warns against commodification, oppression, and injustice, these latter, particularist verses have to be read through the lense of that voice. Yet the Qur'anic egalitarian voice demands that such commodification be overcome.

Our discussion of Qur'anic verses has similarly shown that the vast majority of verses on children are clearly directed against a commodification of children, and instead imbue children with self-worth and dignity; indeed, children are regarded as a gift from God. In light of that overarching voice of the Qur'an, those particularistic verses which appear to negate these rights or return to a commodification must be regarded as reflective of the particularistic circumstances of time and society in which these verses were revealed. Kecia Ali, who deals specifically with the question of female slaves in the Qur'an, likewise suggests: "Treating the Qur'an as a document with some verses bound by context, but others containing broad principles of justice that should take precedence over specific, time-bound commands, is one essential element of feminist and other reformist interpretation of scripture." (Ali, 2006:53). As a matter of fact, Kecia Ali goes a step further by suggesting – basing her argument on the Qur'anic treatment of slavery – that "the Qur'anic text itself requires Muslims to sometimes depart from its literal provisions in order to establish justice" (Ali: 2006, 55). Thus a re-reading of Qur'anic verses that negatively impact the lives of children is necessary, in order to achieve justice for children. In the words of Omid Safi, this work "refers to a relentless striving towards a universal notion of justice in which no single community's prosperity, righteousness, and dignity comes at the expense of another." (Safi: 2003, 3). Safi's notion of community must include the communities of children and youth.

8. The Sunna of Muhammad: Muhammad's Behavior toward Children in His Prophetic Office

In classical understanding of Islamic law, the role model of Muhammad, his Sunna, constitutes the second material source from whence God's guidance for humans can be discerned.

Muhammad's exemplary actions and sayings regarding children are manifold; in their general tone, they support and embellish the Qur'an's positive attitude toward children.

Numerous hadiths portray Muhammad's interaction with children in general, and with his grandchildren Hasan and Husayn in particular, as loving, caring, and considerate. According to different hadiths, Hasan and Husayn accompanied the Prophet even on the minbar (or pulpit); Hasan would climb on Muhammad's back during his prostrations in prayer, and Muhammad showed his affection for his grandchildren with kisses (Wensinck,: 1960, 94; cf. Abu Dawud: 1984, 285). Kindness toward children is repeatedly emphasized in Hadith (Wensinck: 1960, 43).[23] Equity in the treatment of children is encouraged (1960, 43), yet rewards for treating daughters and sisters well are particularly emphasized in hadith (1960, 204).[24]

Compassion toward crying children is also evident in a number of hadith, where Muhammad shortened a prayer upon hearing a crying child (Abu Dawud: 1984, 203). Hadithic literature elaborates on basic Qur'anic injunctions regarding a child's rights to life, sustenance, protection, and education. A father's love for his child is rewarded in paradise (Wensinck: 1960, 43); likewise, a great number of hadith regard the birthgiving of children as meritorious (Khan: 1983).[25] These are but a few, selective hadiths, out of a great multitude of hadiths regarding ideal behavior toward children. Yet, a number of other hadiths exist that are more problematic from a Universal Human Rights perspective. Building upon the Qur'anic verse that God created humans "as a man by nature upright" (30:30), many a hadith states that children are born Muslim, as Islam is understood to be a human's unspoiled original nature. Al-Bukhari, for example, records the following hadith: "[T]he Prophet said, 'Every child is born with a true faith but his parents convert him to Judaism or to Christianity or to Magianism […].'"[26] Likewise, violence against children is not categorically outlawed in hadithic accounts altogether; as Muhammad is reported to have said: "Command a boy to pray when he reaches the age of seven years. When he becomes ten years old, then beat him for prayer." (Abu Dawud: 1984, 125). Similarly, while "pre-arranged" marriage is not outrightly encouraged in Hadithic tradition, and marriage of a virgin without her consent is regarded as invalid, a virgin bride's silence is considered as consent (Abu Dawud: 1984, 561ff). Likewise, while female genital mutila-

---

23 In particular, hadithic literature stresses a parent's obligation toward his or her child: Kindness toward one' relatives in general is prescribed, as the "keeping the ties of kinship" is mentioned with high frequency in hadith.

24 Such an emphasis should be read as reflective of the desire to combat discrimination against girls.

25 Indeed, parents who patiently endure the loss of children are said to be shielded against hellfire, as in the following hadith: „A woman whose three children die will be shielded by them from the Hell fire." On that a woman asked, „If only two die?" He replied, „Even two (will shield her from the Hell-fire)." (Wensinck: 1960, 43).

26 Deceased Muslim children thus are said to enter Paradise, unlike their polytheist counterparts. Yet some Hadith leave open whether polytheist children are condemned to hellfire: "God's Apostle was asked about the (deceased) children of pagans. The Prophet replied, „Since Allah created them, He knows what sort of deeds they would have done." This Hadith allows for the possibility that non-Muslim children likewise might enjoy paradise.

tion, euphemistically called female circumcision, is not expressly encouraged in hadithic literature, there are a few hadiths that seem to be condoning this pre-Islamic practice.[27]

Similar to our observations on the Qur'anic text, we see also in Hadithic accounts of the Sunna of Muhammad that inherent within the "textual edifice of Islam" (Ahmed) there are strong tensions. On the one hand, we find universalizable principles that are fully compatible with the Universal Human rights of Children, but the same edifice also contains particularist injunctions in strong violation of those universal rights. While feminist and progressive Muslim scholars have worked for decades on unearthing the "egalitarian voice" of the Qur'an and Muhammad, similar work by Muslim children's advocates has barely begun. Yet the methodological questions for both struggles are largely parallel; it is hoped that Muslim children's advocates will be able to benefit greatly from the work already under way in feminist scholarship.

In the following, brief remarks I hope to show how an enlarged understanding of the central Muslim notion of Sunna might help to bring about positive results for Muslim children, and how that enlarged notion is already at work in many Muslim communities around the globe.

The concept of the Sunna of Muhammad, central as it is to the development of Islamic law, does not clearly differentiate between Muhammad's childhood, adolescence, and adult life and his prophetic career. While on the one hand Muhammad's function as a role-model for the Muslim community is clearly dependent upon his role as a prophet – in the words of Montgomery Watt, "Muhammad as God's divinely guided exemplar"– and thus his function as the Sunnatic model would only commence upon his reception of prophecy at age forty, Muhammad's pre-prophetarian life also seems to have been regarded as paradigmatic and exemplary by early Muslims. More importantly, for our concerns, is the fluidity of the concept of Sunna beyond the example of Muhammad. While the concept of Sunna did gradually become equated with Muhammad's post-prophetarian exemplary sayings and action, particularly from the 3rd century AH / 9th century CE onward, its original meaning was much broader (Juynboll, 1997). Indeed, the Qur'an itself suggests that while Muhammad's example is paradigmatic (Qur'an 33:21), the examples of other Prophets of old likewise reflect Godly practice (cf. Qur'an 17:77; 33:38; 33:62; 35:43).[28]

27 On the question of Female Genital Mutilation, see, among many others: Anees: 1989, 77–92; Berkey: 1996, 19–38; Hosken: 1981, 3–24; McBride: 2002, 219–244.

28 For further references, please see Rahman: 1989, 52.

9. A Rereading of Sunna: Muhammad as a Role-Model of an Empowered Child

In the various accounts of Muhammad's life (the Sira-Magahzi literature) the hero is most often portrayed in flattering, complimentary terms; his generosity, mild-mannered character, trustworthiness and friendliness are emphasizes in many of these pre-prophetarian narratives as well. Great effort is made by various collectors of these narratives to insist that even in his pre-prophetarian life Muhammad was a sinless, upright, God-fearing monotheist, who was not negatively influenced by pre-Islamic surroundings (Guillaume: 1955, 70ff). The young, pre-prophetarian Muhammad, as much as the adult prophet, actively struggled against oppression, religious persecution, and societal ills of pre-Islamic Arabia. Indeed all sources seem to agree that Muhammad was never touched by, and never engaged in barbaric, Jahilite vices right from the beginning of his life. A few childhood stories relate how Muhammad actively avoided such vices; they show him as highly critical of his surroundings, and indeed highly critical of false Gods and false, illegitimate authorities in his childhood.[29]

It is this face of Muhammad, the critical, if not subversive, child and youth, that traditional Islamic discourse has oftentimes neglected, if not altogether discarded, in favor of an overemphasis on "submission," which is – after all – the root meaning of Islam. Yet Muhammad himself, and even more clearly Muhammad's prophetic predecessors, Abraham and Ishmael in particular, are portrayed in Islamic sources, including the Qur'an, as highly critical of false teachings, oppressive injustice, and illegitimate authorities

10. Abraham and Ishmael

In addition to Muhammad as a Sunnatic / paradigmatic role model as developed in classical, textual edifice of Islam, other prophets of old also occupy an important position in the Islamic *Weltanschauung*.

In ritual life, for example, Abraham, Ishmael, and Hagar play important roles, as their heroic actions are celebrated during the pilgrimage to Mecca, where their paradigmatic lives are reenacted and relived by the pilgrims. Of many of these prophets and prophetesses, the Qur'anic text, elaborated by later Muslim tradition narrates their heroic achievements of childhood and

29 Muhammad is reportedly very proud to have been present at the covenanting of the Hilf al-Fudul, a confederacy established to protect weaker members of the society, in his childhood (cf. Guillaume 1955, 57).

youth. Jesus is said to have defended his mother from accusations of adultery when he was still a newborn baby (Qur'an 19:27ff); and Mary's own childhood is depicted as exemplary (cf. al-Kisai: 1997, 326ff). Likewise, Muslim tradition preserves touching narratives about Hagar and Ishmael, and, most important for our present concern, of Abraham. While Abraham as the father of Ishmael does become the prototypical Muslim in his absolute submission to God's command to sacrifice his son (Wheeler: 2002, 102ff; al-Kisai: 1997, 151–154; cf. Qur'an 37:99 ff), and this Abraham the submitter / Muslim is centrally reenacted in the Muslim pilgrimage to Mecca, it is Abraham the son whose own search for religious truth, and whose rejection of the traditional religious authorities of his time brought about the beginnings of proto-Islam, that is, the religion which the Qur'an calls "Hanifiyya."

Similar to Jewish and Christian narratives about Abraham, the Qur'anic portrayal of Abraham and its post-Qur'anic elaborations in Muslim exegetical literature know Abraham as the son of a polytheist. Already early in his childhood Abraham abandons the polytheistic idol-worship of his family and his people, and becomes a monotheist, as the Qur'an recounts beautifully in Sura 6: 74–81. In several other places the Qur'an (Qur'an 19:41ff, 37:83ff, 29:16ff; cf. Wheeler: 2002, 87ff; al-Kisai: 1997, 136ff) alludes to the story of Abraham disagreeing with idol worshipers, including his own father. In one particular elaboration (Qur'an 21:51–70), Abraham's objection against his own father's belief system and hence Abraham's autonomous rejection of his father's authority is recalled with particular vividness, as well as some humor.

During a religious festival, in which all inhabitants of the city participate, Abraham stays behind in the Temple (or, according to other sources, in his father's idol-making workshop). While he is alone with the idols, he reviles the idols for not eating the food offered to them, and for not speaking. According to one source;

(H)e came up to them, as God said, striking them with his right hand, and began breaking them with an ax which was in his right hand until only the largest idol remained. Then he fastened the ax to its hand and left. When the people returned, they saw what had been done to their idols. It frightened them, and they were amazed by it. They said, Who did this to our gods; he is one of the sinners. Then they remembered and said, We heard a youth called Abraham finding fault with them and mocking them, and we have not heard anyone say that except him. He is one whom we think did that. The affair came to the attention of Nimrod and the nobles and his people, and they said, Bring Abraham before the leaders of the people that perhaps they will bear witness about what we should do with him. When he was brought and his people were gathered against him before their king, Nimrod, they said, "Did you do this to our Gods, Abraham? He said, Nay, their chief did this; so ask them, if they can speak" [Q 21:62–63] He became very angry that you worship these small ones along with him. He is bigger than they; so he shattered them." (Newby: 1989, 69).

Abraham escapes punishment in the fiery furnace by the intervention of God, who protects him from the hot flames and thus vindicates him. I suggest that one of the most popular stories in the Islamic textual edifice, involving Abraham as a youth, can be used as a paradigm to empower Muslim children and youth to stand up against injustice. As the various versions of this narrative recount, Abraham is acting in direct contradiction to his father's beliefs and interests, and thus can be understood as a paradigm not only of perfect submission / Islam, as he is perceived in his father role when he exhibits his perfect willingness to sacrifice his own son, but here, in Abraham's son – role, he becomes a perfect paradigm of the autonomy of a child / youth / son, standing up and acting against the abomination of polytheism and idol – worship, and autonomously proclaims the radical oneness of God.

Let me thus suggest that Muslim children and youth can find empowerment in the childhood and youth stories of Abraham and other prophets and prophetesses of old. Potentially, these stories, which are central to Muslim identity, can empower contemporary Muslim youth who find themselves in struggles with illegitimate authorities, be they Islamists (i. e. Muslim "fundamentalists") or otherwise politically motivated in their violations of children's rights.

Contemporary children's literature in traditional Muslim majority countries as well as in "the West" is already drawing on these role models. A greater exposure of Muslim children to such stories of prophets and heroes who in their childhood stood up against injustices, oppression and wrongful authority will hopefully lead to the development of a widened concept of Sunna and thus find legitimacy in Islamic religious understanding, discourse, and practice.

11. Conclusions

As the aforegoing has shown, the Islamic tradition contains a wealth of resources which can be fruitfully explored to support children's rights as understood by the UN convention of the rights of children. While certain textual sources from the Qur'an and hadithic literature could – on the surface level – be misconstrued to imply the abridgement of the rights of children; a more thorough, contextual understanding of these texts reading particularist verses through the lens of universalizable verses emphasizing the egalitarian, overarching voice of the Qur'an clearly fully recognizes the rights of children. The Qur'anic texts, supplemented with the Sunna of Muhammad, clearly exhibit a strong rejection of the commodification of children: regarding children as a gift from God, the Islamic theological edifice clearly recognizes children's rights, and thus is compatible with the United Nation's Convention of the Rights of the Child.

While the dominant tone of Islamic discourse emphasizes a radical submission (Islam) to the one, true God, such submission is not understood by Muslim tradition to be a passive silencing of the believer's autonomy. Rather, the submitter (Muslim) assents to God's will with an autonomous affirmation; not because s/he is forced to do so (the Qur'an's injunction that "there is no compulsion in religion" (2:256) makes this quite clear), but rather because the believer recognizes God's command as right command, in freedom. Furthermore, the role model of both Muhammad, as well as Abraham the youth, who is recognized by Muslim tradition as the prototypical Muslim, do provide exemplars for the empowerment and autonomy of Muslim children.

Where children are confronted with unjust demands, illegitimate claims of authority, exploitation, violence, abuse, or with threats to their well-being, integrity, mental or physical health, or other rights, Muslim tradition provides powerful theological resources to combat injustice, maltreatment, discrimination, and exploitation of children.

References

Abu Dawud, S. I. A. A. A. S. (1984), Sunan Abu Dawud, English translatrion with explanatory notes by Hasan, A. Vol. II. Lahore, Pakistan.

Adamek, G. (1968), Das Kleinkind in Glaube und Sitte der Araber im Mittelalter, Dissertation, Bonn

Ahmed, L. (1992), Women and Gender in Islam, New Haven and London.

Ali, K. (2006), Sexual Ethics and Islam: Feminist Reflections in Qur'an, Hadith, and Jurisprudence, Oxford.

Al-Kisai, M. i. A. A (1997), The Tales of the Prophets, W. M. Thackston (trans.), Chicago.

Almassian, B. (2002), Male Circumcision in Islamic Culture: A Personal Recollection, The Journal of Religion and Psychical Research 25:4.

Al-Minawi, K. M. (1993), The Child's Rights in Islam, Riyadh.

Anees, M. A. (1989), Circumcision: the Clitoral Inferno, Islamic Culture 63:3.

Arkoun, M. (2002), Islam: To Reform Or To Subvert?, London.

Baligh, (1960), in Encyclopaedia of Islam, Vol. I, Leiden.

Berkey, J. P. (1996), Circumcision Circumscribed: Female Excision and Cultural Accommodation in the Medieval Near East, International Journal of Middle East Studies 28.

Bhandari, N./Karki, M. (ed.) (2005), Voices of Girls and Boys to end violence against Children in South and Central Asia, discussion paper, published by International Save the Children Alliance. Kathmandu, Nepal.

El-Nimr, R. (1996), 'Women in Islamic Law', in M. Yamani (ed.), Feminism and Islam, Legal and Literary Perspectives, New York.

El Jerrari, M. (2002), 'Child Marriage and Islam in India. Morrocco, Pakistan and Egypt' in J. C. M. Willems (ed.), Developmental and Autonomy Rights of Children. Empowering Children, Caregivers and Communitie, Antwerpen, Oxford, and New York.

Erbay, C. (2001), An Analysis of Islamic Law Regarding the Attainment of the Mature Human Element, Hamdard Islamicus 24:1, 11–21.

Esposito, J. E. (2001), Women in Muslim Family Law, Syracuse.

Fitouri, C. (1998), 'Childhood and Youth', in A. Boudhiba, (ed.),The Different Aspects of Islamic Culture. The Individual and Society in Islam. UNESCO Publ., 203–228, Paris.

GILADI, A. (1992), Children of Islam. Concepts of Childhood in Medieval Muslim Society, New York.

GILADI, A. (1995), SAGHÎR in Encyclopaedia of Islam, q. v. Vol. VIII, Leiden.

GUILLAUME, A. (1955), The Life of Muhammad: A Translation of Ibn Ishaq's Sirat Rasul Allah. Oxford.

HASSAN, R. (1992), 'On Human Rights and the Qur'anic Perspective', in L. Swidler (ed.), Muslims in Dialogue. The Evolution of a Dialogue. Lewiston.

HOSKEN, F. (1981), Female Genital Mutilation and Human Rights, Feminist Issues 1:3.

IBN AL-NAQIB AL-MISRI, A. (1991), The Reliance of the Traveller. A Classical Manual of Islamic Sacred Law. Noah Ha Mim Keller, transl., Dubai.

JOHNSON, M.C. (2006), 'The Proof is on my Palm': Debating Ethnicity, Islam and Ritual in a New African Diaspora, Journal of Religion in Africa 36:1.

JUYNBOLL, G.H.A. (1997), SUNNA, in Encyclopaedia of Islam, Vol. XI, Leiden.

KAHN, M.M. (1983), The Translation of the Meanings of Sahin al-Bukhari, Vol. I, Beirut, Lebanon.

KARMI, G. (1996), 'Women, Islam and Patriarchalism', in M. Yamani (ed.), Feminism and Islam. Legal and Literary Perspectives, New York.

KEDDIE, N. R./BARON, B. (ed.), (1992), Women in Middle Eastern History. Shifting Boundaries in Sex and Gender, New Haven and London.

LABABIDY, L. (1996), 'Child and Family in Islam', in C. Coward/P. Cook (ed.), Religious Dimensions of Child and Family Life: Reflections on the UN Convention on the Rights of the Child., Canada.

MA'RUF AL-DAWALIBI, M. (1998), 'The Emancipation of Women: A Continuing Priority', in A. Boudhiba (ed.), The Different Aspects of Islamic Culture. The Individual and Society in Islam, UNESCO Publ., 185–202, Paris.

MCBRIDE, J. (2000), "'To Make Martyrs of Their Children': 'Female Genital Mutilation', Religious Legitimation, and the Constitution", in K. M.Snads (ed.), God Forbid: Religion and Sex in American Public Life, Oxford.

MOTZKI, H. (1986), 'Das Kind und seine Sozalisation in der islamischen Familie des Mittelalters', in J. Martin/A. Nitschke, (ed.), Zur Sozialgeschichte der Kindheit , Freiburg and Munich.

NEWBY, G.D. (1989), The Making of the Last Prophet. A Reconstruction of the Earliest Biography of Muhammad, Columbia.

O'SHAUGHNESSY, T.J. (1991), The Qur'anic View of Youth and Old Age, Zeitschrift der Deutschen Morgenlaendischen Gesellschaft CXLI.

PRUETT, G.E. (1994), As a Father Loves His Children. The Image of the Supreme Being as Loving Father in Judaism, Christianity, and Islam, Bethesda, MD.

RAHMAN, F. (1989), Major Themes of the Qur'an, Minneapolis.

SAFI, O. (2003), 'Íntroduction', in O. Safi (ed.), Progressive Muslims. On Justice, Gender, and Pluralism, Oxford.

SIDDIQUI, M. (1996), 'Law and the Desire for Social Control: An Insight Into the Hanafi Concept of Kafa'a with Reference to the Fatwa of 'Alamgiri (1664–1672)', in M. Yamani (ed.), Feminism and Islam. Legal and Literary Perspectives, New York.

SMITH, J. E/HADDAD, Y. (1982), 'Eve: Islamic Image of Women' in A. al-Hibri (ed.) Women and Islam, New York.

WADUD, A. (1999), Qur'an and Woman: Rereading the Sacred Text from a Woman's Perspective, New Youk/Oxford.

WENSINCK, A.J. (1960), A Handbook of Early Muhammadan Tradition, Leiden.

WENSINCK, A.J. (1986), KHITÂN, in Encyclopedia of Islam, q.v, Vol. V, Leiden.

WARNOCK FERNEA, E. (ed.) (1995), Children in the Muslim Middle East, Austin.

WHEELER, B.M. (2002), Prophets in the Qur'an: An introduction to the Qur'an an Muslim Exegesis. New York/London.

YUSUF ALI, A. (1983), The Holy Qur'an: Text, Translation and Commentary, Brentwood.

Office of the United Nations High Commissioner for Human Rights, "Convention on the Rights of the Child," http://www.ohchr.org/english/law/crc.htm (accessed January 28, 2007).

Construction of Childhood, Interactions and Inclusions

Growing up in a Family with Hindu Values Orientation

USHA S. NAYAR
Tata Institute, Mumbai, India

1. Historical Contexts of India and Their Relevance to the Construction of Childhood

In India religion has a tremendous role in defining childhood and in limiting and supporting the development of children in various spheres. Though we do not know much about the time prior to the religions, it is clear that migration from foreign countries both through invasion and through trade migrations, has resulted in the formation of religions (Buddhism, Jainism, Hinduism, Islam and Christianity initially and other religions later). Sinha (1972) pointed out that "the moral and social qualities that are valued in a society have their roots in religion, philosophy and tradition and are relatively more enduring facts of our existence." (153)

It is essential to keep in mind that these religions differ in the opportunities they give to children in socialization and interactions with the wider world. For example, both Christianity and Islam have provided opportunities to children to attend regular classes in churches and mosques both for formal education and also for religious education and recreation. Hindus and others also had the then existing educational system whereby children from various social classes attended the village school. The major objective of sending children to these schools was learning values that would help them to grow up as a 'good child', which essentially meant an obedient child. This difference in religions' approach to children's involvement continues even today and thus results in differential opportunities for participation (Nayar/Anil Kumar: 2007, 7).

Another factor that had an influence on the opportunities and extent of the construction of childhood was the creation of social classes based on the economic division of society into occupational categories. Subsequent to the migration from middle Asia to India, there was the artificial division of India's people into two categories: Aryans and the native Dravida. In the course of time the latter were made to migrate to the southern parts of the country or were adopted conditionally. The establishment of Aryans in India also saw the division of people according to the occupation they were engaged in. This system was called 'Chaturvarnya'; thus four main caste groups were created:

Brahmin, Kshatriya, Vaisya and Shudra. During the course of time this division became enrooted into the societal fabric and thus became the essential criteria for ascertaining the social status of an individual. The success of the upper class in dividing society based on occupational division (and therefore based on economic status) resulted in marked variations in the living standards of various groups. Further, this has limited the opportunities available to children belonging to various groups because children from a particular caste were only allowed to interact closely with children of the same or an upper caste. The variations were also a result of the cultural differences in the perception of childhood (which here means the differences between the occupational categories and thus created caste and sub-caste groups).

Indian society was until the 20th century characterized by the existence of the joint/extended family system. In this system, a family would consist of people from various generations. Children were viewed as a group to be protected; but there was also a faith that they would grow up as good children because the opportunities of socialization outside the family was limited. However, there was ample scope for interactions with older generations in this kind of family system which was conducive to the 'inheritance' of family and community values down through the generations. The interaction outside family was limited depending upon the social class of the family and the allowed interaction avenues.

The beginning of the 20th century witnessed massive migration originating from southern India to foreign countries like Sri Lanka, Malaysia and Burma in search of jobs. This over time motivated others in the region and elsewhere to migrate to other countries as well as other areas within each region or state. The living standards and the new ideas these migrants brought back to their place of origin has had an impact on the aspirations of others (especially when the continued division of labor, consequent dissatisfaction and the struggle for emancipation by the lower strata of the society began to pick up pace), and created an atmosphere conducive to the nuclearisation of families. This process was characterized by aspirations for a better life, to escape from the problems in joint and extended family systems etc. Therefore, the process of the nuclearisation of families was primarily based on individualism or the growth of individual families and the major aim was self-centered growth rather than societal welfare. This process has thus resulted in imbibing values that are characteristic for an individualistic society. Over the years, children are growing up in families, which have less and less concern for societal welfare as compared to individual or family welfare. Therefore children are also socialized with the aim of becoming successful persons (primarily in material ways) when they grow up.

Another factor that has influenced children's prospects was the development of education in the country especially after obtaining independence.

Before that and for a number of years after that also, the percentage of children attending regular formal education was very low, and this had effects on the extent of participation. However, these out of school children had other opportunities to participate in various activities which schoolchildren never had. Now that the educational system had succeeded in spreading access to education across the country, the major difference has to be found between rural and urban students and also between schoolchildren and children not at school.

Another point in the construction of childhood is related to the gender differences in socialization prescribed by society. Girls were traditionally confined to the house and socialization was limited to those avenues to make her a good housewife in the future. Therefore, they did not get the same opportunities as boys received. Also, the general belief was that it is not necessary to educate girls beyond the essential level. Also important is the preference for sons still existing in many parts of India, which has a dual influence on girls' participation. In families with a preference for sons, the avenues for participation are severely limited for girls whereas in families without any preference (or with a preference for girls), the avenues are far greater.

This chapter focuses on Hindu Values' Orientation guiding children and their childhood.

2. Hinduism's Interactions and Inclusions in the Environment

Hinduism developed from the religious practices of those living on the banks of the river Indus. Hindustan (a name for India) was the 'land of the river Indus' and Hinduism simply their culture. Over three thousand years old, the religion still commemorates a close relationship with the environment. Even today, for most ceremonies, e. g. birth, death, marriage, the five elements of nature (1) Fire (2) Wind (3) Earth (4) Water (5) Sky play a vital role. One also finds representations of these elements in symbolic references of the divine.

To introduce God into a Hindu worldview one must forfeit its traditional definition. In a polytheistic classification Hinduism tends to include rather than exclude religious beliefs. In its philosophical form, God is a divine ethereal force that manifests its presence through energy in this world. What is important is to understand that in practice, Hindu gods merge together to form three heads: Generator, Operator and Destroyer. Brahma, the generator has no form. He is the creator of everything. He is eternally present and often serves as the observer. Vishnu, the operator also represents the protector. He navigates the universe and is responsible for causal effects. Mahesh, the destroyer represents destruction in the universe. He is the closest to Brahma for without destruction there can be no creation. From this, there is no single unified description of Hinduism.

The three gods are intertwined; they are energies of each other. Without a founder, single teacher or a prophet the universal soul is open to interpretation. Just as easily, all interpretations are accepted as denotations of the religion. It has been, and continues to be, influenced by traditions, stories and practices of people from various parts of India and beyond. Since Hinduism does not believe in geographical boundaries of soul, any knowledge or practice from any source is not only welcomed but then also included in the reservoir of knowledge.

The Hindu religion recognizes many religious paths, three of the popular ones are:

- Jnana: The path of knowledge
- Karma: The path of work and performance
- Bhakti: The path of devotion

3. Socialization Process Starts with the Baby in Womb

It is well known fact that parents, families and communities try to transmit their specific beliefs, values, behaviors, essential norms and practices to the next generation. These practices could be related to the concerns of existence itself, survival, protection against possible dangers as well as higher order human development goals of self-actualization and the establishment of socially just societies.

During pregnancy the woman is allowed certain types of foods and forbidden-others to keep the baby healthy. Also, women are encouraged to chant mantras and be involved in reading and listing to scriptures to give spiritual impact on the fetus. There are mythological stories about how the fetus in the mother's womb learns, hence, indulgence in right actions and listening to "good things" would empower the glowing baby in the womb in a positive manner.

"Motherhood" is a virtue that is publicly eulogized. Girls and young women are socialized to develop positive attitudes towards motherhood.

Khanna (2005) a Senior Advocate in the Supreme Court of India prepares the graduating young women in his graduation ceremony address as a chief guest.

> You as women are the ones who are responsible for the destiny of a country and a society. You are the repositories of our past heritage. You are the first teachers as mothers. It is you who teach the young child how to take the first step and the next and the next.

It is you who develop into the child's mind and think those attributes, which make the growing children into great men. (Khanna: 2005, 8).

A newborn in a family with the beliefs and values of Hindu religious orientations is subjected to the experiences that the family has learnt to practice over the generations. Traditions travel longer distances than individual lives.

Because culture, religious beliefs and socialization are so important for human development, there are a number of descriptions illustrating the linkages between what people take up as a way life and their consequences in living it.

4. The Birth of a Child: Perceptions

The birth-rebirth theory in the Hindu religion is determined by 'Karma'. According to Hindu religion the ultimate goal of life is to get to "Moksha" i. e. to be free from the birth and re-birth cycle. Thus, the birth itself is a symbol of 'Karma'. The child comes into this world with its "Destiny" and that is determined by her/his 'Karma' 'good' or 'bad' in the previous life.

The reception of the child is 'gendered' and 'class-based'. Since there is a belief in Hindu families that the 'Son' is the heir; the son performs the last rites of the death of the parents to get them 'Moksha' from this world, the birth of a male child is celebrated and welcomed. A study of the girl in India revealed that the birth of a girl is celebrated by barely two per cent of all the families studied (Anandalakshmy, 1994). The study covered urban areas in many states, including West Bengal, Karnataka and Tamil Nadu.

The 'Son preference syndrome' is deep rooted and embedded in Hindu families and often leads to gender discriminations. With modern, secular, feminist, child-rights based media and other advocacies, this practice particularly in urban educated families is reduced.

Kakar (1978) observes that the gender-role identity of the individual in a mainly Hindu context would integrate cultural, historical and psychological data. Some of the studies of so-called 'middle class Hindus' define women within a matrix of roles that are interpersonal. Her identity is wholly circumscribed by her relationship to others including the right to "birth" in contemporary India.

5. The Importance of Family: A Repeated Message to the Children

5.1. Caste Affiliations are a Distinct Feature of the Construction of Childhood in India

The traditional ceremonies are performed within the family system. The rituals give reassurance that the child belongs to a family. They consolidate the child's and the adult's beliefs that family ties are moral, reliable and able to sustain all social relations for the stability and securing of the child.

> This widening world of childhood employs religious tradition, ritual, family ceremony, social sanction and psychological pressure to shore up family and caste relationships against outsiders and against the future. From the beginning, participation and acceptance in this world entail strict observance of a traditionally elaborated hierarchical social order and the subordination of individual preferences and ambitions to the welfare of the extended family and jati (caste) communities. (Kakar: 1978, 123–126)

The family is the first unit with which the child has contact and the first context in which value systems develop.

In the Indian context, the caste system is of particular relevance. The caste system has two distinct features. Firstly, it shapes the pattern of group actions in terms of determining the traditional orientation, the aspirations and response patterns for the vast majority of the people of India. Secondly, the caste system exhibits strong elements of hierarchy.

As such the caste system determines social status as well as moulding the behavior patterns of the children growing up in a particular family belonging to a particular caste.

Caste regulates communications with the members of its own group and members of other groups; it mediates the form, content and intensity of interpersonal relations. Orthodox Hindu society is thus composed of many interdependent groups. Each group has its own specific function to perform.

Strong religious sanctions lead to the development of family norms which ensure that members of one caste group do not intermingle with members of another caste group. Only in cases of extreme need is a member of one caste permitted to perform duties belonging to a lower caste; and in no circumstances, is a member of a lower caste permitted to perform the duties belonging to the higher castes.

The rationalization which justifies the inferior position of the low castes is based upon traditional Hinduism, according to which the status of different occupations depends upon their connection with tasks considered to be impure and polluting.

These ideas of ritualistic purity and the notion of pollution by way of touch and proximity, which the child learns from his/her parents by observing their interactions with members of this low caste group, determines the rules of behavior.

Thus, "untouchability" which has been illegalised in India, still exists in some pockets. The child gets into "a stigma by caste not by individual; from birth, not from deed performed; it lasts throughout life and cannot be ritually eliminated." (Dushkin: 1961, 166).

There are visible changes in modern India. Children do observe inter-caste marriage, inter-caste interactions, and affiliations too along with the conflicts between groups due to caste. These experiences vary for child to child depending upon where the child is located in metropolitan, urban or rural areas.

To summarize, it can be stated that the inculcation of caste values by the child through observation of familial patterns of interaction, communication and the adoption of prescribed occupation creates a spirit of solidarity with particular groups and isolation or hostility with others. "Caste frustrates the creative power, kills personal initiative, works against the emergence of relationship between individual aptitude, performance and earning" (Jathar/Beri: 1949, 83).

5.2. Children Learn Values Linked with Socio-Economic Class

Socio economic class is yet another parameter that influences the experiences of children. Commitment to traditional, cultural values is more to be found in middle and upper-middle classes of Indian society. The interactions of children amongst their own social class are the reality: unless special efforts are made by parents and significant others to meet across the social classes, children grow with limited social experiences.

Middle-class people value obedience, self-control and self-direction in their children, while working class people are more concerned with training their children in obedience to cultural norms (Kohn et al.:1969).

In terms of temporal focus the lower classes give priority to past events in their value orientations. This happens because of their requirements to engage with the challenges of coping with their survival needs. It is observed that middle classes and upper classes are more taken with the doctrine of Karma and its consequences.

5.3. The Life Cycle of the Child in Hindu Family Value Orientations

The life cycle of a human being is divided into four main stages or ashramas:

1) Brahamacharyashrama – the life of a student, marked by chastity and obedience to one's religious guru, or in a modern context, teacher of knowledge.
2) Gruhasthashrama – the stage to marry, raise a family and perform civic, social duties.
3) Vanaprastashrama –this is supposed to be the period for gaining spiritual maturity and the renunciation of possessions.

4) Sanyashrama – this stage signifies the time an individual reaches old age when the person should have achieved a state of detachment from worldly needs and concerns to follow the spiritual path towards the goal of Moksha. At the same time, the Hindu way of life has played a leading role in the indoctrination of the ideal values of:
   a) Dharma – law, moral duty, right action, conformity to traditional ways of Life.
   b) Karma – inexorable moral law which states that the human soul will receive absolute certainty, the rewards and punishments due to it for its actions. This belief in Karma leads to an understanding of its cosmic causation.
   c) Moksha – to attain liberation by following the path of dharma and karma.

These concepts of dharma and karma inculcate the values of endurance, contentment, submission and withdrawal in the growing child. The children are repeatedly told that these characteristics are necessary precursors of the spiritual perfections leading to Moksha. As described in the texts, Moksha can be understood to mean that a person who has attained this state of mind has gained an all pervasive awareness of the self or "I". The person feels in other "I"s an empathy amplified to the point of complete identification (Tandon: 1981, 22).

The overarching value of Hindus is "Vasudev Kutumbhakam" meaning the whole world is your family, hence, treat everyone with respect and affection. The inclusion of diversity is the guiding principle of the Hindu psyche and children are reminded of it very often in their everyday life.

Keeping this in mind Hindu society attempts at a balance of culture, tradition, practice and belief. It attempts to synthesize these ideas along with communal values involving authority and social hierarchy amongst individuals. A Hindu child is exposed to both a Hindu perspective on social living and communal aspirations in social life.

Various methods of communication are used with children in teaching them to realize a unique self-taught perspective on religion. This thought is appropriated in the liberal design for children to learn and imbibe the values of the general Hindu philosophy to the minute details of rites and rituals. There are innumerable complex and simple rituals and customs that are followed. Two important Hindu customs can be mentioned here. First is the ceremony of Upanayana or the investiture of the 'triple cord'. This ceremony means the introduction of knowledge and marks the initiation into manhood for boys. In other words it signifies the beginning of a regulated, disciplined life of Brahamcharya-studentship of the four stages or ashramas mentioned earlier.

The second example is of girls' marriage. Marriage marks the end of girlhood. Kanyadaan, or the giving away of the daughter in marriage to the man who becomes her husband by following certain procedures, marks a significant event in the life of an Indian girl. After this ceremony is performed, the girl looses her hold and rights on the family of her birth. Kanyadaan (giving away your daughter) by the parents conveys to the bridegroom that the girl's parents have entrusted the well-being of their daughter to her husband. The concept in ritual is explained as

> By reason of the marriage having taken the place of Upanayana it follows that just as in the case of men all the ordinances of the Srutis, Smritis, and Custom become binding upon them after the Upanayana, before which they have freedom of their choice of some actions, but, are unfit for any religious duties meant for the married women. So for women also there is freedom of action before marriage, after which they also become subject to the ordinance of the Srutis and Smritis. (Das: 1962, 43).

The strong oral tradition popular in Hinduism lets this teaching be personalized and individually designed for every child. Along with stories and poems methods such as the 'chanting of mantras' are encouraged for participation in a group feeling of religious togetherness. These efforts are to inculcate in children habits based on the principles and practices of Hinduism.

Stories from ancient Hindu scriptures, the Vedas, the Upanishads, the Bhagavadgita, the Dharamasatras, the epics - the Ramayana and the Mahabharata, and the Puranas are narrated with moral conclusions. Religion becomes the main agency for the intergenerational transmission of Hindu moral philosophy. The religious values are implemented though the teaching of religious leaders, through the narration of stories and parables by members of the extended family and friends (Tandon: 1981).

For children in India the location in terms of social context is an important parameter to construct childhood. While Hindu value orientations are the guiding principles, they are interestingly inclusive of differentials. One such illustration might be interesting. In matrilineal inheritance viz., in Kerala in spite of having a Hindu Value Orientation, son-preference syndrome does not counteract the matrilineal family social systems in other parts of the country.

Also, son-preference syndrome, when it exists, also undergoes change because of demographic pressures. Earlier when there was a large family, there were both girls and boys in the family. The problem became acute, when the norm was a small family with only one or two heirs. Also there is easy accessibility to technology so that the sex of the unborn can be known in advance. The social ill of female infanticide has occurred in India, even in Hindu households which hold to Hindu values of non-violence, respect for pregnancy, motherhood and the belief on Karma.

6. Conclusions

It may be appropriate to conclude that while an attempt has been made to provide an analysis of how the construction of childhood, formal and informal interactions and inclusions are mediated in growing up with Hindu value orientations.

There can be two major perspectives in understanding Hinduism. One where it is popularly understood as a religious institution and the other, that I chose to follow in this chapter, as a value orientations – a way of life. These two perspectives differ in defining the parameters of Hinduism in terms of emphasis on rituals versus philosophy. In both cases, children begin their orientations at an early age and establish within themselves an understanding of the immediate environment that directs the course of life. Both positive and negative assimilation with the environment is a synthesis of religious understanding along with socialization. Hinduism on the other hand chooses to define examples of ritual and tradition over which a negotiable world views. This can be further interpreted to be of static nature that adheres to procedures, norms, rules and regulations. Over the course of time belief stagnates into blind faith which may be the case in the extremes of any religious following today.

The issue is very complex in contemporary India. Undoubtedly, as can be expected in a complex society, wide range of practices from very traditional to modern manifestations of Hindu values are being observed. These range from the strict observance of norms to liberal views for the inclusion of children's own voices, inclinations and wishes.

The dynamics of Indian society with its rich cultural and religious heritage, with greater access to interaction with other cultures in the future, the children will have greater opportunities to empower themselves in their own chosen value orientations. The importance of realizing the dynamics of Hindu philosophy, one that changes and continues to do so in theory, will improve the chances of an ethically tolerant society regarding differences in beliefs and not differences in value orientations.

References

Anandalakshmy, S. (1994), The Cirl child and the Family, New Delhi.

Das, R. M. (1962), Women in Manu and His Seven Commentators, Varanasi.

Dushkin, L. (1963), Special Treatment Policy, The Economic Weekly, October 28, 1961, in K. W. Kapp (ed.), Hindu Culture, Economic Development and Economic Planning in India, A Collection of Essays, Bombay.

Jathar, G. B./Beri, S. G. (⁹1949), Indian Economics, Vol. I, London.

KAKAR, S. (1978), The Inner World-A Psychoanalytic Study of Childhood and Society in India, Delhi.

KHANNA, M. L. (2005), Convocation address, Hans Raj Mahila Mahavidayalaya, Jalandhar (Mimeo).

PEARLIN, L. I./KOHN, M. L. (1969), 'Social Class, Occupation and Parental Values', in A. L. Grey, (ed.), Class and Personality in Society, New York.'

SINHA, D. (1972), The Mughal Syndrome – A Psychological Study of inter generational differences, Bombay.

NAYAR, U. S./KUMAR, A. K. (2007), Child Participation in the Asia-Pacific Region, India. Chapter submitted at the Meeting organized by The China Children & Youth Centre, Beijing & Childwatch International, Oslo (Mimeo).

TANDON, T. (1981), 'Process of Transmission of Values in the Indian Child', in D. Sinha (ed.) Socialization of the Indian Child, New Delhi.

3 The Ethical Impact of Relations and Intersubjectivity among Children

The Child 'as a Child'

A Theological-Ethical Investigation of the Concrete and Relational Giving of a Child

ANNEMIE DILLEN
Katholieke Universiteit Leuven, Belgium

1. Introduction

Children are more and more frequently presented as citizens. Although they do not have the right to vote, they have rights that should be protected and that are listed in the Universal Convention of the Rights of the Child, ratified by almost all countries in the world (except for the USA and Somalia). The idea of children as active agents who not only receive care and protection from others, but who also give to others, is put forward by childhood studies. Paying attention to citizenship for children means clearly also seeing that children can contribute to society. However, this discourse is not without problems. In this chapter, I will focus on some pitfalls when speaking about taking children seriously, 'as children'. I will reflect on paradoxes in child images and argue that the recent theological discourse about treating 'children as children' and valuing the worth of children as such runs the risk of speaking in an essentialist way about children. Speaking about the value of children in general is important, but should be complemented by reflection upon the concrete giving of each individual child. It is only when each child receives recognition for his or her contribution to others that children receive what they need as human persons. This view on the relevance of the concrete giving of children is important in reviewing and developing theories about children's religious education. I will give arguments for this position on the basis of pedagogical and psychological research, but also in relation to philosophy and Catholic theology. I will make clear that seeing children as citizens means taking into account their own particular contributions to society, both as a group and as individuals. Children also give to others concerning religious and spiritual questions and themes. Thinking about the citizenship of children has consequences for thinking about the relation between children and adults within religious contexts. I write as a Catholic theologian, from a Belgian perspective, which influences my own ideas. This religious context also influences my reflection on citizenship and images of children, which can never be 'neutral', but are always influenced by the context and by particular relationships with others. It is the relevance of relationality and a form of mutuality that will be the point to which this chapter is leading.

2. 'Pedagogisation'

Throughout history, a variety of philosophers and theologians have written about children (cf. Bunge: 2001). During the twentieth century, however, children were not a major theme in theology (cf. Wall: 2004, 64–87). In recent years, theology, and not only religious education and catechetics, has been moving towards a more intense study of children. One can distinguish different approaches in theological and especially ethical discussions on children, which can be differentiated by their views on how children should be treated regarding their capacities and needs.

Although the thesis of the historian Aries (cf. Aries: 1960) about the discovery of the child after the Middle Ages is highly controversial (cf. Pollock: 1983; Depaepe: 1999, 21; Boschki: 2003, 280; Hemrica: 2004, 11) we see in it a characteristic of our modern times that children are more often now seen 'as children' with special needs. The Louvain pedagogue Marc Depaepe speaks about 'pedagogisation' (Depaepe: 1999) the movement towards more and more pedagogical treatment of children and 'setting children apart', in pedagogical islands such as schools, youth movements, playgrounds. The current movement towards special care for and attention to children can be interpreted as a way of treating children with respect for their own typical characteristics as children.

At the same time, however, one sees that in actuality society also uses children for commercial aims, such as selling mobile phones, bank accounts or food (Vanobbergen: 2003). This commercialisation of children has some similarities with the idea that children are merely important for society, as opposed to regarding children 'as such'. Historically, various philosophers developed ideas about children with a view to their conceptions of the ideal society, to which children's proper education (and sometimes also eugenetic procreation) should contribute (Wall: 2004, 64f). This philosophy of looking at children first of all from the perspective of society or a global aim is no longer as popular as it once was, but it does continue to exist in actual practice. Children are used both as consumers in a commercialised world and as commodities, which becomes clear in the phenomenon of using children as soldiers (Whitmore/Winright: 1997, 170–175). Dawn Devries speaks about the "instrumental value of children" (Devries: 2001, 164), which we can detect in our society, also for example in the practice child labour. In addition to this instrumental value, Devries also speaks about an intrinsic value of children: treating the child as a child.

3. Children as Children

The contemporary philosophy and intention of taking children seriously 'as children' can, however, take different forms. I distinguish three ways of speaking about 'children as children' – thereby referring to different authors.

A first approach is the 'socialisation' vision. The vision of the famous American moral theologian Stanley Hauerwas is an example of this approach (Hauerwas: 1982, 167–174). Children are vulnerable, and what they need most is initiation into a wider narrative community: first of all a family, but also the religious community of the church. Hauerwas criticises the idea that children should be free to choose their own religion when they become adults. He writes concerning actual social developments:

> Moreover, the family today is not even seen as the bearer of tradition of a nation, religion, or the family itself. As a result children are not raised or initiated by the family to be worthy of carrying forward the work of their ancestors, but rather they are raised to be able to make 'intelligent choices' when they are adults. Perhaps the crassest form of this attitude is exemplified by those parents who raise their children to be able to choose to be 'religious or not' when they grow up. (Hauerwas: 1982, 169).[1]

Further, Hauerwas expresses clearly his view on the needs of children and what he prioritises in the ethical treatment of children. "Intimacy and care are

1 Cf. Hauerwas: 1982, 166. "It is not sufficient to welcome children, for we must also be willing to initiate them into what we think is true and good about human existence. For example, I think we should not admire religious or non-religious parents who are afraid to share their values and convictions with their children. It is a false and bad-faith position to think that if we do not teach them values our children will be free to 'make up their own minds.' What must be said, and said clearly, is that the refusal to ask our children to believe as we believe, to live as we live, to act as we act is a betrayal that derives from moral cowardice. For to ask this of our children requires that we have the courage to ask ourselves to live truthfully." Hauerwas: 1982, 173. "I suspect that we have lost any meaningful reason for why we should have children today – that is, any reason that gives us the skill to know how to raise children once we have had them. As a result our children are anomic, not in the sense that they are raised with no rules, but in that they are raised with no moral role that gives them a status in the community."

indeed important, but equally important is the initiation of children into moral beliefs and institutions which we value" (Hauerwas: 1982, 173). The literature about moral and religious education claims to take children seriously as children, and to offer them an age-appropriate and development-based education. The socialisation approach also influences the (generally more secularised) discourse about citizenship and formation in citizenship values.

A second approach is characterised by the word 'protection'. In addition to the 'socialisation' vision, other theologians also start from the position of the child's vulnerability, but do not give priority to initiation into a community, but to protection against the dangers of our 'risk-society' (Beck), such as violence and poverty. Adults bear the main responsibility for children, and the ethical thinking about children in this context is mainly directed towards the responsibility of adults for children. The moral starting point of this position is 'the option for the poor' or, translated into the context of children, the option for the weakest (cf. Couture: 2000). Adrian Thatcher considers a "liberation theology for children" (Thatcher: 1999, 132–170; Wall: 2004), and in this context he speaks about the importance of the parents' marriage for children. 'Putting children first', as Jesus did, requires caring for children, who are vulnerable, surely when they become victims of a divorce, or when they are born out of wedlock (Thatcher: 1999, 168). Children are not only victims in the context of their family, but also in society in general. This position is a reaction against the phenomena of child soldiers, the commercialisation of children,[2] and other problems mentioned above. The American practical theologian Pamela Couture is one who holds this position, with her theology of children in the context of poverty (Couture: 2000). In this position children's rights are important, mainly the rights of protection and provision, which defend the necessity of proper care for children by families, but also by the society – when the family is not able to give children what they need. Intervention in a family, e. g. in the case of child abuse or neglect, is sometimes necessary in order to help the children and also the parents, who most often only want the best for their child. In this context the subsidiarity principle is important, whereby what can be done on a lower level should be done there, and not by the state, which has first of all a 'helping', subsidising role to play. Parents should firstly be helped to take proper care of their children. Educational advice and empowerment is very important – and putting children in an institution can be only seen as a last resort (Dillen: 2005, 110–121).

A third approach in speaking about the 'child as a child' lays the focus on the child as 'competent subject'. When DeVries uses the concept of the 'in-

2 See for instance Mercer: 2005, 71–116, for a practical theological reflection of children in the consumer cult.

trinsic value' of children, she speaks about a critique against the instrumental value of children (as a cheap labour force or as an economic driving force), but also about the idea that children are not just empty containers to be filled with knowledge.[3] The idea that children are not 'empty containers', but active subjects with their own competence, is one of the main ideas in recent childhood studies. The image of the child as a 'blank piece of paper', a 'not yet adult', is critiqued because children are often presented as incompetent and irresponsible objects of socialisation. They are seen as 'pedagogical projects'. Van den Bergh (Van den Bergh: 1998, 95) calls this traditional socialisation vision 'adultocentric', 'anticipatory', 'functional' and 'deterministic'.

The approach towards children as active subjects is in a certain sense a critique of the socialisation vision, which is the first opinion about treating 'children as children' mentioned above. Socialisation is often seen as a rather unidirectional process, based on a dichotomy between society (as presented by the adult) and the individual (the child) who must internalise the norms of society (Van den Bergh: 1998, 95). Although the socialisation vision pretends to treat the child as a child with his or her own needs, children have a rather passive role in this paradigm and are given little opportunity to use their own competences. Different scholars criticise the 'social mould' vision that is often used in speaking about socialisation and initiation (Knapp: 1999, 55). We find an example of this 'social mould' perspective in a quotation of Gilbert Meilander: "Parents commit themselves to initiating their children into the human inheritance and, more particularly into the stories that depict their way of life. In so doing they 'shape, mould, and civilize' their children." (Meilander: 1990, 143). The risk exists that in the socialisation vision children will not be treated according to what they are now, but what they will be in the future. In that case, the socialisation vision – even when legitimised as being for the sake of children and not for the sake of society as such – has much in common with the instrumental approach towards children, presented above. Children are treated as would-be citizens who need to learn skills seen as appropriate for society in order to have a sense of belonging and to function well in society. If children are only treated in line with the socialisation paradigm, they are only evaluated and stimulated in specific domains, namely those that are important in schools and clubs. A child's other competence – such as skills in family tasks, leadership, emotionally and social maturity, good moral skills, etc. – is often neglected (Meilander: 1990, 95f). The fact that children are

3 "When children see homeless people sleeping in cardboard boxes on sidewalks, they do not ordinarily think about the web of addiction, moral turpitude, failed social policies, and other aspects of the 'big picture' that so often prevent adults from responding with help and compassion to a human being in need. Can we really comfort ourselves as adults, then, with a theory of moral development that says our children, no matter what questions they may raise, are 'pre-moral'?" (DeVries: 2001, 167).

very often seen as incompetent in specific domains means also that they are not socialised into these domains, which fosters their incompetence. It is therefore important that children are not reduced to competence that brings profit and social advantages, like high school results, sporting and music awards (Moyaert/Pollefeyt: 2004, 87–93).

The critique of the image of a child as a 'passive, to be socialised, not yet adult' is based on arguments from psychology and ethical anthropology. Traditional approaches in developmental psychology are put under critique on the basis of the alternative image of children as competent subjects. Traditionally, one thinks that a child is egocentric or 'authistic'. Later the child develops itself, in different stages, following 'nature', leading to a clear goal. Today, in the literature one reads the critique that this traditional view proposes itself as too universalistic and seems to work with a deterministic worldview. Recent theories of developmental psychology look more and more for communication possibilities of young children, because the thinking in phases and in terms of what children can not yet do prevents this exact potentiality of communication (Koops: 1997, 48). Scientists discovered that babies and small children have many more skills than we usually think (Mussen: 1983). Small children may be able to perform certain types of cognitive operations, as well as formulate some types of symbolic representation and abstraction. Young children may not be as fundamentally different from adults concerning the structure of their thinking. At the age of three, they are able to distinguish mental and physical worlds (Koops: 1997, 52) they comprehend that people react on the basis of their own subjective presentations and not so much on the basis of objective facts (Koops/Terworgt: 1994; Rieffe/Koops/Terworgt: 1996; Koops: 1997, 52f). On the basis of simple tests, one can discover that children are able to do much more than what people mostly think. When one shows four-year-old children in an experiment with a biscuit tin that contains pencils instead of biscuits, the children mostly say, after opening the biscuit tin, that they had thought that there would be biscuits in the tin (Rieffe/Koops/Terworgt: 1996, 222; Koops: 1997, 53). Young children are, surely from the age of four, able to see different perspectives and interpretations of reality.

Van den Bergh argues that the tests, used mostly for measuring the self-image of children, are not apt for children under eight years old because they are too abstract (Van den Bergh: 2003, 18f). If children do not succeed in this test, one should not conclude that they have not yet developed a global self-image. But one should also not search to see whether children under eight years old have a global self-image if one already holds the assumption that they 'would not have this self-image'. When one uses adapted methods of questioning, the competence of very young children can become clear.

The image of children as 'competent persons' implies that children should be taken seriously as 'moral subjects'. This becomes clear in the idea that children have rights and can exercise these rights. One could say that the Convention of the Rights of the Child (1989) brings the child back to the people (Koops: 1997, 58). This declaration is a concrete implementation of the idea that young children have much more in common with adults than is usually thought (Koops: 1997, 58). The rights of the child are a clear step towards seeing children as citizens, which is the main subject of this book.

4. Children's Right to Religion

The factor of religion could have an important place within the mainly secular reflection on children's rights and citizenship. In the Universal Convention of the Rights of the Child, article 14, we find the right to "freedom of thought, conscience and religion" and the duty of the states who ratified the convention to respect this freedom (Verhellen: 2000, 197). The second part of this article refers to the role of parents in exercising their right to 'freedom of thought, conscience and religion' regarding their children. "States Parties shall respect the rights and duties of the parents and, when applicable, legal guardians, to provide direction to the child in the exercise of his or her right in a manner consistent with the evolving capacities of the child." (Verhellen: 2000, 197).[4]

The right of a child concerning religion is mostly discussed in the context of the individual child and its freedom. However, religion is an element that is also shaped by the dynamic relation between parents and children. If freedom of religion is only considered an individual right of the child, the child as a competent person is taken seriously, but then the focus lies more on the power struggle in the relationship. I will explain this struggle further at the end of this chapter. Here I can say that if religion is only seen as an individual right, one favours the situation where a child calls his or her parents responsible for (not) having received a religious education. This is in a sense a unilateral relation, exactly as a unilateral religious socialisation (Vergouwen: 2001, 2). If one uses this liberal interpretation of children's rights and religion, there is a danger of a permissive educational style where all the initiative is the child's. Religion is not considered as part of the permanent dialogue and concrete experience of the relationship between parents and children.

---

4 http://www.unhchr.ch/html/menu3/b/k2crc.htm (access: 26 February 2007). The third paragraph of article 14 is: "Freedom to manifest one's religion or belief may be subject only to such limitations as are prescribed by law and are necessary to protect public safety, order, health or morals, or the fundamental rights and freedoms of others."

The German theologian Friedrich Schweitzer recognises that children should not be obliged in their religion, but at the same time he defends the positive right of children to learn to know a specific religion (Schweitzer: 2000). He speaks about the right of children to religion. There should not only be rights of participation or protection against a child's obligation to any religion, but also a provisional right to learn to know a religion. Children have the right to be guided in their religious development, Schweitzer states. This right can be found implicitly in the children's rights convention of 1989 where it deals with the aims of education (article 29) that should be directed to "the development of the child's personality, talents and mental and physical abilities to their fullest potential." (First paragraph) (Verhellen: 2000, 205; Schweitzer: 2000, 132).[5] Also under the third paragraph of article 29 the right of religion can be understood implicitly. In this article we read that education for the child should be directed to

> […] the development of respect for the child's parents, his or her own cultural identity, language and values, for the national values of the country in which the child is living, the country from which he or she may originate, and for civilizations different from his or her own. (Verhellen: 2000, 205; Schweitzer: 2000, 132).

The respect for 'cultural identity' can also imply respect for the experience of the religion of a certain region, Schweitzer writes. However, the 'right to religion' in the sense of 'accompanying in and learning to know' a certain religion is not explicitly adopted in the Universal Convention of the Rights of the Child. Schweitzer pleads for the recognition of the children's right to religion by states and, for example, for giving (and maintaining in) schools the possibility to teach religion. The right to religion can also be made concrete by not hindering, or even stimulating religious communities to teach children religion (Schweitzer: 2000, 133). Also via preschool day care centres, children's right to religion should be guaranteed, Schweitzer writes (Schweitzer: 2000, 133).

The position that a child has a right to religion implies that the religious education of children does not so much serve the church's interests, but children's. In pedagogical texts 'what a child needs to develop itself' is discussed. Most of the time religion plays no part in this. Schweitzer points to the paradox of this idea. One cannot state that a child 'needs religion', because then religion would be reproduced as something 'useful'. The idea of usefulness conflicts with the specificity of religion, which is as such not functional. Nevertheless, religion is not unimportant for a child. In this context Schweitzer uses the expression 'the right of the child to religion' (Schweitzer: 2000, 23–27).

5 See: http://www.unhchr.ch/html/menu3/b/k2crc.htm (access 26 February 2007).

Schweitzer deduces the right to religion from a few questions related to the development of the child, asking for a religious answer. Among them he sees the question: 'who am I and who might I be?' Certain issues call for religious interpretations: a general sense of the whole or the question often posed by children, 'why must people die?' Other questions are the questions about God and security and the questions about the basis of ethical acting. Children also ask why others, even classmates for example, believe in Allah. A child has the right to be helped in searching for answers to such spiritual questions. Saying that a child 'should choose for itself' and therefore parents should not offer religious education in a certain tradition does not meet what Schweitzer understands by the 'right to religion'. For children are not simply equal to adults, who, because of their age and further development, have already had the possibility of contact with religions and to acquiring a certain religion. In order to give children, just like adults, the possibility to make a conscious free choice in the sphere of religion, it is important to make children a concrete offer so that they learn to know a religion from the inside out.

5. A Bidirectional Focus in the Adult-Child Relationship

I mentioned the danger of a unilateral approach in parent-child relations, both concerning the idea of freedom of religion and the idea of socialisation. Some other approaches towards children are more bi-directional. The giving of the child, and not only the receiving, is seen as an important element in theological perspectives. Jeff Astley for instance, writes:

> Faith formation in the family is not all in one direction. One of the significant features of intergenerational education is said to be that adults can learn from children and young people, as well as vice versa. (Astley: 1996, 196).

Astley also specifies what adults can learn from children. He gives two explanations for his finding that adults often become more religious when they have a child. The presence of children in a family conveys to parents a religious message, Astley suggests. Parents are daily confronted with the task of caring for their children and guiding their children. In some sense parents are called to behave like the creating God. Another reason for the growing religiosity of new parents can be found in the fact that children – as very powerless people – appeal to parents' responsibility. Parents can also learn that it is not the power a person exerts that gives him or her value. Astley writes that parents,

> [...] have undergone to some extent a revolution in their system of valuing, insofar as they have come to esteem most highly a person who, in the world's eyes, has no status, power or possessions – that is, a child" (Astley: 1996, 197).

Further on, he explains:

> As we respond to the child-without we are often helped to recognise the child-within, and that allows us to be more accepting of ourselves and to empathise more fully with the behaviour of other children-within-adults. (Astley: 1996, 197).

The presence of children, as powerless people in need of care, can teach parents a 'religious lesson', in the view of Astley. Children also teach parents that perfection is impossible, according to the American moral theologian Julie Hanlon Rubio (Hanlon Rubio: 2003, 152f). Every parent makes mistakes – parents can learn this from their children, even if only by their presence. Children teach parents to deal with the unexpected, with ambiguity and sometimes even with the chaos of life.

6. Biblical Views of Children

In different theological writings, we find the idea that children can give to adults and that education is not a unidirectional process. Often, theologians refer to the 'children's gospel' (Mark 10:14–15; cf. DeVries: 2001, 164) and the biblical image that children can be an example of faith for adults (Astley: 1996, 196; Kähler: 2002). This interpretation of the giving of the child, however, is rather limited. On the one hand, children are rightly respected 'as children', for what they are now, and not only for what they will be. They are not only future believers – the future of the church and society – but also important participants in the present church and society. What it is to be a child, however, has a very specific meaning; for the most part it is to be powerless, weak, dependent, in need of care, open to others and to transcendence and trusting. These characteristics are presented as an example for adults.

On the other hand, there is a risk in presenting the contributions of children to the faith of adults and to the church: this may result in a kind of essentialist reduction. The concrete child does not come into view but stays in the shadow of what 'the child in general' essentially is. DeVries writes:

> Here [Mark 10:14–15, RSV], Jesus not only welcomes children but sets them up as models to be emulated. The value of these children, according to Jesus, is not for the sake of something else but simply for what they are in themselves as children: that is, Jesus holds childhood as intrinsically valuable. (DeVries: 2001, 164).

If one accepts that *childhood* is really presented as intrinsically valuable in this Bible passage, one can still ask whether this also means that *children* themselves are seen as intrinsically valuable. The concrete giving of the child, in specific relations with others, has been moved to the background by speaking about the child as 'model for believing'.

In reading what the gospel of Mark tells us about Jesus welcoming the children, we should try to avoid the danger of 'romanticising' children as such. Throughout Scripture and the Christian tradition, children are often presented as 'gifts' of God, or as a joy for parents. In our contemporary Western society, where the birth rate is very low and children are often seen as very precious and important for their parents, children are also romanticised. Different pedagogical approaches of the last centuries, starting from the perspective of children ('Pädagogik vom Kinde aus') also focus on a beautiful image of the child in general. The practical theologian Joyce Ann Mercer reacts against an all too simple view of the child as a gift, critiquing an essentialist theological reading of the gospel of Mark. She writes about the notion of "receiving the kingdom as a child" (Mark 10:15):

> Some make sense of this phrase and the story from which it comes by referring to an essentialized notion of a child as one who naturally, spontaneously, and passively accepts the kingdom of God. Others read the story through its Matthean version, identifying supposedly childlike qualities such as humility as the requisite characteristics for entering the kingdom of God. I find both of these options problematic because they uncritically assume certain emotional and expressive qualities as essential to childhood and identify participation or membership in God's basilea with the assumption of such features. (Mercer: 2005, 52).

Mercer proposes an alternative interpretation of Mark's story about Jesus and the children. The children in the gospel are children who are not daughters or sons of the adults standing around Jesus, they are 'children in the crowds', the vulnerable, poor and marginalised. Jesus' act of welcoming these children brings us the good news about solidarity with the lowliest people in society, and with children who are not our own (Mercer: 2005, 52).

I agree with Mercer's critique of the essentialist interpretation of the gospel as seeing children as examples of faith. The alternative reading she suggests is very important. However, we could ask if this alternative interpretation does not once again essentialise children. When children are presented as vulnerable, poor and marginalised, and when Jesus' attitude towards them conveys the message of solidarity with the weakest, children are presented as 'models' of poor and marginalised people. Recognising the resilience of these children, and the capacities and struggles of each individual child is surely part of solidarity with children, but is seldom explicitly mentioned as an important attitude in theological and biblical literature. From a theological point of view, taking each individual child seriously, with its difficulties and its capacities, is very important, as each individual child deserves our respect, as being made in the image of God. Seeing a child as a gift not only means recognising general characteristics of the child, those that a child has in common with other children, but also looking at the particularity of this individual child, and the way in which this child can contribute to society, and thus also to the reign of God.

Taking into account each individual child also means listening to children's voices, paying attention to their relations with others. In searching for a biblical basis for such a 'theology of children', we do not find many stories where children themselves enter into dialogue with adults. There are some exceptions, such as the story of the twelve-year old Jesus in the temple (Luke 2:49)[6] and the story of Isaac, who speaks to his father Abraham when climbing the mount Moriah where Abraham wants to bring an offering to God (Gen 22:7)[7]. Theologians often refer to the text of Mark 10:13–16 (parallel texts in Luke 18:15–17, Matt 19:13–15) to speak about children from a biblical and Christian perspective. In this text we read that Jesus entered indeed into relationship with children, embraced and blessed them. The children themselves are not given a voice, however.[8] A reading of the New Testament from a feminist perspective can indicate the role that has been given to women – among others, in the gospel of John dialogue between Jesus and the Samaritan woman (John 4:1–42). In reading the New Testament from the perspective of valuing children in their relational capacity, we do not find such strong biblical stories.[9] The stories where children are given a voice (as Jesus in the temple and Isaac on the way to mount Moriah) are usually interpreted historically in light of an ethos of obedience.[10]

6 Luke 2:49: "He replied, 'Why were you looking for me? Did you not know that I must be in my Father's house?"

7 Gen 22:7 "Isaac said to his father Abraham, 'Father!' And he said, 'Here I am, my son.' He said, 'The fire and the wood are here, but where is the lamb for a burnt offering?" [NRSV]. Within the Jewish midrash tradition, Isaac is not considered as a child, but as a man of 37 years who agreed to be bound. (cf. van de Sandt: 2003, 21f).

8 In Matt 11:16f children are given a voice. They speak for themselves. However this text is a metaphor, that does not deal with real children. We cite the text: "But to what will I compare this generation? It is like children sitting in the marketplaces and calling to one another, 'We played the flute for you, and you did not dance; we wailed, and you did not mourn.'" [NRSV].

9 In the New Testament we find some 'children texts'. One can refer to Mark 10:13–16, 9:33–37 (and parallels in Matt 18:1–5 and Luke 9:46ff) or to children in the miracle stories (Matt 8:5–13, Luke 10:1–10, Mark 9:14–29, Matt 17:14–21, Luke 9:37–43, Mark 5:21–43, Matt 9:18–26, Luke 8:40–56, Mark 7:24–30, Matt 15:21–28). [Schomaker: 2002, 181–192]. Note that in these stories, children are never referred to by their own names.

10 For an interpretation of the sacrifice of Isaac from the ethos of obedience and critique on this ethos, see de Haardt: 2003, 49f. In the Catechism of the Catholic Church the text about the 'fourth commandment' (Honour your father and your mother) refers to the text of Luke 2:51: "[…] and was obedient to them". This text is put after the fourth commandment (Exod 20:12) and before the call to obedience of Eph 6:1–3 [Katechismus, p. 464]. See also Kähler: 2002, 102. "Jesus wird zur Ikone des braven Jungen, wie ihn eine bestimmte Pädagogik haben wollte bzw. will. Zugleich wird er in dieser Zuschreibung zur Verkörperung des unschuldigen Kindes, das seine Tugend in der Beziehung auf den Erwachsenen, den Lehrer, gewinnt. Jesus steht für das eifrige, ja beflissene Lernen, die Akzeptanz der Tradition und den Gehorsam gegenüber der Autorität."

In the New Testament, the child is presented as an example of people who are seen as 'petty'. Small and powerless people are named by the word νηπιος (*nèpios*) (in Latin: *in-fans*, incapable of speaking, literally translated) (for instance Matt 11:16, 21:16, Luke 10:21 and Matthew 11:25) (Schomaker: 2002, 185). The meaning of 'child' and 'infant' are similar in the ancient context, according to the German theologian Schomaker (2002, 185). In this sense, the image of the child in the New Testament was not totally different from its image in neighbouring cultures: children were, according to both the authors of the New Testament and other authors of Greco-Roman antiquity, seen as 'infants', those who were unable to speak for themselves (Kähler: 2002, 105f). In the New Testament however, children are valued because of this infancy. New Testament texts about children cannot easily be applied in our contemporary context or in the theories of recent 'childhood studies'. The New Testament texts call for a critical re-thinking, a 'resistant reading'. 'Resistant reading' means 'reading against the text', or searching for meanings that come to mind by reading and that contrast with what the text initially seems to say. This 'resistant reading' presupposes that one sees 'revelation' as something of the future and which is not fixed in the past. The idea that adults can learn from children in general is an important idea that is expressed in the New Testament texts about children (Mark 10:13–16 and parallel texts), and that needs to be taken seriously. However, the presentation in Mark 10 can also lead to the pitfalls of essentialising children or seeing them only as vulnerable infants. When reading biblical texts from the perspective of children – taking a partial and child-biased position, because of the silenced place children had in the biblical interpretation (Mercer: 2005, 22) – broader ideas about children arise. They are partly inspired by Christian theology (e. g. the idea of the dignity of each child) and partly by human sciences and contemporary ideas (cf. above). It is through the dialogue between these positions that can come alive in a Christian community with the biblical texts that revelation emerges. The texts need to be confronted with the idea of the 'competent child' and the aim, presented by different practical theologians, to educate children in responsible thinking and speaking and a reflexive way about faith (Kähler: 2002, 83–102).

A resistant reading (cf. Reinhartz: 2001, 81–98) of the biblical texts about children with the additional interpretation of respecting the 'child as a child' in (religious) education brings us to a reflection on the concrete giving of children and their individual relational contexts. Children not only 'give' to adults by their 'being' and by being 'a child', but also by their concrete contributions to relationships and by their participation in a variety of activities.

7. Nagy and the Giving Child

The Hungarian-American psychotherapist Ivan Boszormenyi-Nagy speaks about the 'giving child' in the context of his view on parent-child relations and the balance of give and take which plays a role in every relation.

> Even very small children are sensitive barometers; they know when their parents are overburdened with anxiety, guilt and mistrust. Moreover, they want to do something about it. Clinical observation of families gives ample indications of how enormously giving and caring very young offspring want to be toward their massively needy parents. (Boszormenyi-Nagy/Krasner: 1986, 15).

> Yet in our experience, the innate tendency to care about other people is characteristic of very young children rather than limited to parents or parenting figures. Family therapy demonstrates how caring and appropriately considerate three- or four-year-old children can be towards squabbling and mistrustful parents. […] A child whose attitudes and contributions to his parents' well-being are recognized and acknowledged will learn to choose to earn constructive entitlement. He will grasp the rewarding characteristics of caring. Conversely, children whose naturally caring propensities are routinely manipulated and exploited suffer from the most destructive features of chronic parentification. An adult can misuse a child's care for him or her rather than be willing to pay the costs of contributing to the child's autonomous individuation. (Ibid, 78).

Nagy encourages parents to credit their children for their concrete giving. Even when a child is very small, or when a child has a handicap, he or she is able to care in some way for the parents. The laugh of a child and the concrete attempt to help in the household are only some examples of how children can give to their parents. The child can feel when the mother is sad and will try to cheer her up, and when the father and the mother are quarrelling, it is often the child who tries to reconcile them. Also on the level of religiosity, a child can give, for instance by asking pertinent questions, by being quiet in church, by praying as the parents do, etc. It is however, as Nagy says, very important that the parents give the child recognition for giving. If not, the child could be destructively 'parentificated', meaning that the child feels it is necessary to take on the role of the parents, has too much responsibility and does not receive enough recognition for these heavy tasks.

The theory of Nagy is complementary with general ideas about the relevance of children in theories about religious education. Nagy opens our eyes to the concrete giving of each child, and he adds that it is very important for every child that he or she receives recognition for his or her giving. If this recognition is missing, the child is in a certain sense 'indebted' to the world: he or she has given too much, and there is a kind of open account. The danger is then that children can apply this indebtedness in a destructive way and take from others what they need.

Nagy's insight that each child can give, is in a certain sense based on the general view, which we developed above, that children are valuable and that a child 'as a child' is very important. By focussing more on each child as an individual, however, the danger of idealising children can be avoided. It is possible for a parent to discover that his or her child is not this beautiful present as projected by popular literature, media and talk. Speaking in general terms about the value of 'the child as a child' is not very helpful in such a situation when the parent has discovered that children are not angels. An ethical approach to the parent-child relation focuses on the parental task of searching for the child's small ways of giving, even when he or she seems to be unmanageable. By recognising the child for his or her giving, the unmanageable child may become more manageable.

8. The Giving Child in Theories of Religious Education

The idea of the concrete giving of each particular child has implications for existing theories about religious education. When speaking about 'participation' as a model for religious education (Hermans: 2001, 272), it is important to attribute to participation not only the meaning of actively taking part in something, but also of having a voice and the right to have one's own, specific contribution. Adults can learn from children and vice versa; not only can they learn from the general humility and trust of a child, but they may also gain specific insights. For example, when a child remarks on the strangeness of God's creating the world, and His presence in the heart of everyone, as told by her parents, the parents are confronted with a need to think again about their own beliefs. Another child shows an adult that praying need not be difficult. He prays when he sees a cross, and utters spontaneously his sorrows to Christ. Religious education is not just transmission of faith, but can be seen as mutual learning in faith (Nipkow: 1982; Ploeger: 1993, 73f, 97; Lanser: 2002, 129).

This idea of religious education is expressed in the theory of the mutual or transformative learning of faith. This mutual learning of faith is being researched by the Dutch theologian Alma Lanser-Van de Velde on the basis of the theory of Dewey and on the basis of empirical research (Lanser: 2002, 130f). This theory offers a perspective on the interaction between parents and children, although we won't deal with it in detail here. Learning in cooperation with and from each other can be seen as a co-actional process. Educators and children mutually influence each other, and the influence of a child upon the educator also has consequences for the educator's actions and the influence the educator has upon the child. The content of the faith tradition and the faith experience that is the object of the co-actional learning process should be seen in a dynamic way. In the literature about religious education, we find the word 'appropriation' (cf. Becker/Scheilke: 1995) (of the learning person) to indicate that the learning person is making him or herself familiar with what is learned; additionally, this content probably acquires other connotations and interpretations during the learning process;

> Es gehe darum, sich von der Vorstellung eines 'passiv-rezeptiven' Subjects, das vorgegebene Sinnmuster in einem affirmativen und fremdreferentiellen Modus der Aneignung von Sinn übernimmt, zu verabschieden und ein 'aktiv-rekonstruierendes' Subjekt in den Blick zu nehmen, das selbstreferentiell eine je eigene Biographie zu entwerfen und zu realisieren in der Lage ist. (cf. Scholl: 1995, 128).[11]

The concept of 'appropriation' refers, however, mainly to the process in an individual person, and less to the whole process of mutual influencing (Lanser: 2002, 141).

9. Beyond a Struggle of Autonomous Persons: a Call to Responsibility

Co-actional, mutual or transformative learning are each a clear critique of a unidirectional socialisation approach. One could ask, however, if the change from a unidirectional approach of teaching to a bidirectional approach offers something fundamentally different. When adding a move from children towards parents to the traditional line from parents towards children, it is not yet clear how these two lines of interaction are related to each other. In childhood studies, one speaks about a certain autonomy of children. But if two autonomous subjects, parent and child, interact one is confronted with the question of power or equity in the relationship. Some authors clearly criticise the idea of mutual learning, because they are afraid that the active giving of the child means that a child will determine everything in a family or other educational context. Some authors warn against permissiveness and stress the need for giving children clear guidelines and directions.[12] Parental abuse then becomes a possibility, but one can also see this approach as a kind of educative neglect of children (Anatrella: 1998, 295).[13] The alternative is to give parents the authority and to defend a kind of authoritarian parenting.

11 See also: Schmälzle: 1998.

12 See also P. Moreau, La famille, enjeu citoyen, p. 78: "Nier l'inégalité de fait entre l'adulte et l'enfant, et par là refuser, entre l'éducateur et l'éduqué, l'inégalité de statut que justifie pourtant la justice distributive, c'est alors se faire complice de la violence qui s'exerce sur les enfants lorsque, de cette manière, on se refuse à prendre soin d'eux, à les protéger efficacement."

13 "[…] il ne faudrait pas omettre leur abandon éducatif, qui est actuellement le problème majoritaire."

Thereby, one focuses often on the role of the father and the law (Anatrella: 1998, 17–67). For the sake of the children, this authoritarian parenting seems – according to some authors – more preferable than the bidirectional view of the parent-child relationship that tends to give a lot of power to children. This vision, however, is the consequence of a rather dualistic approach of parents and children, whereby 'power' is the central category. Either the parent or the child wins the struggle for power.

We need an alternative view on the relation between parents and children that is not based on a struggle of power between subjects that defend their autonomy and where the autonomy of the one has to be victimised by the autonomy of the other. The sociologist Knapp finds such an alternative approach in the theory of responsibility through and for the other, as it has been developed by Levinas. This alternative approach does not focus on the struggle for power, nor does it contrast the child as an autonomous and active subject radically with the child as an object in need of protection and socialising. This alternative view starts from a positive image of the human being that is characterised by connectedness. The connectedness between people is essentially ethical and directed towards responsibility (Knapp: 1999, 69).[14] The parent-child relation is characterised by heteronomy. In this sense, Knapp's vision of the parent-child relation passes over the modern ideas about autonomy and brings in a certain element of transcendence, namely heteronomous responsibility. Knapp sees the child as 'active' in the sense of sending an ethical appeal to the parent who is called to behave in a responsible way. This view avoids the critique that a multidirectional view on the parent-child relation can lead to educational neglect. The appeal of the child asks for responsibility, and this responsibility is not limited to giving protection and care, but also allows for the participation of children. The concrete responsibility of a parent can be expressed in a democratic education. The basis of this education is not a power struggle or any 'autonomy' theory, but the heteronymous appeal to responsibility.

Levinas' idea about 'continuity' and 'discontinuity' between parent and child further explains the idea of parents' responsibility. Parents have the task of recognising their child as 'the other'. This is also what is expressed in the famous sentence of Kahlil Gibran 'your children are not your children' Gibran: 1946, 18). Levinas points to the complexity of the father-son relationship: "Fatherhood is a relation to a stranger that I am, although it is an other; the relation of the 'I' towards a 'my-self', who is nevertheless a stranger to me […] I do not *have* my child; I *am* in a certain sense my child." (Levinas:

14 "Relations between parents and children, brothers and sisters, husbands and wives, and so on are all grounded in fundamental face-to-face relations that inevitably entail moral responsibility. Levinas calls upon us to dismiss the assumption that familial relations are best understood in amoral terms, or that it is even possible to fully understand parent-child relations in narratives that deny any place at all for a fundamental moral responsibility."

1991, 85f).[15] The son comes forth from the father, and in this sense one can speak about 'continuity', about "a renewal of the father in the son" and a "fusion with him" (Levinas: 1987, 61). But at the same time the son – or more generally the child – is the radical other, who may not be possessed by the father, or the parent. To see the child as the radical 'other' who is not the fulfilment of the parent's own dreams can be interpreted as a stimulus for taking the child 'as a child' (and not as a 'not yet adult') seriously. One could refer to Levinas when demonstrating the relevance of giving 'children their own voice'.

At the same time, those who prefer the 'protection and socialisation' paradigm of children can also find their own philosophical background in Levinas' ideas. An educational vision about responsibility and the ethical appeal that is always present in the parent-child relationship based on Levinas' thought, runs the risk of presenting the child only as very vulnerable and may neglect the competence of the child. In this sense, the vision of the psychiatrist Ivan Boszormenyi-Nagy, whereby responsibility for the child is also central, is more balanced because the giving of the child and the care of the child get more attention. Nagy calls attention to the fact that each child can and wants to give to the parents, by caring, by being happy, by obeying, by taking over certain attitudes, etc. (Boszormenyi-Nagy/Krasner: 1986, 15). A child is vulnerable and should be protected against responsibilities that are too heavy explains Nagy when he develops the concept of 'parentification': the process in which a child is given the role of a parent and receives too much responsibility, which can be destructive for the child's later development. At the same time, it is important that parents also create room for children to 'give to them' and to take up certain responsibilities. If not, the balance of giving and taking is off. A fair relationship between parents and children is one whereby the parents give the child recognition for its giving, and do not claim the giving of the child. Ethical responsibility in the parent-child relationship is not dependent upon mutuality and exact measures of the give and take balance, but it is important to recognise the mutual give and take in parent-child relations to be able to speak about a just relationship and to really behave responsibly.

10. Conclusion

I have developed an ethical reflection on the relevance of taking the concrete giving of children seriously. In some approaches of religious education, children already receive recognition for their concrete giving. I mention in particu-

15 "La paternité est la relation avec un étranger qui, tout en étant autrui, est moi; la relation du moi avec un moi-même, qui est cependant étranger à moi. […] Je n'ai pas mon enfant; je suis en quelque manière mon enfant". See also Levinas: 1987, 60f.

lar the movement of 'theologising with children' (e. g. Bucher: 1991a; Bucher, 1991b; Klein: 2000; Eckerle: 2001; Büttner/Thierfelder: 2001; Wacker/With: 2002; Bucher: 2002; Bucker: 2003; Bucher: 2004), in analogy with doing philosophy with children. The theoretical idea that the naive theology of children should be taken seriously is valuable, but is also an example of a theory that runs the risk of essentialising children. The practice of theologising with children, however, treats children seriously as individuals, and 'little theologians' (Dillen: 2007). It is this serious consideration of the child's own particular contribution concerning religious communication that I want to defend.

References

Anatrella, T. (1998), La Difference Interdite. Sexualité, Education, Violence. Trente ans après Mai 68, Paris.

Ariés, P. (1960), L'enfant et la Vie Familiale sous l'Ancien Régime (Civilisations d'hier et d'aujourd'hui), Paris.

Astley, J. (1996), 'The Role of the Family in the Formation and Criticism of Faith', in S. C. Barton (ed.), The Family in Theological Perspective, Edingburgh.

Becker, U./Scheilke, C. T. (ed.) (1995), Aneignung und Vermittlung. Beiträge zu Theorie und Praxis einer religionspädagogischen Hermeneutik. Für Klaus Goßmann zum 65. Geburtstag, Gütersloh.

Boschki, R. (2003), Beziehung als Leitbegriff der Religionspädagogik. Grundlegung einer dialogisch kreativen Religionsdidaktik (Glaubenskommunikation Reihe Zeitzeichen, 13), Ostfildern.

Boszormenyi-Nagy, I./Krasner, B. R. (1986), Between, Give and Take. A Clinical Guide to Contextual Therapy, New York.

Bucher, A. A. (1991a), Gottesvorstellungen in der kindliche Entwicklung, in Lebendige Katechese 13, 19–24.

Bucher, A. A. (1991b), Gott ist ein Mensch für mich... Gottesbilder im Grundschulalter, in Katechetisc Blätter 116, 331–335.

Bucher, A. A. et al. (ed.) (2002), Mittendrin ist Gott, Stuttgart.

Bucher, A. A. et al. (ed.) (2003), Im Himmelreich ist kein Sauer. Kinder als Exegeten (Jahrbuch für Kindertheologie, 2), Stuttgart.

Bucher, A. A. et al. (ed.) (2004), Zeit ist immer da. Kinder erleben Hoch-Zeiten und Fest-Tage (Jahrbuch für Kindertheologie, 3), Stuttgart.

Bunge, M. (ed.), (2001), The Child in Christian Thought, Grand Rapids, MI.

Büttner, G./Thierfelder, J. (ed.) (2001), Trug Jesus Sandalen? Kinder und Jugendliche sehen Jesus Christus, Göttingen.

Couture, P. (2000), Seeing Children, Seeing God. A Practical Theology of Children and Poverty, Nashville, TN.

De Haardt, M. (2003), 'Abrahams Offer: Prototype van Gehoorzaamheid, Prototype van Geloof? Over Gender, Monogenese en Monotheïsme', in R. te Velde (ed.), Doen wat God wil: Zegen of Ramp? Over Ethiek en Religie in het Licht van Abrahams offer, Budel.

Depaepe, M. ([2]1999), De Pedagogisering Achterna, Aanzet tot een Genealogie van de Pedagogische Mentaliteit in de Voorbije 250 Jaar, Leuven-Amersfoort.

Devries, D. (2001), 'Toward a Theology of Childhood', in Interpretation 55, no. 2, 161–173.

Dillen, A. (2005), Het gezin: à-Dieu? Naar een Contextuele Ethiek, Theologie en (Godsdienst)Pedagogiek van gezinnen Vandaag. Unpublished PhD – Faculty of Theology, K. U. Leuven, Leuven.

Dillen, A. (2007), 'Theologising with Children: A New Paradigm for Catholic Religious Education in Belgium and New Challenges for Catholic Schools', in G. Grace & J. O'Keefe (ed.), International Handbook for Catholic Education, New York, (in press).

Eckerle, S. et al. (2001), Gott der Kinder. Ein Forschungsprojekt zu Bildern und Gottesvorstellungen von Kinderen, Münster.

Gibran, K. (1946), The Prophet, New York.

Hanlon Rubio, J. (2003), A Christian Theology of Marriage and Family, Mahwah, NJ.

Hauerwas, S. (1981), A Community of Character. Toward a Constructive Christian Ethics, Notre Dame, NI.

Hemrica, J. C. (2004), Kind-zijn tussen opvoeding en Recht. Een Grondslagenonderzoek naar Kindbeelden, Antwerpen-Apeldoorn.

Hermans, C. A. (2001), Participerend leren. Grondslagen van Religieuze Vorming in een Globaliserende Samenleving (iko-reeks, 1), Budel.

Kähler, C. (2003), 'Wenn ihr nicht werdet wie Kinder … Kindsein als Metapher im Neuen Testament', in R. Lux (ed.), Schau auf die Kleinen … Das Kind in Religion, Kirche und Gesellschaft, Leipzig.

Klein, S. (2000), Gottesbilder von Mädchen. Bilder und Gespräche als Zugänge zur kindlichen religiösen Vorstellungswelt, Stuttgart.

Knapp, S. J. (1999), 'Facing the Child. Rethinking Models of Agency in Parent-Child Relations', in C. L. Shehan (ed.), Through the Eyes of the Child. Revisioning Children as Active Agents of Family Live (Contemporary Perspectives on Family Research, 1), Stamford, CT.

Koops, W./Terworgt, M. M. (1994), 'Vroegkinderlijke Psychologische Theorieën. Een Overzicht van Actueel Onderzoek', in P. Steerneman/H. Pelzer (ed.), Sociale Cognitie en Sociale Competentie bij Kinderen en Jeugdigen, Leuven.

Koops, W. (1997), 'Het Moderne Kind als Kleine Volwassene', in H. Baartman et al. (ed.), Gezinnen onder Druk. Over Veranderende Ouder-Kind Relaties, Kampen.

Lanser, A. (2002), Geloven Leren. Een Theoretisch en Empirisch Onderzoek naar Wederkerig Geloofsleren, in Praktische Theologie 29, no. 2, 127–142.

Levinas, E. ([4]1991), Le temps et l'autre, Paris.

Levinas, E. (1987), Ethisch en Oneindig. Gesprekken met Philippe Nemo. Introduced by R. Bakker (translated from the French by C. J. Huizinga), Kampen-Kapellen.

Meilander, G. (1990), 'A Christian View of the Family', in D. Blankenhorn et al. (ed.), Rebuilding the Nest. A New Commitment to the American Family, Milwaukee.

Mercer, J. A. (2005), Welcoming Children. A Practical Theology of Childhood, Saint Louis, MO.

Moyaert, M./Pollefeyt, D. (2004), 'De Pedagogie tussen Maakbaarheid en Verbeelding', in Ethische Perspectieven 14, nr. 1.

Mussen, P. H. (ed.) (1983), Handbook of Child Psychology. Volume II, New York.

Nipkow, K.-E. (1982), Grundfragen der Religionspädagogik. Band III: Gemeinsam Leben und Glauben Lernen, Gütersloh.

Ploeger, A. K. (1993), Inleiding in de godsdienstpedagogiek, Kampen.

Pollock, L. A. (1983), Forgotten Children. Parent-Child Relations from 1500 to 1900, Cambridge.

Reinhartz, A. (2001), Befriending the Beloved Disciple. A Jewish Reading of the Gospel of John, New York.

Rieffe, C./Koops, W./Terworgt, M. M. (1996), 'Vroegkinderlijk begrip van mentale processen. The Child's Theory of Mind', in J. D. Bosch et al. (ed.), Jaarboek Ontwikkelingspsychologie, Orthopedagogiek en Kinderpsychiatrie, Houten-Diegem, Bohn Stafleu Van Loghum, 216–236.

Schmälzle, U. F. (1998), 'Von der Vermittlung zur Aneignung. Überlegungen zum Paradigmenwechsel in der Katechese', in F.-P. Tebartz-van Elst (ed.), Katechese im Umbruch. Positionen und Perspektiven. Für Dieter Emeis, Freiburg im Breisgau-Bazel-Wenen.

Schöll, A. (1995), '"Hermeneutik der Aneignun". Sozialwissenschaftliche und Empirische Vergewisserungen', in U. Becker/C. T. Scheilke (ed.), Aneignung und Vermittlung. Beiträge zu Theorie und Praxis einer religionspädagogischen Hermeneutik. Für Klaus Goßmann zum 65. Geburtstag, Gütersloh.

SCHOMAKER, F. (2002), Die Bedeutung der Familie in Katechetischen Lernprozessen von Kindern. Eine Inhaltsanalytische Untersuchung von Konzepten zur Hinführung der Kinder zu den Sakramenten der Beichte und der Eucharistie, Münster, Lit.

SCHWEITZER, F. (2000), Das Recht des Kindes auf Religion. Ermutigungen für Eltern und Erzieher, Gütersloh.

THATCHER, A. (1999), Marriage after Modernity. Christian Marriage in Postmodern Times, Sheffield.

VAN DEN BERGH, B. (1998), 'Kindbeeld in Context. Wisselwerking tussen de Maatschappelijke en Wetenschappelijke Benadering van Kinderen', in Ethiek en Maatschappij 4, 92–115.

VAN DEN BERGH, B. (2003), 'Kinderen, Opvoeders en Maatschappij: Verkenningstocht of Verplichte Wandeling?', in L. Ackaert et al. (ed.), Kom je dat thuis eens Vertellen? Visies van ouders en Kinderen op het Dagelijks Leven in het Gezin, Leuven-Leusden.

VAN DE SANDT, H. (2003), De Vroegjoodse Receptie van Genesis 22: Twee Perspectieven, in R. te Velde (ed.), Doen wat God wil: Zegen of Ramp? Over Ethiek en Religie in het Licht van Abrahams Offer, Budel.

VANOBBERGEN, B. (2003), Geen Kinderspel. Een Pedagogische Analyse van de Vertogen over de Commercialisering van de Leefwereld van Kinderen, Gent.

VERGOUWEN, C. G. (2001), Een Hemelsbrede Gelijkenis. Geloofsopvoeding in Godsdienstpsychologisch Perspectief (Studies op het Terrein der Godsdienstpsychologie, 9), Kampen.

VERHELLEN, E. (^{4}2000), Verdrag inzake de Rechten van het Kind. Achtergronden, Motieven, Strategieën, Hoofdlijnen, Leuven-Apeldoorn, article 14.

WACKER, M.-T. /WITH, R. (ed.) (2002), Gottes Kinder. Jahrbuch für Biblische Theologie, Neukirchen-Vluyn.

WALL, J. (2004), Let the Little Children Come. Child Rearing as Challenge to Contemporary Christian Ethics in Horizons 31, nr. 1, 64–87.

WHITMORE, T. D./WINRIGHT, T. (1997), 'Children: An Undeveloped Theme in Catholic Teaching', in M.A. Ryan/T.D. Whitmore (ed.), The Challenge of Global Stewardship. Roman Catholic Responses, Notre Dame.

http://www.unhchr.ch/html/menu3/b/k2crc.htm

Rethinking Human Rights in Light of Children

John Wall
Rutgers University, New Jersey

It was only in the twentieth century that the notion of "children's rights" gained widespread usage and official sanction such as in international charters and declarations. Previously, "human rights" were typically thought to extend only to adults, children occupying a private realm of family distinct from the larger political order. The Enlightenment architects of modern human rights theory – John Locke, Jean-Jacques Rousseau, and Immanuel Kant – explicitly argue against children possessing public rights on the grounds that children as yet lack the moral autonomy to be able to hold them without doing themselves harm.

The recent intensification of interest in children's rights around the globe arises from a historically changing sense that children are not just parts of families (however broadly understood) or even objects of state aid but also distinctive and participating social citizens. That is, children engage in social practices and have just as much a stake as adults in social constructions of wealth, health care, gender, class, and the like. In the wake of industrialization and its sharp "separate spheres" of public and private life, there is now a worldwide movement to integrate children in more meaningful ways into the public arena.

This movement for children's rights, however, has not been without its ambiguities and its critics. Ambiguities include the fact that children – and especially younger children – generally rely on rights being granted to them not by themselves but by adults; that children may not be as well able as adults to stand up for and defend their public interests and liberties for themselves; and that, as a result, the analogy often cited to women's rights may not entirely make sense. Critics argue that most children still lack the moral capability to possess at least many public rights (such as voting); that treating children as rights-bearing individuals obscures their vulnerabilities and dependency, thus ignoring what makes childhood distinctive; and that, especially as argued in my own country, the United States, the children's rights framework undermines the more crucial importance to children of families, setting up a conflict between the rights of children and those of parents.

This paper uses postmodern Christian resources to argue that children do indeed deserve public rights but that considering children's rights requires a fundamentally new rethinking of the language of human rights overall. Traditional modernistic groundings of human rights leave out children inherently, because they are based on the distinctively adult-centered point of view of an individualistic rationality. Postmodernity offers a more child-centered alternative foundation of human rights because it bases ethics instead in diversity and otherness. Children are just as "other" as anyone else. However, postmodern ethicists have not, in general, considered the question of how social ethics should be shaped in light of children. As a result, I appropriate Christian ethical resources to tap into deeper historical senses of otherness that, when interpreted in creative new ways, allow it to include children and children's rights centrally.

This complex hermeneutical procedure of refashioning ethics in the face of children is far from alien to Christianity. This religion, after all, traces its origins to the transforming birth two thousand years ago of an infant. The self-reflective gesture of thinking from the point of view of childhood I call "childism," in analogy to similar hermeneutical gestures of feminism, womanism, environmentalism, and even humanism, all of which childism (in fact though not in name) arguably predates. Placing children at its center has informed and challenged both Christian and other ethical and theological norms throughout history in conflicting and sometimes surprising ways. Here I argue that this complex tradition of Christian ethical childism should be reshaped once again so that human rights, in light of children, are understood not as furthering autonomy but as concrete markers for creative societal decentering in loving response to each other.

I illustrate the need for a new interpretation of human rights of this kind around some of the key children's rights documents that have been created throughout the twentieth century. These can be seen as struggling gradually toward a similarly "childist" point of view. I also engage the childhood studies field among sociologists, anthropologists, historians, lawyers, and others, which is partly responsible for framing and interpreting the most recent children's rights document, the United Nations' 1989 Convention on the Rights of the Child. Christian ethicists and church leaders have not engaged in these discussions as deeply as they should. This dearth of religious ethical reflection is especially evident in the United States, whose failure to ratify the 1989 Convention (alongside only Somalia) is attributable in large part to the concerns of Christian groups.

However much rights language is not the only way to speak ethically about children, failing to address children's rights will continue to hurt children themselves, both in the United States and worldwide. The solution is not to abandon the discourse of human rights, which can and has taken many meanings in history. It is to transform it in light of children so that the many difficulties of globalization, cultural pluralism, and market individualism in today's world may be addressed in a more fully child-centered way.

1. Childism in Christianity

The Christian moral tradition has reshaped itself in light of children in at least three distinctive ways. These can be termed "bottom-up," "top-down," and "dialectical." Such historical forms of childism do not succeed one another over time but have gained relative prominence at diverse times throughout the two thousand years of Christian thought and practice. They do, however, share certain fundamental moral questions, including most prominently these three: What does childhood teach us ontologically about the nature of human "being"? How does considering childhood redefine a society's common teleological purposes or aims? And how does the lens of childhood help to reinterpret human deontological responsibilities toward one another? These are questions respectively, in theological terms, of faith, hope, and love. Answers to them have provided a vast array of different and sometimes contrary perspectives on children, as well, therefore, as diverse interpretations today of the meaning and significance for children of human rights.

The "bottom-up" approach frequently takes as its touchstone Jesus' proclamation in all three synoptic gospels that "unless you change and become like children, you will never enter the kingdom of heaven." (Matt 18:3–5; Mark 9:33–37; and Luke 9:46–48). Each distinct human being enters the world in infancy with its own unique good gifts from God. Sinfulness derives not from children but from the corruptions of larger collective society. In children we discover the purest and most immediate "image of God" in the world – God incarnated in humanity – to which adults should aspire in their hope to become genuine "children of God."

Thus, for example, second and third century theologians like Clement of Alexandria, Origen, Tertullian, Cyprian, and Gregory of Nyssa all encourage adults to imitate children's moral simplicity, freedom from desire, sexual purity, and indifference toward worldly status and wealth (Bakke: 2005).[1] The Eastern Christian thinker John Chrysostom sees in children's purity from worldly passions and resentments "the height of true wisdom." (Bakke: 2005, 78). Thus also, in modernity, Jean-Jacques Rousseau refashions such an argument around the more secular lines that children present society with uncorrupted "noble savages" who love themselves and others fully (*amour de soi*) rather than merely for self-gain (*amour-propre*) (Rousseau: 1979). The founder of modern Protestant theology, Friedrich Schleiermacher, declares in his many writings on children that children are "the pure revelation of the divine," since they incarnate natural "gifts" for joy – indeed children are the true "gift" of Christmas – and "baptize" adults into God by show-

---

1 For larger discussions of religious figures' views of children see Bunge: 2001; Browning/Bunge: forthcoming 2008.

ing humanity what is truly meant by its "feeling of absolute dependence" on the divine (Schleiermacher: 1989, 15, 29; 1990, 36, 39, 45, 55; 1991). In the twentieth century, the Catholic theologian Karl Rahner sees in children humanity's aim of "eternity," "openness," and "validity in God's sight." (Rahner: 1977, 33–50).

In the United States, such a view of children profoundly shapes moral beliefs about both children and society: from children's own intense sentimentalization as pure and good; the enormous value placed on the private haven of the family against a corrupted public realm; American "nationhood" as expressing a nostalgic wholesome childlike "natality";[2] and a strong ethos of market capitalism that assumes inner individual desires to be ultimately better than outer societal restraints. It also deeply shapes how Americans in particular think of human rights. As legal theorist Barbara Bennett Woodhouse has pointed out, the United States' founding Constitution and its subsequent interpretation are built primarily around so-called "negative" or liberty rights, rights to state and social *non*-interference. In contrast, "positive" rights to state and social aid and welfare, whether for children or for adults, remain relatively suspect. Why? Because on a bottom-up view of the human good, the collective public realm itself is presumed largely corrupt. Government is more likely to be the problem than the solution, especially in relation to the private home, and so its role should be limited chiefly to protecting the negative rights of individual liberty.

The irony of this childist perspective is that in the process of humanizing childhood as good it also profoundly dehumanizes it. In a similar way to women and minorities, it tends to place children on such an ethereal pedestal that it ends up justifying their larger public marginalization. If children are *models* of the good, then beyond negative or liberty protections, adults and societal institutions owe them very little. This irony helps to explain why children in early Christianity, for example, were highly valued but also frequently left behind by parents seeking to become martyrs, or sometimes even encouraged to become martyrs themselves. It also allows the wealthiest country in the world, the United States, to romanticize children in politics and mass media while, in contrast with other developing countries, denying them basic common goods like guaranteed health insurance and consistently sustaining the highest rates of child poverty. Children as "images of God" can be driven to the extreme of removing children from concrete earthly concern.

In contrast, a "top-down" tradition of Christian childism, more frequently derived from Paul's letters and the prior influence of Plato, has insisted instead that children enter the world as embodiments of human unruliness or

2 See Levander: 1998

original sin. Children should not be left to their own devices but require strong community and society disciplining into reason and morality.

Thus, Paul says one must "put an end to childish ways" in order to overcome the passions of the flesh and live according to the grace of the spirit (1 Cor 13:11). This echoes in a way Plato's two major writings in social ethics, *The Republic* and *The Laws*, which had argued extensively, five hundred years earlier, that child rearing is the key to turning humanity's animal brutishness into reasoned social order (Plato: 1961, 1379). Likewise, the neo-Platonism of Augustine in the fourth century sees in children the embodiment of human being's original sin: their violent disregard for others and narrowness of pride, faults we should strive to root out as we grow up toward God (Augustine: 1961, 27). David F. Wright has even argued that Augustine's creation of the doctrine of original sin is significantly in part an effort to explain the widespread early Christian practice of infant baptism, which did not entirely square with the then prevailing notion of infant purity (Wright: 1987, 51).[3] Reformation Protestants like Martin Luther and John Calvin similarly suggest that in childhood we find humanity's "seeds of sin" which need disciplining by God's grace enacted through a powerful church, society, and state in order not to grow into "fruits of sin." (Calvin: 1960).[4] The eighteenth century founder of Methodism, John Wesley, who wrote voluminously on child rearing and education and created many successful schools and orphanages, claims that children need their wills broken from infancy and in school "ought never to play" so they can learn rigor and discipline (Wesley: 1975, II.5,3:370).[5] And even the pietist Enlightenment thinker Immanuel Kant, in a non-theological way in his little known last published work titled *Education*, describes rational moral autonomy as the victory of "cultivation" or *Bildung* over children's heteronomous "animal" desires (Kant: 1960, 11, 6).

Such a view is today enjoying something of a resurgence, particularly in conservative and fundamentalist movements in the United States and globally that are concerned with a perceived corrosion of social order and children's moral upbringing. On the whole, this top-down tradition has stood at the forefront of opposing the application of human rights to children. It sees children as unready for the public responsibilities that human rights entail. However, it also yields an at least implicit, and sometimes explicit, notion of the rights of parents, families, and religious communities. These are again "negative" rights, but in this case to raise one's children free of public interference and according to one's own particular moral and traditional values. The danger, however, is a different form of children's dehumanization: the notion that

3 Quoted in O.M. Bakke: 2005, 241.

4 For commentary on Calvin's view of children see Pitkin: 2001, 167.

5 See also Minutes of the Methodist Conferences (London: John Mason, 1862), 1:164.

children must be socialized *into* morality because they lack an intrinsic moral sense of their own. It is difficult to think of children as possessing their own voices and agency in the world when one's focus lies principally in their needs for clear moral disciplining. At its extreme, this form of childism, like its opposite above, both humanizes and dehumanizes children in the very same movement.

Different again is a third "dialectical" childism that is neither bottom-up nor top-down but relational or developmental. On this view, children begin life neither innocent nor sinful but neutral or in potential. Human nature begins in childhood able to develop gradually, through social relations and particularly attachment to parents, into increasingly rational, moral, and responsible participation in society.

This tradition arises in Christianity from syntheses of biblical norms chiefly with Aristotelianism, often via Islam. Aristotle himself, disagreeing with his teacher Plato, sees children's animality as not so much unruliness as inherent natural potential. While children remain incapable of full virtue or happiness, in Aristotle's view, they nevertheless can *develop* reason, morality, and civilization through natural emerging processes of social relationality (Aristotle: 1947a; 1947b). Similarly, the medieval theologian Thomas Aquinas's "natural law" ethics is both reflected in and reflective of his view that children develop through four natural seven-year stages of increasing reason and morality. In the first seven years of life a child is an "irrational animal," but in the second can learn from others, in the third can begin to think for himself, and finally around twenty-one gains the full "use of reason" as also thinking along with others (Aquinas: 1948).[6] A different kind of dialectical perspective arises in John Locke's secular Enlightenment theory of children as "white pages" or "wax" able to be written on or molded over time by adult education into scientific and moral reason (Locke: 1989, 105; 138f). In this, Locke differs from his Enlightenment successors Rousseau and Kant, even if all share the aim of social reason, in viewing children as starting out morally neutral. More recently, Catholic subsidiarity theory has interpreted child rearing dialectically as furnishing children's moral development with concentric circles of family, church, community, and state support so that children may grow toward participation in the larger common good.

Today, this dialectical or developmental kind of childism has its greatest influence, especially in the United States, through developmental psychology. A child on this view, broadly speaking, does not begin life morally good or evil but rather increases gradually over time, through interaction in family and society, in moral and social capabilities. In terms of human rights, dialectical childism tends to yield a more "positive" notion, especially for children, of

6 For Thomas's developmentalism, see Traina: 2001.

rights to active state investment and aid. This is because it recognizes a need for deliberate and energetic public investment in children's lives if children are eventually to develop into productive members of the public world themselves. Children are owed such things as health care, education, and economic support because these are vital for children's dialectical emergence into full social citizenship. Likewise, society should actively promote children's welfare through children's rights because society itself will function with a progressively increasing rationality and morality in the long run.

Many of the sociologists and anthropologists who formed the field of childhood studies in the 1980s in Europe have pointed out the paradoxical nature of such a view (James/Prout: 1990). The argument is that the developmental perspective grants children positive human dignity and rights chiefly from the angle of that which children are *not yet*, namely developed adults. It does not view children as full social participants in their own right. While Europeans have traditionally provided children with high levels of positive rights, they are increasingly concerned with granting children greater social agency and rights rather than mere social potential. Among some Christian ethicists, the more bottom-up notion of children as "images of God" has been used, similarly, to argue that children are not just potentially moral creatures but moral creatures through and through.[7] As we have seen, Aristotle and Locke both in fact argue *against* children's citizenship rights on account of their relative lack of developed moral reason. Again, as in the other two historical forms of childism, the effort to humanize children, in this case by attending to their complex developmental growth, can lead by itself to children's subtle dehumanization.

2. A Hermeneutical Ellipse

This history provides many resources for rethinking human rights today, but it also raises serious questions. The first question is how social thought may incorporate a more fully childist methodology. That is, how is it possible for societies to reshape the very human rights on which they are founded from the point of view of those who can less powerfully reshape human rights for themselves?

My response is that human rights discourse includes children when it is constructed through what I call a "hermeneutical ellipse": a hermeneutical circle of historical interpretation, as described for example in Paul Ricoeur

7 See, for example, the British Anglican theologian Thatcher: 1999, 132–170; Marshall/Parvis: 2004.

and Richard Kearney, but decentered or disrupted by the "second center" of "others" like children who cannot speak up as fully for themselves.[8] An ellipse is a circle with two centers rather than one, like the orbit of the Earth around the Sun. Human rights grounded in this way are bottom-up and top-down at once without being merely dialectical. They are constructed and tested through a distorted or asymmetrical circle by humanity as other than itself.

To see this, it is worth recalling that "hermeneutics" itself has a complex developmental history. Not coincidentally, Schleiermacher is the originator of both the modern theology of childhood and modern hermeneutics. Schleiermacher has written more on childhood than practically any other Christian theologian in history. And, in the early nineteenth century, he moved hermeneutics beyond mere techniques for the exegesis of classic texts (especially scripture) into a general method of human social understanding. He does this by adapting Immanuel Kant's critique of pure and practical reason to argue for a new hermeneutics as the practice of "divining" behind human linguistic expressions the mysterious "genius" or "subjectivity" of the individual author. Similarly, childhood for Schleiermacher serves among other things as a divine gift from God to the world that epitomizes this subjective hermeneutical mystery. Hermes as the messenger of the gods takes his purest and most complete form in each new baby that enters the world. Hermeneutics divines the kind of inner natural wisdom or intuition that each of us still in some way retains from childhood despite the inevitable corruptions and distortions of language and society. Thus, childhood becomes a vital hermeneutical concern in Schleiermacher in part because it embodies the kind of sacred human inwardness that hermeneutical understanding overall seeks to approach. This child-centered, or at least child-inclusive, approach mirrors hermeneutically what we saw above is Schleiermacher's connection of children to the theological grounding of "the feeling of absolute dependence."

While I do not share Schleiermacher's romanticism about either hermeneutics or childhood – his valorization of inner subjective purity – I do believe we can profit from once again rethinking religious and ethical hermeneutics in relation to children. This possibility has been obscured by subsequent developments in hermeneutics itself. In the early twentieth century, Wilhelm Dilthey insisted against Schleiermacher that the proper object of hermeneutical interpretation is not the hidden subject behind language, but rather *language itself*, as the means by which humanity expresses itself in history. Because history and language are dominated by adults, however, the relation of hermeneutics to childhood becomes that much more difficult to establish. On this account, children will never have the same hermeneutical agency or voice as adults, but rather, insofar as they are not yet as linguistically competent, remain out-

8 For a fuller description of this childist methodology see Wall: 2006, 523–548; 2004, 160–184.

side the hermeneutical circle. Subsequently, Martin Heidegger argues that hermeneutics should *oppose* empirical inquiry by describing *Dasein*'s pure phenomenological "being-in-the-world." His student Hans-Georg Gadamer interprets this to mean that the proper object of hermeneutics is "historically effected consciousness" or human understanding as it is always already constituted by historical traditions (Gadamer: 1992, 265–307). These developments, however, only further obscure the relation between hermeneutics and childhood. While children share historical being-in-the-world with adults, they do not share the same historically effected consciousness and capabilities by which it may be subject to deliberate hermeneutical interpretation.

Fortunately for our purposes, a significant step forward has been taken by the more recent hermeneutical phenomenology of Ricoeur, which, while it never explicitly addresses childhood, insists on a fuller interpretive circle. According to Ricoeur, the historically effected interpretation of human being-in-the-world cannot be carried out apart from the larger circular "distanciation" or critical test offered by empirical reflection on actual experience. Such distanciation occurs whenever one enters any linguistically structured world of a "text," whether that text is a piece of literature or an empirically constructed scientific observation. One important means of such self-reflective "distance" on one's received historical assumptions is through the social and psychological sciences, which help us avoid merely imposing our values directly on current experience and instead allowing values and experiences mutually to shape one another (Ricoeur: 1981, 43–62, 131–144).

Such a self-critical hermeneutical circle has two advantages for the social ethics of childhood. First, it includes both "child" and "adult" perspectives as sources of meaning: pre-reflective historical horizons that shape adults' and children's worlds alike, prior to explicit self-interpretation; and reflective textual and scientific modes of reflection that are more distinctively adult and which children (and indeed adults themselves) only increasingly develop. Children may even, Jerome Berryman has used Ricoeur to suggest, be able to explore this pre-scientific world *more* authentically than adults through deep capacities for symbolism and play (Berryman: 1991). But adults (at least in principle) are on the whole more fully capable of making critical arguments about their tradition-constituted values by subjecting them to textual and evidence-based reflection. This is why only adults should be held accountable to full legal responsibility. Yet the distinction between "adult" and "child" here remains a matter of degree rather than kind since it does not eject children from the hermeneutical circle altogether.

But second, and more importantly, a hermeneutical circle of this kind shows, methodologically, how children (as well as adults) may be studied as at once participants in their shared social worlds and distinctive objects of empirical inquiry. For adults, these two sides of the hermeneutical circle can (or may not) operate as one: We belong to a moral history that we can also interpret self-consciously for ourselves. But for children, this relation or tension of belonging and reflection is relatively less expansive. Children bring their own interpretive perspectives to their worlds. But the younger the child, the less she or he brings to this interpretation socially distanciating capabilities such as scientific observation, falsification of assumptions, cultural comparison, testing against experience, relation to history and literature, and accounting for others' diverse points of view. This is why children require educations. As a result, children's well-being in general depends to a higher degree than adults' on empirical understanding and response from the adults and society around them. The younger the child, the more she or he depends on others for a fully critical hermeneutical circle of social interpretation.

This hermeneutical circle requires further modification, however, if it is to answer to the full challenge of childism. This modification reflects my own and others' sympathetic revisions of Ricoeurian hermeneutics in an even more fully "postmodern" direction. Childhood raises to an especially sharp degree the problem of what Emmanuel Levinas, Jacques Derrida, John Caputo, Sallie McFague, and Richard Kearney have called the interpretation of "otherness." "Otherness" refers to the sense in which each singular human being is ultimately *irreducible* to any understanding, narration, or construction of them whatsoever. Levinas claims that no other is fully reducible to anything "said" about them, but is always also its own transcending or infinite "saying" beyond language and meaning. The other is a self-transcending "face" of the Wholly Other (Levinas: 1981, 46). Levinas, along with Derrida and Caputo, believes this means abandoning the false promise of a self-closing hermeneutical circle altogether so as to disrupt it endlessly.

This extreme otherness, however, would once again leave children out in the cold, now not as non-autonomous selves but as others failing to receive a sufficiently concrete response from selves and society. A child as purely "other" asks of me only the negative response that I *not* do her violence. Kearney and McFague offer a more nuanced and revised Ricoeurian interpretation of otherness in which the other interrupts the ordinary hermeneutical assumptions of self and society but only to reorient and reconstruct them anew. McFague calls such a hermeneutical circle "metaphorical" in the sense that "good metaphors shock, they bring unlikes together, they upset conventions, they involve tension, and they are implicitly revolutionary." (McFague: 1982, 17). Kearney describes the relation of self and other as involving a "diacritical hermeneutics" characterized by "a hermeneutical retrieval of selfhood through the odyssey of otherness." (Kearney: 2003, 18f).

From a childist point of view, the hermeneutical circle requires the self's and society's constant decentering or stretching in the manner of a hermeneutical ellipse. Children demonstrate more sharply than perhaps any other group the necessity for societies to interpret themselves around both ongoing centers of historical meaning and, in tension with these, second centers of historically excluded others. The decentering comes from the fact that children cannot as powerfully recenter societies for themselves, but rely profoundly upon others to do so. Such, however, is the case to some degree for us all, for societies are collections of others ultimately irreducible to one another. Children are the most easily marginalized segment of society because they are more prone than any other group to having their "saying" capabilities overshadowed by what is "said" by others about them. Likewise, the study of children is of necessity originated and conducted not by children themselves but by adults, even in the laudable efforts of social scientists to include children's participation in research, which is still initiated, guided, and interpreted ultimately by grown-ups. The underlying problem is not how to make children equal societal and research participants. It is how to interpret the meaning and status of children as others when children more than any other others cannot fully represent their own otherness themselves.

The study of human rights should likewise not expect children's social problems to be resolved by simply providing children equal rights to adults. Rather, it relies on a hermeneutical ellipse primarily initiated by adults in which children are allowed to make an impact in their very distinctiveness and singularity. This requires societies to interpret themselves through a second decentering or asymmetrical moment. Children's experiences must be allowed to disrupt and constantly open up the interpretive horizons adults bring to them. Ricoeurian "distanciation" must be radicalized into a hermeneutical "decentering" in which traditional ethical assumptions are open-endedly tested through the lens of empirical, textual, and moral difference.

Oddly enough, such a task returns us in a certain sense to Schleiermacher's divination of the child (and humanity) as gift. Children demand from adults an interpretation of not only their sameness to adults but also their irreducibility and even mystery. However, through a more sophisticated hermeneutical circle based on a reinterpretation of Ricoeur, this gift need not become romanticized – which is itself a form of children's marginalization. Rather, children's gifts of meaning to the world may be provided concrete interpretive responses by adults and society through the hard, tireless, and ultimately endless work of better understanding children's diversely other voices and experiences. And so, ultimately, should such a hermeneutical ellipse – taught us by children – shape how societies interpret the human rights of adults as well.

3. Human Rights in the Image of a Creator

Normatively, a new and fourth childist conception of human rights can be imagined, on this basis, that is neither bottom-up, top-down, nor dialectical but rather circular or elliptical in a similar way (Wall: 2005).

This can be done by reexamining one of the central symbols in both human rights and child-related discourse, even for secularists like Locke and Kant, namely the Gen 1:26–27 affirmation of humankind as an "image of God." While this symbolism is a staple in much of Christian childism throughout history, it requires still further re-interpretation if it is to avoid history's various possibilities of children's dehumanization. The notion of children as images of God informs perhaps the most extensive effort in recent times to rethink children's rights from a Christian perspective, namely Kathleen Marshall and Paul Parvis' argument that children's rights derive from their bodily existence as "incarnating" God in the world. This argument is grounded significantly in Irenaeus' early Christian theology of the Word made flesh: "At the end of the day children have rights because they have human bodies. And that means, from a Christian point of view, that they are made in the image of the Word who took flesh and came into the world." (Marshall/Parvis: 2004, 324). My own contribution is to read the Genesis symbolism in such a way that considerations of childhood transform human rights in a further postmodern hermeneutical way. Just as feminism has transformed contemporary ethical understandings of, for example, relations and responsibilities, so also, but in different ways, should childism transform human rights.

Feminists like Elizabeth Johnson and Sallie McFague have used this "image of God" symbolism to speak of God's and humanity's possibility for "bodying forth" into an ever more concretely inclusive social world. Similarly for Marshall and Parvis, this grounds human rights in embodiment. Childism can take this notion even further by highlighting humanity's concrete social *creativity*. Humankind in its origins is an image of a Creator who created this world over mythic time (in seven days), in narrative speech ("And God said …"), and even as wanting and needing a human image of itself. To be an image of *this* world-Creator God is interpreted in the story's own next line, Gen 1:28, through God's very first command in the Bible to humanity: "be fruitful and multiply." This suggests, among other things, that the Bible itself interprets humankind as an "image of God" in the first instance through the lens of childhood.

Narrowly or literally read, the command to be fruitful and multiply calls human beings to create or pro-create children, perhaps in analogy to God, as worldly images of ourselves. But such a reading cannot, of course, apply to children themselves. Children up to a certain age – and for the ancient biblical writers, children by definition – cannot yet biologically reproduce. So the more literal interpretation of this command includes children but only as its objects, not also as its subjects or participants. (And, it seems safe to say, few would also extend this literal interpretation of the command to adolescents capable of fulfilling it).

It is possible instead, however, to interpret Gen 1:28 more accurately and meaningfully by interpreting it symbolically or mythically. In this case, it may be read as a command to imitate God through *social reproduction*. The symbol of "reproduction" suggests the self-creation of one person into two (or two people into three). Morally speaking, it suggests the creation of new relations and society with those who are other. The larger moral command is to create our own shared worlds of meaning in relation not just to ourselves but also to one another, such as through culture, communities, families, traditions, economics, politics, and so on. In this case, children do in fact belong as images of God in their remarkable capabilities for play and pretend, energetic imagination, transforming the lives of parents and others around them, participating in symbols and culture, and embracing and finding wonder in the surrounding world.

The capability for this broader kind of social fruitfulness and multiplication is invested in us precisely in our status as "children" of God. Human beings can bring their own primordial imaginations and play into recreating their already given social worlds anew. Children possess this capability in abundance since they enter their social and cultural worlds with fresh eyes and perspectives. At the same time, like the rest of us, they are capable of turning this creativity into destruction as they refuse to share with others, do not respond to otherness, and lack social expansiveness. Genesis, from a childist point of view, commands both children and adults alike in the face of this possibility for destruction to grow in social creativity instead. Genesis calls for humankind's growing moral generativity.

Human rights grounded in the image of *this* Creator are calls to recreate and transform our broken social relations. What is commanded is not a particular moral narrative but rather the exercise of a more inclusive narrative capability. We are commanded, as images of the world's original Narrator, ourselves *to narrate*. This capability, shared by children and adults alike, is realized morally to the extent that a person's or society's given history is transformed in the direction of a more fully inclusive humanity (in the image of a fully inclusive God). Not only are children also capable of this defining human practice, but from birth they serve as its greatest exemplars. They more than anyone face the struggle, in the face of fragmentation and corruptibility, of creating meaningful worlds in relation to others. But it is adults and adult social institutions who shoulder the greater responsibility, for they can in principle through time exercise this capacity for social reproduction in more expansive and other-inclusive ways. All human beings narrate their relations to one another, even if adults possess on the whole the hermeneutical experience and resources to do so more widely and other-responsively.

Human rights in light of children are then neither just negative "bottom-up" liberty protections, nor "top-down" bulwarks for family or traditional values. Nor are they only "dialectical" entitlements to positive societal aid. They function in a more complex "elliptical" way as markers by which societies recreate themselves in fuller responsibility to otherness. They name those both bottom-up protections of freedom and top-down infusions of goods that in combination enable the transformation of human relations in more loving, just, and inclusive directions. That is, each human right recognizes a "second center" around which social affairs should revolve, a concrete point through which the voices and experiences of "others" should be welcomed into a more fully shared social world. As ultimately both negative and positive at once, human rights open up a creative and transformative social space in which each other is able to be more dynamically included.

In a parallel way to feminism, childism may then evolve beyond children's "first wave" rights to basic citizenship and "second wave" rights to equal social agency to "third wave" rights to their own distinctive experiences and struggles transforming the very fabric of social meaning. Children should not have to become just like adults in order to be admitted into society. Rather, adults should recognize what is distinctive about children and expand social meaning to include it, even the social meaning of adults themselves. In this way, societies are ever more primordially humanized.

Children remind us that to be made "in the image of God" is not simply to bring a pure and unsullied innocence into the world. Nor is it something utterly lost in the original sin of the Garden of Eden that can only be recovered through strict moral and spiritual disciplining. Rather, as fallen images of God, all human beings, including children, are engaged in a struggle to create meaningful human relations responsible to one another. Children may engage in this struggle in relatively less expansive and powerful ways as can adults. And they may, as a result, hold relatively more limited social responsibilities in this sense. But, children as images of their Creator just as much as adults deserve the "right" as fellow human beings to impact and shape the creation of their shared social worlds. This right underlies, from this childist Christian point of view, all other rights to bottom-up protections of social agency and top-down provisions of social support. It is their primordial *raison d'être*. In light of children, human rights are calls for a more fruitful and multiplied social reproduction. They are markers for the creation of an ever more other-inclusive society.

4. Reinterpreting International Children's Rights

This hermeneutical or elliptical conception of human rights for children can be illustrated by rethinking the historical significance of the twentieth century's great international documents on children's rights and particularly the United Nation's 1989 Convention on the Rights of the Child.

The usual argument for this 1989 Convention is primarily bottom-up: children should be recognized as full social participants in and of themselves, just as have women and other groups previously. The focus is on the language of children's "agency." It is also secondarily dialectical: children in addition have special developmental needs like education that require deeper positive social support. What is principally rejected is a top-down view that sees children as passive receptors of adult socialization. This rejection is why critics tend to see the Convention as undermining the socializing roles of families, communities, and traditions; as giving children too much power over parents; and even as relativizing local cultural values through a new form of colonization by European values of individualism. However, these criticisms miss the Convention's important larger purpose: namely, to affirm children as not only members of families and communities but also full social citizens in their own right. The argument that children need more than rights does not make their human rights any less important.

What is truly distinctive about the 1989 Convention, however, can be seen by comparing it to the two major international agreements about children that precede it and on which it is built: the League of Nations' 1924 Geneva Declaration of the Rights of the Child and the United Nations' 1959 Declaration of the Rights of the Child. The latter is grounded to a large degree in the United Nations' foundational document, written in the wake of the horrors of World War II, the 1948 Universal Declaration of Human Rights.

The 1924 and 1959 children's rights Declarations contain, respectively, five and ten rights. These rights are almost entirely "positive" rights to society's active aid and welfare. They include such rights as adequate nutrition, health care, education, the love of a family, and priority in aid relief. In larger historical terms, these are primarily "dialectical" rights to present and future-oriented development (though they include also a minimal recognition of "top-down" rights to family and community values). This largely positive rights orientation is made clear in the statement common to the preamble in both Declarations that "mankind owes to the child the best that it has to give." This statement, significantly it turns out, is absent in the 1989 Convention.

In contrast, the longer 1989 Convention contains approximately 34 distinct rights. About ten of these are similar kinds of positive rights, including in addition an adequate standard of living and state promotion of children's best interests. But a greater number, around 24 depending on how you count them, are "negative" or liberty rights, that is, rights to state and social *non*-interference. Such rights are virtually absent from the earlier children's rights Declarations. They are the rights that cause the most controversy among critics of the Convention and at the same time are the most assiduously defended by its proponents, especially in the field of childhood studies. They include the very first right of the convention, that of non-discrimination (which is the one negative right also found in the 1959 Declaration, though not in 1924). They include also rights to such things as freedom of expression, privacy, non-coerced separation from parents, and freedom of culture and religion. These negative rights are in essence bottom-up rights. They make space for children to shape and interpret the world around them as they see fit to do so for themselves. Beyond needs for external socialization and welfare support, children should even more importantly – if the number of the different kinds of rights is an indicator of importance – be guaranteed their own social agency and voices.

Controversies around the 1989 convention can be traced, then, to deep and centuries old fault lines concerning the nature and status of children in society. While the 1989 Convention builds on the earlier Declarations of 1924 and 1959, it also rests to a significant degree on a radically different historical view of children: as good gifts to a corruptible society rather than corruptible beings in need of society's beneficence.

At the same time, however, a fuller and more elliptical childism allows for a fuller interpretation of the 1989 Convention's true historical significance. For the Convention's usual bottom-up justification obscures the fact that in reality it continues to rest in significant part on the positive rights dimensions of the earlier Declarations. What is truly groundbreaking about the 1989 convention, we can now see, is not its bottom-up affirmation of children's liberties – which have excited writers on children throughout history – but its *mixture* of liberty or negative rights with welfare or positive rights. This mixture is to my knowledge historically unprecedented and uniquely able to be captured by the language of human rights.

This means, among other things, that the Convention does not exactly follow the feminist or liberationist model of the right to social agency – even if it shares much with it – but responds to children somewhat distinctively. Adults in general are owed fewer state rights to such things as an education, a loving family, relief priority, or promotion of their best interests. To a larger extent than children, adults should secure such positive goods and benefits for themselves. Children in particular – or to a higher degree – require bottom-up and top-down rights at once; that is, a clearer rights circularity. But, as children teach us, this circularity underlies adults' rights as well. Social liberties are ultimately supported by basic social goods, which in turn are best distributed and interpreted through the most inclusive possible social liberties.

Were one to design a new convention on children's rights more adequate to this fully elliptical complexity, it would include a clear articulation of the interdependency of negative and positive rights and a strong and full mixture of them. It would furthermore include a limited but important element of the top-down negative rights of families and cultures to educate children into particular cultural values. Though each of these three historical foundations of children's rights are to some extent detectable in the 1989 Convention, they could be drawn out more fully. In the end, children's rights documents can hope to respond to children as children only insofar as they embrace an elliptical other-responsive structure.

Children's rights are in the end the most concrete and vivid illustration of the primordial human right to take part in social reproduction. What children ultimately call for from society is an active-passive response to their so easily marginalized otherness. Children are not little adults, non-adults, or merely developing adults but socially generative human beings. The interaction of liberty preservation and welfare provision allows children to participate as images of their Creator in the dynamic cycle of interdependent social creativity. Each right constitutes a concrete social marker around which children should be welcomed as their own centers of society. Likewise, a human right in general should be understood as a response to each other in their capacity as a contributor to the generation of society.

Let us take just one example of how such rights might be applied: to the situation of children's health care provision in the United States. This right is currently interpreted in this country chiefly as a negative right to participate in the health care free market. While the elderly enjoy a positive health care right to state welfare, this right is in fact gained through their larger negative right to demand it freely at the ballot box. The assumption that health insurance is a social liberty rather than a social duty explains why 8 million children have no form of health insurance at all while the elderly are guaranteed public health insurance universally. The United States as a society does not extend or stretch itself toward full health care insurance and provision for children because even children's greatest social liberty would still not allow them to gain it for themselves.

From a more fully childist point of view, the right to health care should be understood elliptically as both a liberty and an aid. Both children and adults, but children especially, require active societal support if they are to be able to receive adequate health care. Children show that the right to health care is a right to a socially creative response to otherness. Societies do not naturally provide health insurance by the ordinary processes of freedom and exchange, but must decide to extend health insurance to those at their public margins. This decision is for an increasing rather than decreasing social reproduction, a greater rather than lesser inclusion of the perspective of others, a wider rather than narrower decentering of social creativity. Like all human beings, children call for a certain basic level of social generosity in order to contribute toward social generativity themselves.

5. Conclusion

Human rights so understood in light of children are finally not just an accommodation to secular values but one of the most powerful ways to express the depths of Christian love. Childism will ultimately agree with Paul in 1 Cor 13:13 that between faith, hope, and love, "the greatest of these is love": For it is love to which humanity is ultimately called by children as the very littlest in its midst. Love in this sense does not mean simple self-sacrifice, but neither can it be reduced to mere attachment or equality. Children also love in return even as they call for others' loving superabundance. The larger problem raised by considering children is how to love creatively or decenteredly, how to respond to one another in a way that in the process also transforms ourselves and our societies. From a childist point of view, love commands an asymmetrical or elliptical responsibility endlessly to expand toward one another, both the least and the greatest, just as the Creator responds with endlessly expansive love for all humanity as his children.

This socially creative love is a common thread throughout an otherwise diverse Christian childist history. When Chrysostom and other early theologians wonder at children's innocence and simplicity, they are in part calling adults to respond to children in loving self-transformation. Schleiermacher's interpretation of childhood as divine incarnation, however overly romanticized, asks a corrupt world to change through love and become renewed. At the same time, when Augustine insists on children's original sin, the purpose is in part to awaken adults and society to the superabundant moral and spiritual investment that children (and the rest of us) therefore require. Calvin and others' interpretations of children as unruly brutes can be read as ultimately made in the service of sharpening adults' own senses of responsibility for society's transformed regeneration. In these and other ways, otherwise quite opposed Christian ethical perspectives on childhood share a command to love one another creatively and inclusively in the image of an ultimately all-loving Creator. This, among other things, is what children teach us.

Human rights in light of children are, or should be, incarnations of God's transforming love in the world. They are imperfect human creations, but they can still unsettle and decenter human social horizons in ways that open them up to the voices and experiences of each other. Children are the greatest tests of this kind of love because they require societies' greatest fruitfulness and multiplication. The difficult gesture of childism requires nothing less than continuing self- and social transformation, the endless task of expansive social reproduction. By interpreting human rights in this way, we may hope that seemingly intractable problems like children's global poverty, lack of health care, and all manner of social neglect and violence may be provided more fully child-centered solutions. The language of rights may then give voice to the primordial possibility that, as children of God, human beings may grow toward their own infinitely irreducible humanity.

References

AQUINAS, T. (1948), Summa Theologica, trans. Fathers of the English Dominican Province, New York.

ARISTOTLE, ([2]1947a), 'Nicomachean Ethics', trans. W. D. Ross, in Aristotle, Introduction to Aristotle, revised and enlarged, R. McKeon (ed.), Chicago.

ARISTOTLE, ([2]1947b), 'Politics', trans. B. Jowett, in Aristotle, Introduction to Aristotle, revised and enlarged, R. McKeon (ed.), Chicago.

AUGUSTINE, (1961), Confessions, trans. R. S. Pine-Coffin, New York.

BAKKE, O. M. (2005), When Children Became People: The Birth of Childhood in Early Christianity, Minneapolis, MN.

BERRYMAN, J. W. (1991), Godly Play: An Imaginative Approach to Religious Education, Minneapolis, MN.

BROWNING, D./BUNGE, M. (ed.) (forthcoming 2008), The Child in World Religions, New Brunswick, NJ.

BUNGE, M. (ed.) (2001), The Child in Christian Thought, Grand Rapids, MI.

CALVIN, J. (1960), Institutes of the Christian Religion, J. T. McNeill (ed.), trans. F. L. Battles, Philadelphia.

GADAMER, H.-G. ([2]1992), Truth and Method, German original 1960, revised, trans. J. Weinsheimer/ D. G. Marshall, New York.

JAMES, A./PROUT, A. (ed.) (1990), Constructing and Reconstructing Childhood: New Directions in the Sociology of Childhood, New York.

KANT, I. (1960), Education, trans. A. Churton, Ann Arbor, MI.

KEARNEY, R. (2003), Strangers, Gods, and Monsters: Interpreting Otherness, New York.

LEVANDER, C. (1998), Voices of the Nation: Women and Public Speech in Nineteenth-
Century American Literature and Culture, New York.

LEVINAS, I. (1981), Otherwise than Being, or Beyond Essence, French original 1974, trans. Alphonso Lingis, Pittsburg, PA.

LOCKE, J. (1989), 'Some Thoughts Concerning Education', in J. W. Yolton/J. S. Yolton (ed.), The Clarendon Edition of the Works of John Locke, New York.

MARSHALL, K./PARVIS, P. (2004), Honouring Children: The Human Rights of the Child in Christian Perspective, Edinburgh, Scotland.

MCFAGUE, S. (1982), Metaphorical Theology: Models of God in Religious Language, Philadelphia, PA.

PITKIN, B. (2001), "'The Heritage of the Lord': Children in the Theology of John Calvin," in M. Bunge (ed.), The Child in Christian Thought (Religion, Marriage, and Family), Grand Rapids, MI.

PLATO, (1961), The Laws, in E. Hamilton/H. Cairns (ed.), The Collected Dialogues of Plato, Princeton, NJ.

Rahner, K. (1977), Ideas for a Theology of Childhood in Theological Investigations, Volume 8, trans. D. Bourke, New York.

Ricoeur, P. (1981), Hermeneutics and the Human Sciences: Essays on Language, Action, and Interpretation, J. B. Thompson (ed. and trans.), New York.

Rousseau, J-J. (1979), Emile: Or, On Education, trans. A. Bloom, New York.

Schleiermacher, F. (1989), The Christian Faith, H. R. Mackintosh/J. S. Stewart (ed.), Edinburgh.

Schleiermacher, F. (1990), Christmas Eve: Dialogues on the Incarnation, New York.

Schleiermacher, F. (1991), The Christian Household: A Sermonic Treatise, Lewiston, NY.

Thatcher, A. (1999), 'Theology of liberation for children in' in A. Thatcher, Marriage after Modernity: Christian Marriage in Postmodern Times, New York.

Traina, C. L. (2001) 'A Person in the Making: Thomas Aquinas on Children and Childhood', in M. J. Bunge (ed.), The Child in Christian Thought, Grand Rapids, MI.

Wall, J. (2004), Fallen Angels: A Contemporary Christian Ethical Ontology of Childhood, International Journal of Practical Theology 8.2, 160–184.

Wall, J. (2005), Moral Creativity: Paul Ricoeur and the Poetics of Possibility, New York.

Wall, J. (2006), Childhood Studies, Hermeneutics, and Theological Ethics, Journal of Religion 86.4, 523–548.

Wesley, J. (1975-), Sermon 96, 'On Obedience to Parents', in W. R. Ward/R. P. Heitzenrater, The Bicentennial Edition of the Works of John Wesley, Nashville, TN.

Wright, D. F. (1987), 'How Controversial was the Development of Infant Baptism in the Early Church?' in J. E. Bradley/R. A. Mueller (ed.), Church, Word, and Spirit: Historical and Theological Essays in Honor of Geoffrey W. Bromiley, Grand Rapids, MI.

The Sense of Belonging

The Importance of Child Participation in the Ritual Life for the Recreation of the Culture of the Indigenous Peoples

YOLANDA CORONA/CARLOS PÉREZ
Metropolitan Autonomous University, Mexico

Illustration 1: The "little dances" of the children in honor of Saint Peter.

1. Introduction

The last decades have witnessed a mobilization process of indigenous peoples in search of recognition that has had a strong impact on an international level. During an initial conference in Barbados in 1971, several social scientists called for the recognition of the historicity the indigenous peoples, as well as of their nature as political actors with the right to participate in the construction of their own destiny. Although legal recognition of the human rights and basic liberties of the indigenous peoples has not yet been attained, to a certain extent these have succeeded in gaining an international presence. This is evident, for instance, in the proclamation whereby the year 1993 was declared the International Year of the World's Indigenous Peoples, in the establishment of the International Decade of the World's Indigenous People in 1994, and in the creation, in the year 2000, of the Permanent Forum on Indigenous Issues within the Economic and Social Council (ECOSOC).

Traditional indigenous peoples have resisted several centuries of domination and extermination thanks to a series of reproductive and recreational cultural strategies that may be clearly observed in their bonds with children and young people. This article presents a fragment of the findings of the research we are conducting on the children's situation in Tepoztlán, Morelos. Tepoztlán is a small town of approximately 15 000 inhabitants, located near Mexico City. In the last decades, Tepoztlán has undergone an accelerated process of modernization; nevertheless, it has been able to preserve its traditions and forms of collective organization.

We refer specifically to child participation in the ritual life, stressing its importance as a culturally significant practice whereby these peoples convey to the new generations a sense of belonging to the community and a way of viewing the world that favors collective bonds and reciprocity relationships, both of which have been essential to their survival. In order to provide a wide context for our findings, we will initially present a brief discussion of the modernization of the political systems and their impact upon indigenous peoples, and the continual struggles of these to attain recognition of their rights and their culture, both of which are included in the present-day debate on cultural citizenship. We then proceed to describing the ethnographical research on the resistance movement in the town, whose findings confirmed the close relationship existing between the political and the ceremonial life. In the final part of the article we point out the ways in which the new generations participate in and appropriate the cultural logic of their community as a result of their inclusion in the ceremonial life.

2. Modernization and the Indigenous Peoples

Doubtless, the modernization of political systems and the eager efforts to become integrated into an economic globalization process were the prevailing tendencies in most of the world during the twentieth century. This allowed a large number of nations to adopt governmental systems advocating a representative democracy which favored definitions of citizenship that implied a homogenous society where all the citizens appeared to enjoy the same rights.

The need of states to shape national identities in order to integrate the various groups that constituted them necessarily implied the negation of cultural differences among them. However, in spite of these efforts, the modern societies of the beginning of the 21st century are as yet far from being regarded as homogenous and uniform. Diverse groups with very ancient historical roots and heritages coexisting within them to the present day are demanding recognition and claiming their right to difference.

In the case of Latin American countries, national and cultural integration has faced many conflicts due to the fact that the nation state model from the West does not fit the historical reality of the American countries because it is based on a different identity from that which brought forth the modern European states. We must not forget that, as Bartolomé points out, all the Latin American states precede contemporary nations and were previously shaped according to the idea of a national collective entity because they were constituted upon the basis of heterogeneous – often indigenous – communities whose integration was sought according to an imaginary concept of nation determined by the characteristics of the dominant political elite (2006: 137). This reminds us of the fact that, before the notions of citizenship or of nation in the modern sense were proposed, societies in this continent were organized and ruled according to communal social organization forms that abided by a condition of belonging inherent to their historical traditions.

Certainly, the modernization processes had different effects on the indigenous peoples, because, as Gros suggests, they also implied the break-up and destruction of a social order of colonial domination that kept various groups subjugated by means of severe mechanisms of economic, ideological, social, and political control (2000: 173). Access to broader educational opportunities also afforded the indigenous peoples a greater awareness of their cultural differences and allowed the emergence of a new ethnicity expressed in collective mobilizations directed toward the recognition of their rights as culturally differentiated communities.

Thus, where the principle of citizenship might be assumed to point to an integration process, we observe an effect in the opposite direction, with the resurgence of local identities and movements in defense of native cultures in a number of emerging countries – social movements which visibilize ethnic minorities or culturally differentiated communities that reappear on the present-day scene demanding to participate in matters that affect them.

As Bartolomé has stressed, the political struggles of the various indigenous peoples in our continent have not implied the building of a state apparatus of their own but their "recognition as collective agents before national and international collective entities" (2006: 147). This may be understood as a demand the indigenous peoples of a citizenship allowing them to belong to the national collective entity but also to belong to their community of origin.

Guillermo de la Peña has given to the possibility of maintaining a differentiated cultural identity and social organization within a State the name of "ethnic citizenship" (1999: 23). This proposition is similar to the notion of cultural citizenship put forward by Renato Rosaldo since 1994 in an attempt to obtain recognition of the right to difference of the Latino communities in the United States. The author stresses the recognition of their sense of belonging and their rights, expressed not only in a formal or legal sense but also in the application of public policies and social cost policies to these communities that have been traditionally marginalized because they belong to a cultural group other than the dominant one. According to this author, cultural citizenship should include respect and support of those everyday practices of the groups which allow their cultural reproduction.

The debate on the collective rights of socially differentiated groups within democratic states has also been approached by Kymlicka (1995) from the notion of multicultural citizenship that multiethnic states should adopt. This is particularly important for Latin America, where there is a current population of forty to fifty million indigenous people belonging to 400 ethnolinguistic groups, most of them within Mexico. The indigenous population rate in this country is twelve to fifteen percent of the total population, *i. e.*, approximately twelve to fifteen million people. Other countries like Bolivia, Guatemala, and Peru, have a smaller number of indigenous people, but these constitute respectively 56 %, 43 %, and 40 % of their populations.

Under these conditions, the presence of ethnic groups and, above all, of the cultural diversities this implies, give us an idea of the great challenges that the Latin American nation states must face in order to recognize their multiethnic nature. Although we shall not cover in detail the complexity of the various views on the relationship between citizenship and cultural diversity, we must point out that there is a difference between the propositions of Rosaldo (1994), Kymlicka (1995), and other authors – whose discussions refer to the individual rights of differentiated communities – and those of Latin American theorists such as Bartolomé (2006), Reina (2000), and De la Peña (1999), who also refer to the recognition of the indigenous peoples as collective agents.

The case of Mexico is a good example because the issue of the autonomy of indigenous peoples has evinced a profound dilemma. On the one hand, the sectors most identified with the process of integration into the global economy attempt to modernize their political systems without considering the demands for autonomy that are already under discussion at Congress. On the other hand, the peoples, ethnias, and communities demand recognition of the fact that the country is a plural nation with various living cultures struggling for a form of citizenship that does not exclude their origin before considering unconditional observance of integration patterns.

In Mexico, as in other nations with a strong presence of cultural minorities, resistance struggles and the demands of traditional indigenous peoples appear within the context of globalization as a sound box for broader demands, such as the defense of human rights or of the environment, or demands for justice and freedom, which equally concern other social groups.

The indigenous rebellion headed by the Zapatist National Liberation Army (EZLN) in 1994 in our country at the very time when the government was celebrating the setting in motion of NAFTA is a paradigmatic example, because it evinced the profound split existing between the dominant sectors and those sectors that have been marginalized throughout history. Since then, we have witnessed a movement for the reassessment of indigenous cultures and participation by indigenous peoples in the national political life staking their claim to difference and asserting their own cultural values.

In this sense, we may see that it is precisely the struggle of marginalized groups for the recognition of their rights that allows a broadening of the exercise of citizenship. This is in consonance with the approach of Van Steenbergen (1994), who regards citizenship as a strategy for empowerment and for the inclusion of underprivileged sectors, and brings us closer to the proposition by Chantal Mouffe (1999) in the sense that citizenship is related to the antagonism and dispute between actors, stances, and views of the world aspiring to recognition of their demands. This last proposition helps us to understand some of the expressions of social life in our country, since there is a continual tension between the official notions and standards of citizenship – which appear to include the indigenous peoples – and the continual struggles by the latter for the recognition of their demands and their rights. It is worth asking ourselves whether representative democracy in our country – where there are no representatives of the indigenous peoples at Congress – is not in fact a form of expropriation that sets itself up as the only valid form of political participation in order to minimize the other possible ways of influencing public life.

For this reason, traditional indigenous peoples are forced to resort to their organizational forms in order to exert pressure upon the state so that their voice may be heard in relation to matters affecting them directly. In the next section we shall briefly describe the struggle of the inhabitants of Tepoztlán in the last years in defense of their land in the face of the threat implied by mega projects that others have attempted to impose upon them.

3. Local Context of the Discussion: the Resistance Movement of the Tepoztecans

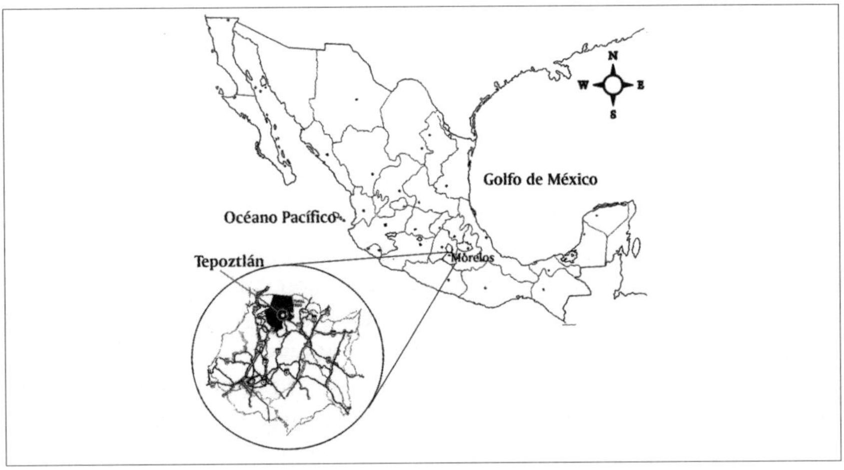

Illustration 2: Tepoztlán localization.

Starting in 1994 and for a period of five years, the Tepoztecans were the agents of a resistance movement opposing the construction of a major tourist project centered on a golf club but also including 600 residences, tennis courts, an area for hotel services, restaurants and shops, a heliport, and a corporative high-technology park. All these were planned to be built in an area of 187 ha (462 acres approximately).

The investors made sure to underpin their project with the ruling class and the public officials involved in the granting of the corresponding permits and licenses. They never took the trouble to survey the opinion of the locals concerning the project but assumed that these would be benefited by a greater availability of job vacancies. However, opposition to the golf club by the population was based mainly on the defense of the region's natural resources, because the town has suffered from a scarcity of water throughout its entire history.

The people's response to the project was to immediately dismiss the municipal president and those local authorities that had supported the investors without the consent of the people. Communal organization forms were taken up again by the people in order to designate new local authorities, and a representative was elected for each neighborhood. In later political ceremonies, symbols and values of the Mesoamerican tradition deeply rooted in their identity were given clear expression. After five years of conflict and intense organized protest in which a Tepoztecan died in a repressive action from the government, the people of Tepoztlán succeeded, and the project was cancelled.

This type of conflict is typical of our times when the predatory tendency of globalization allows private consortiums the appropriation of the natural resources of a community, through privatization, or through making them available to national and/or foreign investors, or through their promotion as tourist or "eco-tourist" locations, where supposedly the interest of the native population would be taken into account and the quality of their life would improve; however, in reality, these projects regard these people only as cheap labor.

This two-faced discourse of the modernization wave is precisely what has made an impact in the towns of Mexico, causing them to lose their land and their local identities in an unequal struggle. All these practices have generated great tension and conflicts in the determination of who is in charge of the resources. In many towns it has manifested as cultural resistance movements which are basically one side of an ancient process of social re-appropriation of the natural world and the preservation of resources. In the midst of these efforts made by the communities in order to survive, we may observe some very interesting strategies that strengthen their values, traditions and cultural referents.

At this point we must note that, although the communities' defense of the lands, the springs, and the woods have existed for many centuries, one of the characteristics it has acquired through globalization is its placement within a solidarity information network that deprives it of its exclusively local nature and adds it to the movements and struggles of various parts of the world that are rebelling against policies of resource management which disregard the inhabitants of the affected place.

In our research we have emphasized the great importance of the bonds of exchange and reciprocity which are generated in the ceremonial life as the basis and support for the collective response in resistance movements. Although we had witnessed the various religious ceremonies and rituals for more than six years and were acquainted with a long history of movements in this town against several modernizing projects, we had not realized the extent to which the force of tradition and the relevance of the historical bonds with their ancestors are rooted in the hearts of the population.

The five years of struggle by the Tepoztecan people made it possible for us to observe the existence of a historic memory displayed in a cultural fabric that brought forth pre-Hispanic elements, conferring on them a new meaning and blending them in to those political and social behaviors that became habitual throughout the duration of the movement. For us, the origin of the strength of a small town that enabled it to stop a project endorsed by the political ruling class and supported by national and foreign investors who flaunted before public opinion thousands of millions of investment dollars, was still a mystery.

In previous analyses (Corona and Pérez: 1999, 2002), we have suggested that one of the essential elements that made the success of the resistance movement possible was the manner in which the force of history made itself present, because seemingly political ceremonies gained new meanings as acts that legitimized very ancient traditions, values, and beliefs. We agree with Frank when he says that legitimization means:

> […] to be able to make reference to a value that proves undisputable from the intersubjective perspective, and, strictly speaking, only what is regarded as sacred – *i. e.*, as all-powerful and unassailable – can be intersubjectively undisputable. (Frank: 1994).

For this reason, we may say that it was the mythical religious sense and the value of the sacred that afforded the movement of political resistance a greater potential, for it was evident that the Tepoztecan people were willing to die for the cause they championed.

According to Guillermo Bonfil Batalla, there is among the indigenous peoples a culture of resistance that manifests itself, on the one hand, in the preservation of their own cultural spaces, and, on the other, in a distrust of extraneous propositions (1994: 190–200). The author proposes that the historical experience preserved by collective memory has made it evident to them that the changes promoted by the dominant culture have undesirable consequences for the interests of the community and generally mean a reduction of their autonomy and of their decision-making ability.

Nevertheless, it is possible to find a will to persist:

> […] expressed in a tenacious resistance in order to preserve their decision-making ability and their cultural heritage; in a continuous, selective appropriation of alien cultural elements that they find adequate to overcoming domination, and in the exercise of an unceasing creativity allowing them to forge new cultural elements or to modify the former ones in order to adjust their culture. (Bonfil Batalla: 1994, 195).

Thus, for this author, the persistence of these groups responds to a threefold process of *resistance*, *innovation* and *appropriation*, activated through historic memory, which leads them to acknowledge that externally imposed changes seldom bring them benefit and generally act against the common interest. This could explain why in many communities like Tepoztlán, their own history and cultural elements have become weapons in the struggle against extraneous projects that may imply a disintegrating influence upon the community. Another strategy that has made their survival possible has been the bonds they establish with the new generations in order to strengthen their values, traditions and cultural referents.

4. The Inclusion of Children: the Sense of Belonging

In towns like Tepoztlán, people usually think that the best way for children to learn is by doing things or participating in processes as opposed to merely listening to verbal instructions or receiving directions. The way the community is organized allows for all generations to meet in special social spaces. This was also seen at the time of the resistance movement, when life in the town changed completely. Barricades were built for protection, meetings took place continually in front of the municipal palace, and night-time became very important because of the need for night shifts in strategic locations in order to guard the town. In this situation, girls helped women to prepare hot beverages and food for the guards, young men formed groups and joined the adults, and the little ones went to bed late and remained playing while waiting for the adults to return.[1]

Children were present in demonstrations and movements and were once subjected, together with elderly people and with women, to an illegal arrest – almost a kidnapping – during a march to celebrate Zapata's anniversary, when two trucks from a long convoy going out of town were stopped in order to prevent the president from being disturbed by Tepoztecans while he was presiding over a ceremony.

What happened in Tepoztlán during the resistance movement has to do with a formative process, occurring in everyday life through childhood, that brought about many different and very intense experiences and had a strong impact on the subjectivity of the local children. We may think that this was a case of a true "resistance pedagogy" whereby the children found themselves totally immersed in the collective organization, and which enabled them, on the one hand, to acquire social and political knowledge, and, on the other, to deepen their relationship of belonging with their community in the midst of a struggle for its resources.

As we mentioned before, the results of the initial stage of our research show that ceremonies and rituals are basic to the preservation of models of collective action in this town, and therefore we focused on investigating the manner in which the new generations appropriate these models.

In recent anthropological research (cf. Good: 2001; Barrientos: 2001), an effort has been made to change from viewing people as passive agents or as victims of the imposition of larger power structures to regarding them as agents continually seeking to influence the destiny of their own social group.

---

1 We would like to emphasize the fact that in villages like Tepoztlán, children and adolescents are not barred from participating in political life, as is the case in certain urban, middle and high-class situations, where, in an attempt to protect them, children are confined to their home environment, and their views are limited to the events of their family and school life.

However, although this is the view held by many of the surveys carried out in traditional indigenous communities, children are still considered to be passive agents who merely internalize the cultural contents conveyed to them by the adults. In the research we have developed, we emphasize the active role of children and young people in the appropriation of the values and cultural practices of their locality, and we have chosen child and youth participation within the ceremonial life as the core theme of our analysis.

We used an ethnopsychological approach for analyzing the manner in which adults bring about child participation in ceremonies, the way in which communal attitudes and values are appropriated by them, and the meaning that participation in religious festivals has for the children. We use the categories *guided participation* and *participative appropriation* of Barbara Rogoff from a socio-cultural perspective (1993), as well as the processual historical approach of Catharine Good (1994).

5. Children and Ceremonial Life

An important aspect of the research we have been carrying out is centered on the observation and the ethnographical description of various aspects of the ritual cycle of festivals and of the ceremonial life. This cycle not only includes religious festivals but also the festival of the patron of Tepoztlán – "El Tepozteco" (The Tepoztecan)[2] –, who, according to a legend, is the son of the Wind God and a maiden from the town.

Barabás and Bartolomé state that:

> Religion is an exponential realm of culture, exceptional among others because it is where the categories of understanding, manifesting themselves in singular organizational forms of social and cosmic reality, are constructed. (1999:16).

Some anthropological studies on "popular Catholicism" have stated that in the ethnic religions there is no separation between the mythical complexes and the rituals referring to natural forces or potencies and/or to the examples of the Catholic Church.

In the last decades, researchers analyzing different religions in Mexico have shown that there are several aspects relating to the Mesoamerican tradition in which symbolic referents may be found in the religious ceremonies that are not exclusive to a particular area but are shared by many groups in the south-central area of Mexico (cf. Good: 1988; Broda: 2001; Barrientos: 2001).

---

2 For more information about the Tepozteco visit the website: http://www.sonoma.edu/users/w/wahrhaft/tepoztlan/Articles.html

Illustration 3: Girls weaving palm leaves for the "fiesta".

With regard to child participation in festivals and in the ritual life, it is important to clarify that the town of Tepoztlán has been characterized by an intense ceremonial life: Lewis (1951) reports a cycle of 49 festivals, while Eugenia Echeverría (1994) states there are 56 festivals around the year. These numbers include festivals where the whole town participates as well as the festivals organized by each neighborhood. The number of celebrations is really higher, as not all villages and communities belong to the same municipality. Children are always present in the festivals and, in fifteen of these, children have a particular role, performing in scenes designed specifically for them.

There is a system of implications, agreements and conventions in these festivals whereby various members of the community participate in a collective activity integrating them all. In these situations we may speak of *the transference of responsibilities*, where the younger members of the group acquire increasing abilities enabling them to participate more intensely in the festivity.

It has been found that in the ceremonies where the children play a specific role, they participate in different activities: in ninety percent of the cases, girls and boys performing as "shepherds" offer their chanting and dancing. There is a clear gender division where the girls have a prominent role in festivals dedicated to divine entities of female gender (women saints, virgins), and the boys, in those of male saints, Christ and the Warrior Patron of the town. In some celebrations children carry the images during a procession; in others they are musicians, they carry banners or ceremonial implements, are in charge of decorations or weave various objects made of palm leaves.

We would like to put forward what is a key aspect of the ritual life in Tepoztlán, according to our research – namely, the fact that relations take place in open and amplified spaces; these spaces are open and amplified in a two-fold sense:

In physical terms, for the children the festival extends beyond the church grounds and includes the adjoining lands, the nearby streets and those houses in the neighborhood that host different aspects of the festival organization. Both girls and boys can move around freely in the various settings and have great freedom to choose whether or not to participate in these activities.

In terms of participation, an attitude of great tolerance on the part of the adults in regard to the children's behavior has been observed; according to them "the children cannot be forced to participate, it is necessary that they enjoy doing so".

Festivals demand a great amount of work and resource management. There is a complex organization of this work through what is called in Nahuatl "*cuatequitl*", or collective voluntary work, in which children participate at their own pace. In the absence of any coercive attitude or pressure for them to do their work, children are allowed to find the tasks they like best, always in coordination with others.

The children themselves, in their attempts to participate in the dances or in the festival activities in general, inform the adults about the appropriate level of participation they can have and bring about changes in the role that the parents or stewards play during the process of the festival. They become acquainted with the various activities, the rhythms of the chants and dances, and the ceremonial tasks, and in this way progressively acquire greater confidence and therefore a greater control over their performance. This allows the transference of certain responsibilities according to their abilities. We may point out, on the one hand, the sensitive attitude of the stewards, who give the children a great amount of freedom, and on the other, the desire of the children to control the situation in a more independent way. It is interesting to observe the continuous efforts the younger ones make to improve and to participate in an appropriate way. In this regard, the company of other children who perform the activities properly is a source of motivation. They continually observe what others do and, in this environment of endless interaction there is a flowing collaboration with their peers that enables them to construct together the specifics of the dance.

At this point it seems appropriate to remind the reader of a statement made by Barbara Rogoff regarding the need to acknowledge the active nature of observation and listening (1993: 263). Children are actively interested in understanding the social contents by focusing on better-skilled children who perform a culturally meaningful activity; they always seem to be interested in capturing every detail of that particular activity.

Relationships implying different levels of asymmetry in terms of knowledge and abilities take place in those activities specifically organized for the participating children. This in turn implies the existence of communication and of a shared effort in which adjustments are continually made among the participants.

A type of interaction implying a subtle assessment among the various participants and a series of "adjustments" in response to signals that peers offer so as to point out improvement in capacities and abilities may be observed especially in the dances. This shows the active participation by children in guiding the support of adults or peers with greater knowledge, adjusting it as they develop their own skills. It is important to consider that not only do children with less ability improve but also those with greater skills develop due to their mutual commitment – in their attempt to teach others what they know, they necessarily improve their own understanding of the whole process they are trying to facilitate.

Another important concept that applies to the ceremonial life is that of *participatory appropriation*; this refers to the process through which individuals can transform their understanding and responsibility within the group through their participation. An interdependent relation with their partners and adults is emphasized, where the changes children experience transform at the same time their roles in relation to others who contribute actively to the social organization. According to Rogoff (1993:248), the term *appropriation* questions the notion of a boundary between a person and the external world, "[…] because someone who participates in an activity is part of this activity and can not be separated from it."

It is interesting to point out the differences existing between the relationship established with the children in the context of the ceremonies and those occurring in other contexts, *e. g.*, at school. For example:

- The nature of their participation is voluntary ("*cuatequitl*").
- Three generations participate, and the children are not divided by age.
- Relationships occur in a larger space including the church, the land surrounding it and the adjoining streets. In all these scenes the children move freely.

Almost all the religious celebrations provide a space where the entire neighborhood can be together, integrating three generations in all their activities: grandparents, parents and children can be seen playing different roles and performing different tasks that contribute to the festival.

As for the organization, the elders seem to be in charge of inviting and encouraging the younger ones to participate in the dances. They also tell stories about the life of the patron saint, the Tepoztecan, or the town, and speak to others about the reasons for performing these dances, the proper way to do

Illustration 4: Elders, mothers and children contribute together to the festival organization.

them and what might happen should people neglect performing them or perform them unwillingly, illustrating this with stories about what has happened in previous years in that regard. This is an important contribution to the building of a collective memory about the festival and its role in the lives of the townspeople.

Parents are in charge of making the costumes and dance implements. They have to take the children to church and help the younger ones directly with the steps of the dance. They must provide food for the attendants to the dance and money or goods to help in the various aspects of the festival.

Sensitizing and encouraging the younger children are basically tasks for the mothers. They start by taking their babies in their arms so that the very little ones can become familiar with the rhythms and the chanting; they help the toddlers to practice some dance steps when safety allows for it, and they offer help to the little ones who have just been integrated into the group of dancers. Once the children have agreed to participate in the festival, they offer their time for rehearsal during the month prior to the festival, as well as the work of chanting and dancing during the celebration.

The children and young adults start to become integrated into different responsibilities; all the "*mayordomos*"[3] from the neighborhood are present

3 Stewards of the celebration.

during all three days, accompanied by their sons and daughters and grandchildren, who make ornaments by weaving palm leaves, or act as hosts for the visitors, taking care of endless details. Mothers, who bring food to offer at the festival or at the rehearsals, are generally helped by their sons and daughters. Also, the young relatives of the steward of the dance often help in its organization.

As may be observed in the description of the manner in which children and young people participate in culturally significant activities in this town, the cultural logic of this community allows the daily re-creation of values, symbolic contents and organizational forms that are central to building their identity. The entire community shares social and political spaces that allow the new generations to strengthen their sense of belonging and to identify with the issues of the town and the strategies for their solution. From our perspective this sense of identity and belonging is essential for the development of citizenship

6. Final Thoughts

As has been described before, we can see that in the organization of festivals where the children play the main role, a great deal of time, work and resources are invested around them. We may also witness a series of exchange relationships.

If we take into account that many Tepoztecan families do not have a high income, we can say that we are in the face of a town interested in investing not so much in material goods but in their own culture. This validates the proposition by C. Good, who regards traditional indigenous peoples as "cultural investors" among whom a great generosity can be observed (1994). This generosity can be considered a strategy to extend and consolidate social relations through an investment of personal goods and work. This has to do with what the author describes as "a cultural primordial imperative of having some kind of exchange with others." (Good: 1994, 145).

In the analysis we have described, our point of departure is the assumption that the peoples have a society design implying a permanent education process expressed in terms of everyday situations. These are related to a latent educational function which may or may not have explicit pedagogical purposes but which promotes the sense of belonging to the community. The festivals of patron saints and the ritual life of Tepoztlán are part of the local everyday life and therefore are essential factors in the strengthening of the identity of the children and young people.

We have emphasized particularly the organizational and relational aspects learnt by the new generations during their participation in the ritual life, rather than its religious and symbolic contents. As we said before, surveys carried out in Tepoztlán show that the political and religious spheres are not separate; on the contrary, activities associated with the ceremonial, ritual, and religious life constitute the basis – and allow the strengthening – of the collective organization set in motion during the political movements.

Evidently, these people exercise a form of citizenship based on a different cultural logic from the one proposed by the State and related to the following aspects:

- A notion of belonging to a collective entity nourished by the intense ceremonial life as well as by reciprocity relationships.
- The intentional use of historic memory and of the indigenous past both in public discourse and in political activities.
- The inclusion of new generations in collective political, religious or social activities.
- A relationship with the natural world that refers to a symbolic construction regarding the sacred, as well as a shared conceptual framework in the use of and the relationship with the earth.

In 1998, Professor Miguel Leon Portilla spoke about "the modern Mesoamericans" referring to those indigenous peoples of Mexico who have been able to remain present and to preserve their customs and ways of community life in the modern world. He stated that in spite of having been excluded from the political, social and economic life of Mexico, and of living in conditions of marginality, scarcity and even extreme poverty, they have been able to maintain their creative ability and their decisions about change. This has allowed them to raise their voice in the last years to claim the right to be in control of their own destiny and the chance to be included in the life of Mexico with a greater degree of autonomy.

From our perspective, the expression "modern Mesoamericans" implies that the participation of these peoples in the political life requires a reaffirmation of their difference in order for them live in a country with such a great cultural diversity.

References

Báez, J./Broda, J. (2001), Cosmovisión, Ritual e Identidad de los Pueblos Indígenas de México, Serie Biblioteca Mexicana, Fondo de Cultura Económica and Consejo Nacional para la Cultura y las Artes, Mexico City.

Barabás, A./Bartolomé, M. (1999), 'Los Protagonistas de las Alternativas Autonómicas', n. d., text for discussion at the ENAH workshop.

Barrientos, G. (2001), 'El Cerrito Tepexpan: Sustentador de Vida. Ritual y Reproducción Cultural de Mazahuas y Otomís en el Altiplano de Ixtlahuaca'. Thesis for a Master's Degree in History and Ethnohistory. ENAH, Mexico City.

Bartolomé, M. (2006), Procesos Interculturales, Del Siglo XXI, Mexico City.

Bonfil Batalla, G. (1994), México Profundo, una Civilización Negada, Mexico City.

Corona, Y./Pérez, C. (2002), 'Childood and Cultural Resistance: The Participation of Children in Community Resistance Movements' in N. Del Río, The Vulnerability of Mexican Children in a Globalized World. UNICEF, Mexico City.

Corona, Y./Pérez, C. (1999) Tradición y Modernidad en Tepoztlán, Historias y Leyendas de un Pueblo en Resistencia, Taller de Investigación de Psicología e Instituciones, No 7, UAM- Xochimilco, Mexico City.

De la Peña, G. (1999), Territorio y Ciudadanía Étnica en la Nación Globalizada, in Desacatos 1. CIESAS. México.

Echeverría, E. (1994), Tepoztlán, ¡Qué viva la Fiesta!, Mexico City.

Frank, M. (1994), El Dios Venidero. Lecciones sobre la Nueva Mitología, Barcelona.

Good, C. (1988), Haciendo la Lucha: Arte y Comercio en los Nahuas de Guerrero, F. C. E., México.

Good, C. (1994), "Trabajo, Intercambio y la Construcción de la Historia: Una Exploración Etnográfica de la Lógica Cultural Nahua", Cuicuilco, Nueva Época, Vol. 1 (2): 139–153.

Good, C. (1996), 'Las Fiestas Religiosas en la Construcción de la Cultura: Procesos de Identidad entre los Nahuas del alto Balsas, Guerrero'. Paper given at the Identity and Region Symposium, Tepoztlán, Morelos, Octubre. Published as "La vida ceremonial en la construcción de la cultura: procesos de identidad entre los nahuas del alto Balsas, Guerrero", in: J. Broda/C. Good (ed.) Historia y vida ceremonial en las comunidades mesoamericanas: Los ritos agrícolas, Mexico City.

Good, C. (1997), "Las Fiestas Religiosas en la Construcción de la Cultura", Identidad y Región, Tepoztlán, Morelos, Octubre.

Gros, C. (2000), 'Ser Diferente para ser Moderno, o las Paradojas de la Identidad. Algunas Reflexiones sobre la Construcción de una Nueva Frontera Étnica en América Latina', in L. Reina, Los Retos de la Etnicidad en los Estados-Nación del Siglo XXI, México.

Kymlicka, W. (1995), Multicultural Citizenship, Oxford.

León Portilla, M. (1998), 'Los modernos mesoamericanos', Supplemento Masiosare, La Jornada, March 8th, 1998.

Lewis, O. (1951), Life in a Mexican Village: Tepoztlán restudied, Urbana.

Mouffe, C. (1999), El Retorno de lo Politico, México.

Reina, L. (2000), Los Retos de la Etnicidad en los Estados-Nación del Siglo XXI, México.

Rogoff, B. (1993), Aprendices del Pensamiento. El Desarrollo Cognitivo en el Contexto Social, Buenos Aires.

Rogoff, B. (1997) 'Los tres Planos de la Actividad Sociocultural: Apropiación Participativa, Participación Guiada y Aprendizaje', in: J. Werscht/P. del Río/A. Alvarez (ed.), La Mente Sociocultural: Aproximaciones Teóricas y Aplicadas, Madrid.

Rosaldo, R. (1994), Cultural Citizenship and Educational Democracy, Cultural Anthropology, vol 9, no. 3, 402–441.

Rosaldo, R. (1999), "Ciudadanía Cultural, Desigualdad, Multiculturalidad", Invited lecture given at the "The Right to Cultural Identity" Seminar, at the North-Western Ibero-American University [UIA], Tijuana, Baja California.

Van Steenbergen, B. (1994), The Condition of Citizenship, London.

Villoro, L. (2002), Estado Plural, Pluralidad de Culturas, Biblioteca Iberoamericana de Ensayo [Ibero-American Library of Essays], Mexico City.

Weisberg, R. (1974), Political Learning, Political Choice and Democratic Citizenship, Englewood Cliffs.

The Givenness of Intentionality

Merleau-Ponty's Phenomenology of the Body as a Way to Understand the Spirituality of Children

Marta Maria Espeseth
Oslo, Norway

Nobody had taught Marte how to play the drum. She had experienced drum playing with its rhythms and sound, by watching and listening and walking in the Constitutional Day processions through the years. As she grabbed hold of the drumsticks, she started to play the drum. With her body she had grasped the meaning of drum playing. The body has the potential to incorporate and act through instruments, says the French philosopher Maurice Merleau-Ponty (1908–1961), and according to him, Marte incorporated the drumsticks into her body as she transplanted herself into the drumsticks. In that act she dilated her being-in-the-world and changed her existence. She realized her potential for relationship with the world and the people around her.

What is the connection between a girl playing the drum, and our topic about spirituality, religion and citizenship? Within the context of this book we deal with ways of interpreting spirituality that strengthens the position of children in modern, civil society. If our aim is to improve the lives of children, we have to seek an understanding of faith and spirituality embodied in the life world of childhood. We need to seek an understanding where dignity of children is something other than a reward for citizenship. We need to see the dignity and citizenship as inherent in children's life, as something constitutionally given, as something that is already there. Likewise; religion ought to be seen not as a condition for dignity, but as a way of living maintaining dignity and citizenship.

The works of Merleau-Ponty, especially his main work *Phenomenology of Perception* (2003), but also some shorter texts of child psychology and of religion, underline the phenomenological impact on the dignity of children (Merleau-Ponty 1964a, 1964b, 1973). The phenomenology of Merleau-Ponty read together with the story of Marte, whom I got to know, having been her teacher for some years, makes it even clearer by showing us the givenness of intentionality. With the eyes of cognitive psychology, neural psychology and scientism, Marte is an autistic child with deficiencies and disabilities, who most people find very difficult to understand and communicate with. With Merleau-Ponty's existential phenomenology we do not see the autistic child isolated and with no interest for life outside herself. We see a child who is aware of her common life with others, and a child who is intentionally directed towards the world and other people. When Marte is seen with the eyes of phenomenology, we can see a child with identity, knowledge and competence, with her own will and intentionality. The phenomenological reading of Marte and Merleau-Ponty opens up the potentiality of intersubjectivity expressed by a child with severe handicaps afflicting perception, communication, language, motion and understanding. By focusing on Marte, this very special child, it is the basic, ordinary and common human features that emerge. In the eyes of phenomenology, Marte is a child who lives her life expecting to be a citizen. Her form of life is in a way a quite special one, but still, in another way, her life is also a very ordinary life. Her intentionality and direction towards the world of other people, is paradigmatic for every human being's life directed to each other. In the intentional movement towards the world and others, I will suggest that we find the beginnings of spirituality, and it is to this directed intentionality that I later want to link religion and citizenship of children.

1. Marte and Merleau-Ponty

1.1. The Skipping Rope

It's good to have Marte there when playing with the skipping rope! The children in the school yard loved the skipping; Marte held one end of the skipping rope, the adult or another child held the other, and they made it swing in a high arc. That was Marte's activity every break during the school day.

Merleau-Ponty writes in the beginning of *The Body* that we are linked to our surroundings by *intentional threads* (Merleau-Ponty: 2003, 83). For Marte the skipping rope was that kind of a thread. It had always been a challenge for the adults around Marte to find activities for her to take part in together with other children. Children are supposed to play and jump, scream and wave, laugh and sing. They are supposed to love being together with other children. While their bodies are constantly moving, they are examining themselves and one another, learning about the world and their connection to it. Not necessarily with reflected words and long explanations, but by directed looks and intentional movements. "It is through my body that I understand other people, just as it is through my body that I perceive 'things'." says Merleau-Ponty (2003, 216). That is exactly what they are doing, the children constantly moving and acting to sense, interpret and understand each other, the game and the things. They throw their intentional threads around them; they mingle in and out, weaving their threads together in tight networks. Marte was not like the other children. She never threw herself spontaneously out into the world of a playing childhood. She never screamed or ran laughingly to meet other children. Very carefully she could perhaps move in their direction, but suddenly she stopped, turned around, went another way or stood there, at a safe distance from the lively children. When they gave her the end of the rope, she came closer. As the children wove their intentional threads together, Marte kept holding her end, turning the rope, feeling the movements in her wrist and sending her impulses through the rope as she received the impulses from the person at the other end. She was a part of it, in her own way, and through it she visualised what Merleau-Ponty calls "*the intentional arc*" (2003, 157, 182).

> […] the life of consciousness – cognitive life, the life of desire or perceptual life – is subtended by an 'intentional arc' which projects round about us our past, our future, our human setting, our physical, ideological and moral situation, or rather which results in our being situated in all these respects. It is this intentional arc which brings about the unity of the senses, of intelligence, of sensibility and motility. (Merleau-Ponty: 2003, 157).

In my interpretation religious belief and spirituality could be understood as phenomena subtended by this intentional arc, as one of the respects in which human life is situated. Thinking with Merleau-Ponty, I understand *the intentional arc* to be another expression for *the field of perception* that we are all in. Here the borders between subject and object, body and mind, between me, the world and the other, are unclear. The expression underlines how human beings are directed to the world and one another, and how this interconnection can be understood. Within the field of perception, spirituality emerges from intentionality and intersubjectivity.

In illness the intentional arc "*goes limp*", it "*gives way in the patient*", says Merleau-Ponty, while it in the normal subject endows experience with its full degree of vitality and fruitfulness (2003, 157, 182). The fact that Marte was an autistic child with a mental disability exerted an influence on her total being, her motion and cognition, her speech and her communicative abilities. Perhaps we could say that her intentional arc had gone limp or that it was given away, if a diagnostic description like that existed. Marte was, undoubtedly, an unusual child, and she required special care to live a good life. At the same time, she showed us what is common and fundamental in all human life. She was linked to the world with her intentional threads. She wove her threads into the closely woven fabric of existence, into a network of relationships. Some of her threads were not especially strong, some of them quite invisible. And they were very difficult to identify and examine through medical and psychological tests. But some of the threads were strong and visible. Those, who experienced them at their best, were perhaps the children skipping the rope: those who became a part of Marte when she included them under her intentional arc. She had found her own way of understanding other people, her own way of perceiving things.

Under the skipping rope that built an intentional arc, the children jumped in and out, laughing and singing, flying and floating. They were with Marte, and she with them. With the rope she projected around them her past, her future, her human setting. Her intentional arc was not given away.

1.2. The Drumsticks

Was it possible for Marte to play a music instrument? She showed us her musicality in short glimpses: in the way she listened to music, and by singing segments from her hundreds of favorite tunes. When other people tried to sing together with her, or encourage her to sing along with them, she stopped and started to do something else. In school we tried different kinds of instruments together with Marte, and got to know her musical taste and preferences. Most of the instruments she turned away from, without any specific interest. But when she held drumsticks in her hands, something happened! Marte played. She played the distinct roll of drums on whatever was available: on the table and the shelf, on tins and boxes, on anything! She held the drumsticks, lay them on a surface, and made exactly the small movements with wrist and fingers that are required from a drummer marching and playing in the seventeenth of May parade. We gave her a drum, so that we could play together; Marte on the drum, her teacher on the piano.

In Merleau-Ponty's analysis of the habit (2003, 164–170) he underlines the power of the body to acquire habits like for example typewriting, dancing and using the white cane of the blind. The origin of habit is neither the intellectual analysis of different motional components and how they are to be put together, nor the blind and mechanistic way of reacting and responding to certain types of stimuli. The habit is neither a form of cognitive knowledge nor an involuntary action, but knowledge of the body. That bodily knowledge comes forth when bodily effort is made, and it can not be formulated in detachment from that effort (Merleau-Ponty: 2003, 166).

Nobody had taught Marte how to play the drum. She had acquired the habit of drum playing by exerting a bodily effort over the sticks and the drum. She had experienced drum playing with its rhythm and sound, by watching and listening, and by walking the seventeenth of May parade throughout the years. When she got the drumsticks in her hands, when she moved them towards the drum, she could play. "The acquisition of a habit is indeed the grasping of a significance." says Merleau-Ponty (2003, 165). With her body Marte had grasped the significance of drum playing.

The body has the potential to incorporate and act through instruments. Merleau-Ponty uses the blind man and his white stick as one of several examples. When the blind man uses the stick to explore his surroundings and to orient himself through the streets he is walking, the stick has ceased to be an object to him, and it is no longer to be perceived for itself. The point of the stick has become an area of sensitivity, extending the scope and active radius of touch, and providing a parallel to sight. The stick is not a foreign object between him and the world, but has become a part of his own body. To get used to a stick is to be *transplanted* into it, or conversely, to *incorporate* it "into the bulk of our own body", according to Merleau-Ponty (2003, 165f). "Habit expresses our power of dilating our being-in-the-world, or changing our existence by appropriating fresh instruments." (Merleau-Ponty: 2003, 166).

Marte dilated her being-in-the-world and changed her existence by appropriating the drumsticks. She transplanted herself into the drumsticks, and she incorporated the drumsticks into the bulk of her own body. In that act she extended her scope and active radius of being in touch with the world. She did not give a "normal" response to other people's request. Very often she turned around and went away, but now she was participating. For Marte, with her autism, it often seemed to be hard and meaningless to interact in social and musical relations. She enjoyed listening to music, and she enjoyed singing excerpts from songs her father and others close to her had been singing to her. But she never did the two things at once; she never performed her music or sang her songs together with anyone. The music around her was one thing, the music within her another. With the drumsticks, all that changed: with the drumsticks she could participate in a musical relationship; she could make music together with other people. The music within her and the music around her became one stream, and she was in that stream together with other people. The rhythms of the drum, the rhythms of her body, and the rhythms of other people's bodies became the rhythms of one body, the rhythms of the living, vibrant world. In that way she changed existence when grasping the drumsticks.

In the phenomenon of habit Merleau-Ponty finds that we have to revise our notion of understanding and our notion of the body. Understanding is not to subsume a sensory datum under an idea, or to explain the body as an object. It is the body that understands in the acquisition of a habit, and this bodily understanding is a "perpetual movement towards the world." (Merleau-Ponty: 2003, 167). Merleau-Ponty gives an example:

> When I put my hand to my knee, I experience at every stage of the movement the fulfilment of an intention which was not directed at my knee as an idea or even as an object, but as a present and real part of my living body, that is, finally, as a stage in my perpetual movement towards the world. (2003, 167).

When Marte grasped the drumsticks and played her drum rolls, she fulfilled the intention of being in movement towards the world. Her understanding of the world was not of the sharp intellectual kind. Her handicaps resulted in a lack of tools and strategies for conventional communication by means of planned and conscious action and logical, reasonable language. She understood by her intentional act of playing the drum. In the musical stream she experienced herself as being in movement towards the world, and the world did not frighten her. According to Merleau-Ponty, her understanding was intentional: "To understand is to experience the harmony between what we aim at and what is given, between the intention and the performance […]" (2003, 167).

Playing the drum was Marte's way of understanding, of communicating and handling, her being-in-the-world with others. It was possible for Marte to play together with a group of people, not only with me, and it was possible for her to be a part of an ensemble! We tried in several ways. Once I asked a trumpet player, another time a saxophonist and a bass guitar player. I knew that if they met Marte with a lively and enthusiastic "Hi! Now we are going to play together!" Marte would for sure back out. She would turn around, go to the window, seek for a way out of the situation; or she would move backwards, until she safely felt the wall against her back, knocking her hands together, repeatedly uttering small phrases to avoid the expectation that she play. So I instructed them to act quite indifferent, not meeting Marte with intense eye contact or effusive, hearty greetings. They were told just to be there and do their things. They did so, and Marte played together with them.

1.3. The Inhabited Room

Marte moved away, the glance of her eyes moved beyond, her hands moved towards each other in steady, rhythmical bumps. Her lips and throat moved while she was talking. She turned around, looked out the window, out of the room, or she stood with her back towards the wall and looked into the room. We thought it was her way of dealing with requests and expectations which she was not for the moment ready to meet. It wasn't always like that. Sometimes she could meet us with a rascally glance, directly asking for us. She could smile and say something that made us answer with a smile. Then we knew that she was ready to meet us and the rest of the world.

We must avoid saying that our body is *in* space or *in* time, says Merleau-Ponty. "It *inhabits* space and time." (2003, 161). It seemed to us that Marte felt her space threatened when too much attention was paid to her. Her room became too small, and other people came too close to her. Like many people with autism, she turned aside, both avoiding touch and keeping eye contact. Marte's kind of sensitivity was different to ours. Perhaps we took up the room in a way that kept Marte away from the space she needed around herself. Her way of taking up space together with others, was to seek support from the walls and the windows.

In the same way that the body exists *here*, it exists *now*. And as the body is not only *in* space, but *inhabits* space, it is not only *in* the time, but *inhabits* the time. The positions and the movements of the body express the bodily structures of both space and time.

> I am not in space and time, nor do I conceive space and time; I belong to them, my body combines with them and includes them. The scope of this inclusion is the measure of that of my existence [...] (Merleau-Ponty: 2003, 162).

How strong was Marte's grasp of time and space? Did she embrace time and space, or did she flee from them, or even more: Was she displaced from time and space? I don't think she fled, but I am sure that she embraced them. She belonged to time and space; she was inherent to them. But sometimes she had to work hard to take hold of them, not to be displaced, not to lose her inhabiting of time and space. She moved to the window to make sure that she was not locked up, and to show us that her room had openings to the world. She moved to the wall to feel it against her back, to ensure herself and us that her body took up space, and to remind herself and us that this was her space, and that her room had some walls that necessarily ought to be there. She showed us how her body was combined with time and space, how they were included in her body, and how mobility is basic intentionality. She locked her hands, bumping her knuckles against each other to embrace her own bodily space, to acknowledge her being there. At the same time she protected herself by keeping a distance to others in the large space outside. She stepped back to tell us that we had to slow down and lessen our movements. We shouldn't be so hasty and not come so close. We ought to talk less to hear her better. She wouldn't meet our eyes before we had put away the objective analysing look and put on the open and wondering look, the look which was sensing more than knowing for sure, wondering more than explaining. By her intentional movements in time and space, she told us very concretely what Merleau-Ponty expresses: "The time and space which I inhabit are always in their different ways indeterminate horizons which contain other points of view." (2003, 162).

Marte reminded us of opening up other ways to see and perceive. She reminded us of the indeterminate horizons of other points of view; open points of view and wondering over the common humanity of both usual and unusual children and their ability to claim citizenship just by being there, embodying time and space.

1.4. Telling the Story of Life

Marte did a lot of chatting – single words and short phrases of all kinds. Walking beside me, or looking out the window, bumping her hands together, all these words and phrases came. She had snapped them from people around her, and now she was testing and tasting them, repeating and playing with them. The small phrases came streaming: What time is it? Go to the class room, go to the class room; Humpty, dumpty...; what time is it?

One day, in the middle of word stream, Marte says "Mina is dead". I was looking at some photos which I hadn't seen before. Marte was standing there, a couple of meters away from me. One of the photos showed Marte's mother and a little girl in a pushchair. Marte must have caught a glimpse of the picture, despite the distance to me and the photo. At that time I didn't know the story behind the picture: A couple of years before this event, Marte's little sister Mina died suddenly. Newly employed and recently arrived to the small town, I hadn't heard this story before.

We often wondered why Marte said what she said; why she was saving words and phrases then to repeat over again. Was it an expression of conscious thought and meaning from her side, or was it blind reflection, parrot language or echo speech? Did she just produce a meaningless stream of word-like sounds?

Words have a meaning, says Merleau-Ponty. Speech doesn't presuppose thought, it completes it. This is a main point in Merleau-Ponty's thinking of the body as expression, and of speech (Merleau-Ponty 2003, 202–232). Merleau-Ponty's phenomenology is arguing with two different sets of theories, so called intellectual, idealistic theories, and empiric or mechanistic theories. Neither of these two alternatives is sufficient to understand speech, and what they have in common is that the word is not the bearer of its own meaning and thus it has no inner power. In empiric and mechanistic theories, the words are just results of psychological, physiological and physical mechanisms, of objective causality. In intellectualistic and ideal theories, words are just the external signs for inner recognitions, and these inner recognitions could even take place without the words. In both empiricism and intellectualism language is but an external accompaniment of thought.

1.4.1. "What Time is it?"

All the questions of time, did they really bear meaning? Did they really fulfil Marte's thought? How did her thoughts look like then? We couldn't see any signs of interest in time, nor did we believe that Marte could have any possibility of understanding time, or any conception about hours and minutes. Getting to know Marte better, I sensed nuances in her speech. I could differentiate between speech with meaning and intention, and meaningless repetitions of, for me, incidental words. I answered her questions patiently and kindly, one or four times. But if she went on asking, I overheard her or tried to change the topic of our conversation. "If speech presupposed thought […] we couldn't understand why thought tends towards expression as towards its completion." (Merleau-Ponty 2003, 206).

The ability of thinking logical and reasonable is often what the psychologists and special pedagogues deal with, testing and training children with mental disabilities. Speaking and acting become measures of intellectual capacity, of thinking. The functionality of Marte's acting and speech was not of the best kind, and lots of lacks came clear. The Merleau-Ponty way of interpreting Marte's words and deeds make us focus on other aspects than lacks and disabilities. There is another way of understanding the connection between speech and thought than that of speech presupposed by an independent thought. The thought is tending towards expression; it needs to be spoken to be completed. It is all the same, whether thought and speech are highly developed by a great intellect, or they find other ways than the intellectual to come forth.

> A thought limited to existing for itself, independently of the constraints of speech and communication, would no sooner appear than it would sink into the unconscious, which means that it would not exist even for itself. (Merleau-Ponty: 2003, 206).

Marte was striving with speech and communication. She was tending towards expression to complete herself, her words and deeds, and to reach out to other people as they reached out to her. She used the words she had about people and things, names and nouns of children and their toys, people and their cars. She named persons she met and things she saw, again and again. "The denomination of objects does not follow upon recognition; it is itself recognition." says Merleau-Ponty (2003, 206). Marte had to denominate objects repeatedly to strengthen her recognition, and she wanted me to be a part of her recognition. By questioning me abut what time is it, she tried to make a meeting place of her and my world. She couldn't risk her recognition of life by being silent and sink into the unconscious. She risked the constraints of speech and communication to recognise the intersubjectivity between her and other people.

About the intersubjectivity of speech Merleau-Ponty says that "[t]here is, then, a taking up of others' thought through speech, a reflection in others, an ability to think *according to* others, which enriches our own thoughts." (2003, 208).

As I reflect phenomenological in Marte, taking up her thoughts, I recognise that she already had taken up my thoughts, reflected in me. A piece of philosophical writing, yet imperfectly understood, "discloses to me at least a certain 'style'", and I begin to understand it "by feeling my way into its existential manner." (Merleau-Ponty: 2003, 208). That certain style of hasty people, always on the run to reach something, always pushing Marte to hurry up, became in her speech thousands of repeated *What time is it?* Her style had felt its way into existence in my field of perception, and there I sensed its meaning. I couldn't interpret anything that she not already had carried into me by her tone and accent, by her existential manner of words and phrases that she chose to perform.

1.4.2. "Mina Dead"

I had sorted and classified Marte's speech. Some was speech *without* thought, some was speech *with* thought; some was spoken, but not thought, some was thought and then spoken. Merleau-Ponty dissolves the distinction between thought and speech as he says that "The orator does not think before speaking, nor even while speaking; his speech is his thought." (2003, 209). Then follows a comprehensive reasoning which ends up with the statement "Thought is no 'internal' thing, and does not exist independently of the world and the words" (2003, 213). The thought belongs to the world and between people. There it is born, while it is expressed. Speech is not something exterior to thought; not the clothing of thought, but the body of thought. The spoken word becomes the presence of thought in the phenomenal world because the word within itself carries and contains its own meaning, because it is embodied meaning. Beneath the conceptual meaning of the words, there is a primordial layer of existential meaning. This existential meaning is not only rendered by the words; it *inhabits* the words and is inseparable from them (2003, 212).

When Marte's little sister Mina dies, everyone around Marte was concerned about what this would do to Marte. How was Marte's experience of loosing her little sister? How could she understand that Mina was dead? What did sorrow mean to Marte? Was she mourning? How could she express her sorrow? It is relevant for professionals working with disabled children to ask questions about the impact of lost and sorrow, and the people around Marte got counselling to deal with these questions.

"*Mina dead.*" Marte told me the story only this single time, as she caught a glimpse of the photo of Mina together with their mother. Marte's parents and teachers had told Marte that Mina was there. They had been together with her, looking at pictures, talking together in Mina's room, visiting the grave yard. Marte understood that I was new, that there was something I didn't know. I had never been together with Marte talking about Mina. There was a lack in our relationship, and Marte wanted to tell me the story to make up for the lack. The story was short, only the period of two words, grammatically incomplete, but with the whole meaning intact. The words of Marte had to layers of meaning: The informative layer with the conceptual meaning of the words, telling me that Mina is dead, and beneath that, the existential meaning of her words, what it meant to Marte and to me that Mina was dead. Here I meet Marte's style and personality, her affective world; her *existential mimicry,* to be in the words of Merleau-Ponty. Beneath the story of Mina who is dead, I meet Marte telling me about herself as the big sister to Mina. She is not indifferent and unconscious. She has lost her little sister, and she has to tell me that in very clear, short words. "*Mina dead*" was not a grammatically incomplete period from a girl short of linguistic skills; it was words *inhabited* with existential meaning.

"The spoken word is a gesture, and its meaning, a world." says Merleau-Ponty after he has discussed the relationship between thought and expression (2003, 214). The gesture, like speech, is the body's own expression. The living, intentional body is *in* the world, directed *to* the world, *together* with people and things, as perceiving them. The look is also a gesture, and Marte's look was at the photo of Mina in the same moment that the photo showed up. The very short glimpse Marte must have had of the photo, by Merleau-Ponty called *a sense-giving intention,* released Marte's story. This new sense-giving intention becomes known to itself "by donning already available meanings", meanings that come out of previous acts of expression. Those disposable meanings link up, and "a fresh cultural entity has taken on an existence." (Merleau-Ponty: 2003, 213). Marte's story was such a fresh cultural entity. Thought and expression are simultaneously constituted, and this simultaneous constitution is made possible by our *cultural store,* of language and speech, put at service according to what Merleau-Ponty calls an *unknown law*. Marte had received words and stories from her family at home, and from the people around her in the small town. She had got a cultural store that made her able to creating her own story and incorporating others into it. She was speaking "within a world already spoken." (Merleau-Ponty: 2003, 214).

The sense-giving intention which sets in motion a person's speech, is not an explicit thought, says Merleau-Ponty, "but a certain lack which is asking to be made good." (2003, 213). Marte was telling the story of Mina out of the asking for a lack to be made good. As Marte's look was at the picture of Mina, it was Marte who was with Mina and Mina with her. Mina also belonged to the relation of intersubjectivity made of Marte and me. When she told me the story, she took hold of me and Mina and presented us to each other. I took up the sense-giving intention which had set in motion the story, not in a process of thinking, but synchronized with Marte in our common *change of existence.*

> Just as the sense-giving intention which has set in motion the other person's speech is not an explicit thought, but a certain lack which is asking to be made good, so my taking up the intention is not a process of thinking on my part, but a synchronizing change of my existence, a transformation of my being. (Merleau-Ponty: 2003, 213).

Marte made a gesture to involve me in her world by telling me the short story of "*Mina dead*". Marte's world was a world of Mum and Dad and Mina, of grandparents and neighbours, and of other citizens of the small town she lived in. I was invited to be a citizen of Marte's world, as she already was.

1.5. Singing the World

In a way Marte recorded songs, rhythms and tunes, as she recorded words and phrases, and she "played the record" for us again and again. What she preferred most of all, was listening to music and singing. Her father, a competent all round musician, and we who were together with Marte, often sang to her; a countless number of songs of all kinds, as we tried to get her singing along with us. She never answered our untiring encouragement of her to sing, although we knew that she was good at singing, and that she knew the songs.

Spontaneously she sang hundreds of tunes, on key, with good articulation and beautiful voice. She was never singing on request, and never together with anyone. The songs came spontaneously when she herself was ready to sing.

There is a *power of expression* in language and speech, which we have recognised through Marte's repeatedly asking of what time it is, and in her short story of "*Mina dead*". This power of expression is well known in the arts, for example in music, says Merleau-Ponty. The musical meaning of the sonata is inseparable from the sounds that carry it. The musical meaning enters the notes and the sounds and becomes one expressional act. This intimate relationship between expression and meaning is easy to overlook in language and prose, while in arts as painting, music and poetry it becomes clearer.

The constituted language has words with conceptual and definite meanings, which follows conventional rules and is to be described within a grammatical system. Beneath the constituted language there is the bodily origin of language, the system of expression where we find the emotional and gestural meanings of the words. The words, vowels and phonemes are but "so many ways of 'singing' the world." says Merleau-Ponty (2003, 217) in his very extensive phenomenological analysis of language and speech. The difference between languages, how they sound and what kind of sounds they are dominated by, can be explained in many ways, and Merleau-Ponty do not regret linguistic knowledge and research. But what is important to underline is for Merleau-Ponty that "we need to seek the first attempts at language in the emotional gesticulation whereby man superimposes on the given world the world according to man." (2003, 219).

> The predominance of vowels in one language, or of consonants in another, and constructional and syntactical systems, do not represent so many arbitrary conventions for the expression of one and the same idea, but several ways for the human body to sing the world's praises and in the last resort to live it. (Merleau-Ponty: 2003, 218).

The poetry invites us to experience the sensibleness of the words. The words are felt in the mouth, in the finely tuned muscles in tongue and lips, between moist surfaces and textures. Marte strove with the intellectual meaning of the words, but she really had a grasp of the words' bodily and sensible meaning. It was good to play with words that tickled the mouth. All the words said by the people around her, which were so difficult to understand the significance of, received meaning when Marte took them into her mouth, when she interpreted them with her own body. The words received an even clearer meaning when she sent them out into the world as song. Talk words come out in sliced up streams of air. Song words come out on a continuous airstream, on a bow of intentional breathing. I feel how the words, the sounds and breath are fastened to the body when I sing. The vowels, consonants, and words received new meaning when Marte sand them. In speech they often became dry and meaningless, in the song they hung together and became an unbroken bow between Marte and the world, Marte and the people around her. She sang the world. She interpreted herself in the world, and the world in her. The song was the invisible intentional strings that created life connections and meanings.

2. Spirituality of the Living Body – the Givenness of Intentionality

Marte is waving the skipping rope, playing the drum, acting and speaking in her own manner. She is telling her stories and singing her songs. There is nothing extraordinary about it; it is just ordinary daily life activities taking place anywhere. In my reading of Merleau-Ponty together with stories of Marte, I have shown what can come out of a phenomenological interpretation of a child and her way of living. Even though Marte is a child who keeps the world on a certain distance, she shows us her expectation of belonging to the world and to the people there. The expectation of belonging to society isn't a subject of teaching, training or construction in Marte's life. It is already there. The expectation of being a citizen is inherent in the whole of Marte's directedness towards the world and other people, in what we may call *the givenness of intentionality.*

Merleau-Ponty is the philosopher of the living, intentional body, and unlike most of western philosophers, he starts with the body and the perception, and not with the thinking and reasoning. The living body is our way of *being* in the world and being *to* the world. When Merleau-Ponty asserts that we are our bodies, it is not an expression of a reductionism in the view of human life, but rather the opposite. The living body can not be reduced to anything other than itself, for it is already something other than itself, indeed it is our whole being-to-the-world. Nothing can transcend the living body, because the living body is it self transcending. If there is a mystery of life, if there is anything magical in our being, the mystery and the magic is inherent in the living body as intentionality and intersubjectivity.

The wonder of the living body is what Merleau-Ponty deals with in his very detailed phenomenological analysis of the body in all its modes, whether it is the body as perceiving and acting being, or as thinking, feeling and speaking. In my earlier work (Espeseth: 2004), and in the first part of this chapter, it is the statements of existential character following his phenomenological analysis, that make us see Marte with a dignity that is already there, and with her expectation of citizenship as something given. The body as incarnated intentionality in all its modes, and the body incarnated with its surroundings, is what emerge from the reading of Marte and Merleau-Ponty. It comes forth, almost with the regularity of a liturgy, and sometimes in a style that is close to poetry and to religious and spiritual expressions. Incarnation and intentionality may be the connection between a girl playing the drum, and the spirituality and religion of children.

The givenness of intentionality as an interpretation of spirituality, and spirituality as embodied in children's own way of acting and being in the world should emerge as a general conclusion of what I have been working out through this chapter

Spirituality and religion are never main themes in Merleau-Ponty's phenomenology. But the questions of spirituality and religion are set in play both in his work on the phenomenal body, and in his work on social and political issues. We have seen it in the previous part, in the givenness of intentionality as embodied spirituality. Now we are going to question the role of religion within a social and political context. For Merleau-Ponty the anchor of existence in the living body is problematical, or at least ambiguous, together with the belief in God. When Merleau-Ponty says something about God, he seems to do it in connection with his critique of Descartes and objective thought. He places the idea of God together with the impossible idea of an objective thought, both above and apart from human life and the world of perception. Objective thought, as well as belief in God, is a threat against the intentional, living and perceptual body and the intersubjectivity of human relations (e. g. Merleau-Ponty: 2003, x–xiii, 231, 418, 425; 1964b).

In the essay "Faith and Good Faith" from 1948 (1964a), Merleau-Ponty deals with the ambiguity of religion. It is easy to cite religious texts or individual acts which promote freedom and oppose the interest of established regimes. But it is even easier to find texts in the same traditions which are hostile to freedom. Merleau-Ponty refers to the discussion between the believer regarding his religion as liberating and progressive, and the non-believer regarding the same religion as reactionary and deliberating. This kind of discussion doesn't make any difference. The two of them have no way of understanding each other; the discussion collapses when the subjective world of faith and lived experience meets the world of objective principals and ideas. For Merleau-Ponty it seems important to bring in another viewpoint to the discussion of religion and freedom. Merleau-Ponty seeks to understand faith as a phenomenon, as something given, not as an object one can only react from a distance. He is concerned with the ambiguity of faith, both as a spiritual way of life, and as a social phenomenon. The ambiguity of faith as a spiritual way of life corresponds to its ambiguity as a social phenomenon. Although he is very critical to the impact of church through history, and to the belief in God as an eternal universal logic force, he wants to give Catholic faith its due by studying some of its sentiments. There has to be something more about the question than on the one side the inner experience of faith and truth, and on the other side the total denying from an outside position.

Merleau-Ponty asserts that the great contradiction in catholic belief is that of both an interior and an exterior God. He cites the words of St. Augustine; '*Turn inward*' and '*truth dwells within the inner man*', and he points on the postulate of finding God when turning away from things. In this interior God Merleau-Ponty doesn't seem to find a God of freedom, but an ideal Father-God, invulnerable and of another world: "Our fate here matters little in the other world because God is worthy adoration no matter what." (Merleau-Ponty: 1964a, 174). This kind of religion makes man suppressed by renouncing his claim on his life. In Merleau-Ponty's word this approach to God makes religion reactionary, and for our sake the dignity and citizenship of children will be of no interest.

"The Incarnation changes everything", Merleau-Ponty continues. "Since the Incarnation, God has been externalized." (Merleau-Ponty: 1964a, 174). Here is the crucial connection to the phenomenology of the body; it reopens the question of the distinction between the body and spirit, between interior and exterior. There is another way of striving with the relationship between body and sprit, between interior and exterior, than that of objectivity and idealism.

> He (*the externalized God of Incarnation*) was seen at a certain moment and in a certain place, and He left behind him words and memories which were then passed on. Henceforth man's road toward God was no longer contemplation but the commentary and interpretation of that ambiguous message whose energy is never exhausted. (Merleau-Ponty: 1964a, 175).

The meaning of incarnation is that "God is no longer in Heaven but in human society and communication [...]" (Merleau-Ponty: 1964a, 177). Merleau-Ponty asserts that incarnation is not followed out in all its consequences, and that Trinity is not regarded as a dialectical movement. This is a problem for religion regarding it to be truly rooted in human society and communication. The church has through history gone lost by worshiping the Son in the spirit of the religion of the Father, instead of seeing that the religion of both the Father and the Son are to be fulfilled in the religion of the Spirit, and by that understand that God is with us now and forever, everywhere. In the established church the religion of the Father lives on in the religion of the Spirit:

> Behind the incarnate Spirit there remains that infinite gaze which strips us of all secrets, but also of our liberty, our desire, and our future, reducing us to visible objects.

When infinite knowledge has already settled everything, love changes to cruelty, and the Incarnation turns into suffering because it is incomplete, and Christianity becomes a new form of guilty conscience, Merlau-Ponty argues.

Merleau-Ponty questions liberty and sincerity to be the over all general values of manhood, and he works out the relationship between sincerity and commitment, and that of liberty, faith and responsibility.

> From the moment we do something, we turn toward the world, stop self-questioning, and go beyond ourselves in our action. Faith – in the sense of unreserved commitment which is never completely justified – enters the picture as soon as we leave the realm of […] ideas and have to deal with the existing world. (Merleau-Ponty: 1964a, 179).

There is a great ambiguity in his thinking, and perhaps just this ambiguity is important to take notice of in the discussion about religion and the citizenship of children. My point here is that thinking with Merleau-Ponty on the citizenship of children in modern society, both religious and civil, underlines the importance of embodiment, of remaining *true to incarnation.* In our context remaining true to incarnation might be understood as recognizing the dignity of children as something already given, as something inherent to all respects of children's life.

References

Espeseth, M. M. (2004), Uvanlige barn og profesjonelle hjelpere. Kropp, fortolkning og dannelse. Maurice Merleau-Pontys fenomenologi om kroppen som bidrag til dannelse hos profesjonelle innenfor habilitering og spesialpedagogikk, Master Thesis, The Faculty of Theology, University of Oslo.

Merleau-Ponty, M. (1973), 'Expression and the Child's Drawing', in C. Lefort (ed.), The Prose of the World, trans. J. O'Neill, Evanston.

Merleau-Ponty, M. (1964a), 'Faith and Good Faith', in M. Merleau-Ponty, Sense and Non-Sense, trans. with a Preface by H. L. Dreyfus and P. A. Dreyfus, Evanston.

Merleau-Ponty, M. (1964b), 'The Metaphysical in Man', in M. Merleau-Ponty, Sense and Non-Sense, trans. with a Preface by H. L. Dreyfus and P. A. Dreyfus, Evanston.

Merleau-Ponty, M. (2003), Phenomenology of Perception, trans. C. Smith, London/New York.

4 How to Look for the Impact

Initiation to Adulthood

The Challenge of Modernity, the Paradox of Ritual, and the Gifts of Confirmation in a Norwegian Context

Jone Salomonsen
University of Oslo

1. Human Becoming and the UN Convention on the Rights of the Child

Processes of modernization and globalization have engendered a world in which inherited customs and traditions are questioned and destabilized, and where the individual's right to choose a way of life that coheres with her own conscience and cultural taste is becoming a stated norm. This vision of human potential and freedom is beautiful and necessary, although it is not easily matched in the concrete life worlds of people, nor is it completely true. It is predicated on the assumption that what is inside, in the heart, is purer and less corrupted than what is forced from the outside, from social structure and imposed processes of kinshipping, gendering and ranking. Yet, modernization and globalization are not internal states of heart or mind. To the extent that they are, they are powerful social facts that nobody really is in a position to choose as individuals. For example, if your heart desires that you choose an anti-modern life style, in accordance with tradition and the way of your ancestors, you may have no choice at all.

This painful combination of constraint and promise inherent in any version of modernity also affects children and youth. As an aid in the development of policies intended to advance their wellbeing within the present political state of affairs, the international community issued the UN Convention on the Rights of the Child in 1990.

The significance of the Declaration of Human Rights for the freedom of individuals and of societies cannot be overestimated. And to grant full humanity to children and extend the notion of rights to also include them is a most important rhetorical and legal step in the efforts of adults to protect the young and vulnerable from violence, neglect and commodification. Still, I want to take hold of an aspect of modernity's measures for the child as expressed in the Convention on the Rights of the Child, and ask if the existential horizon for adult becoming in late modernity really is applicable in full to children: is the child born a modern adult in miniature, yearning to make independent choices and exercise her liberal rights, or must she first be made a person according to some tradition in order to be some/body at all? Does freedom from custom and tradition give meaning if you never had one in the first place?

The stated point of departure for the UN charter is the best interest of the child (§ 3). A child, it says, has inherent dignity and inalienable rights, similar to an adult. For a full and harmonious development of her or his personality, a child should grow up in a family environment. Not in *any* family environment, but in an atmosphere of happiness, love and understanding. This harmonious family – nuclear or extended – is proclaimed to be the basic group in society. States that sign the Convention are thus obliged to help families provide appropriate direction and guidance in the child's exercise of her rights, although in a manner consistent with her evolving capacities (§ 5). The major means to help families help their children develop "good personalities" are education (§ 29) and educational material from the mass media (§ 17). In addition, children have the right to spiritual development and to learn according to their culture (§ 27). If brought up in the freedom and spirit of these ideals, the child will be fully prepared to live a responsible, individual life in a free society.

However, this imaginary child is not perceived as *initiated* into adulthood or into modern citizenship through the hard labor of people or social institutions, neither is her presumed individuality and spirituality seen as resulting from the struggle to transform what is given and to craft a personal path. She has simply *evolved*, slowly and naturally, with the pleasant aid of her good guardians and the spirituality of traditions, into a grown manifestation of the qualities already and mysteriously inhabiting her soul. What, then, are these inborn, natural qualities of every child that may be alienated but never destroyed? According to the UN charter, they are the spirit of peace, dignity, tolerance, freedom, equality and solidarity.

This language is not only derived from the utopian goals of Western civilization. It is also derived from the language of pure religion, that is, religion castrated of social structure and ritual and the cycles of necessity and repetition, and turned, instead, into an abstract vision of the spiritual development of all humans from a state of being *dependent*, weak, children in a family, to a state of having become *separate*, strong, individuals in community.

This universalist and idealist construction of the human person and her living context should be questioned. I will question it for its evolutionist anthropology, that is, for how it envisions human becoming as a uni-linear movement *from* dependence, which is lower, *to* separation, which is higher, but also for its simplistic notion of family, reducing family relations to that of the classroom, only recognizing family as a fundamental group *in* society, not reflecting how kinshipping – in fact – *constitutes* society and does so without mercy, both in regard to material and symbolic realities.

To sustain my argument that modernist, evolutionist anthropologies are reductive and not very helpful to explain how children actually grow into citizenship, I shall discuss the significance of religious ritual and the practice of confirmation of young people in the Christian church.

2. The Implied Anthropology of Ritual Theory

There are many theories of ritual, and some will certainly agree with evolutionist anthropology and state that to leave ritual as such behind, to grow out of its authority and compliance with tradition, is in itself a sign of becoming mature, of having separated and become an adult.

But there are other options than looking at ritual as a childish and inferior way of thinking and meaning-making. An alternative is to look at ritual as a mode of acting, taking place through a symbolic interaction between ritualized bodies and a ritualized space that in and of itself has the ability to craft a form of communication that otherwise cannot be said. According to the late American ethnologist Barbara Myerhoff, ritualization is – among other things – an act of response to the founding paradox of the human life situation, which is that we simultaneously and forever are separate and yet interdependent (Myerhoff: 1986, 109–135). Every person exists distinctly and separately from all other people, yet she is always intertwined and totally dependent on fellowship. Thus, the silent and sometimes indirect communication of ritual is 'We are indeed and in this very instance One Body. But you were born alone and you must die alone, and at the threshold you may be asked: Who are you? What did you bring?' The paradoxical situatedness of humans between separation and dependence is in particular orchestrated in rites of passage, often aiming at a reformulation or reinterpretation of dependence into solidarity, of separation into freedom.

Barbara Myerhoff also argues that rites of passage try to reconcile another paradox, namely that humans simultaneously are both nature and culture, and that no person, therefore, is just born, but from the very first day of her existence – or even while still in her mother's womb – is also made. To be made means to be given (or attributed), in a systematized and ritualized way, prescribed gender roles, social positions and normative life expectations just as persuasively as if they were in-born. This is made quite explicit in religion. For example, the biblical creation narrative in Genesis 1, with its double definition of humans as sexually differentiated twins, may be read as the beginning of social stratification, of dominion and subordination. But it may also be read as a ritual proclamation that "woman" and "man" do not spring from anything natural but are God's creation, taken to mean that cultural creativity as such is divinely ordained and necessary, indeed, was carried out in an exemplary way by Godself as s/he created chaos into an ordered and meaningful cosmos and thus constructed the human "house" and the human "tasks". That God, really, is a force of culture, not of nature. In a direct extension of this ordering, creating, divine activity we find Christian baptism, a ritual in which a person born is re-figured or re-created into God's adopted child, that is to say, to a Christ-like person. Such a person is symbolically grafted into the body of Christ and therefore has *received* a complete life horizon other than the one presumably *given* by nature. The cultural act of Baptism has revealed what natural life is meant to be.

3. Confirmation in Denmark-Norway as Case

There is no ritual without a body of cultural and/or religious knowledge, and this knowledge may seem painfully repressive if we only look for stated theological content, for what the ritual doxa proclaims to be about. However, to give an example of the profound paradox of growing up negotiated in ritual, namely that freedom is the other side to interdependence, I will present a particular case: Christian Confirmation in a Norwegian context. I will discuss how this rite – which in the Christian tradition is regarded as the next step after Baptism – could become a traditional Norwegian Maturity Rite and why this presumably anti-modern tradition has become so popular, even though it to a large extent pacifies the confirmand, imprints upon her religious dogma, and forces her to engage in an expensive gift-exchange between kin, friends and kindred. What are the enduring, hidden gifts of confirmation to a young person or to a society that try to cope with the dilemmas of becoming human in late modernity?

To start sketching an answer I will start out with a short summary of Confirmation as a historical rite in our hemisphere. When King Christian VI, absolute lord over Denmark and Norway (1730 – 1746), was to celebrate the two hundredth anniversary of the Evangelical-Lutheran reform in the North, he was advised by his officials to introduce obligatory Christian confirmation for all the state's potential citizens, that is to say, for young people. This happened in 1736, and turned out to be a particularly important tool in absolutism's supposedly positive purpose to enlighten the people and deliver them from paganism, superstition and immorality, as well as to create a more stratified but also more unified society. The key to unity and obedience was to bring people up from various regions and classes to the same norms and beliefs – to live according to the same custom and tradition. Just as all inhabitants of the Danish-Norwegian kingdom were commanded to be baptized, that is to say, to be Christian, now they were commanded to be confirmed. No-one could any longer inherit or own land, marry, be a godparent or witness in court without first being confirmed. If young people did not do their duty as a citizen by the age of nineteen, or their parents held them back, they risked prison or penitentiary.

Forced confirmation was carried forward by Calvinist theological influence and the pietistic revivals of the 1600s and 1700s, and equivalent stories can be found in most reformed states in Europe and America. In these countries, which at the time also had state churches, confirmation became the direct preliminary to public elementary schools. Christianity was this school's main subject and the confirmation questioning on the church floor was this school's exam. In Norway, a school reform came in 1889, and only then was the school system transferred from being classified as a church responsibility to being classified under the state. For 150 years, then, school attendance and confirmation training had been more or less the same thing.

The upper classes did not need confirmation in order to gain access to book learning. But for ordinary people it opened doors that the absolutist lords had hardly intended: allowing people to break the reading code and teaching them to eat of the tree of knowledge is not possible without also giving a new basis for reflection on good and evil, which sooner or later will open up for new thoughts and convictions concerning who and what the divine is, who or what a person is, and of one's own worth and dignity as an individual. This is the biblical paradise story turned on its head in a nutshell, which means that confirmation training – which originally, and by virtue of its authoritarian, catechetical character exclusively represented just another form for disciplining Adam and Eve – in fact and ironically has brought them back into the garden. This was never Christian VI's plan, nor that of his clergy. But this is a very likely development with regard to reforms and good intentions coming from the above, intended to advance the wellbeing of those below or create for her or him a truer, more God-fearing and enlightened life. Reforms and interventions are never transparent. They can just as easily advance a deep will and demand for autonomy in the subjects to be reformed and, therefore, raise in them a call for another policy, another praxis, different from the reformer's intention.

With the emergence of modernity, the forced religious foundation for the unity of the Norwegian state was replaced with humanist ideals and eventually with the conception of universal human rights. My point, however, is that modernity and the idea of individual freedom cannot be seen – at least in Norway – independently of the completely un-modern and forced linkage between Christian confirmation and the gaining of civil rights. The state and the state church created a disciplinary institution whose purpose was to initiate young people to adult life and full civil rights in conformity with the morality of pietism and the church's doctrinal teachings, and thus lead them out of the shadowy existence of a pagan way of life. At the same time, and by virtue of its discipline, the seed was already sown for a completely new possibility for commoners to formulate a self-proclaiming revolt against this institution and all other forms for domination. It manifested itself systemically in the shape of Norwegian nationalism and the break with Denmark in 1814, and a hundred years later, in 1905, through the dissolution of the union with Sweden and the final proclamation of Norway as a sovereign state. The church in no way led the process, but contributed all the same, indirectly and involuntarily, through the institution of confirmation and the emergence of the elementary school. Schooling, education and a chance for self-reflection are in other words not primarily faith-forming, tradition-preserving- resources that give access to an in-group, but primarily unpredictable sources for new knowledge and new forms of social structure to emerge.

My main point is to make clear the historical irony that an institution meant for discipline, and which sprang from an equally disciplining religion, actually came to foster the yearning for freedom and autonomy. Religious education was meant to install in people correct belief and correct moral behavior. In addition it opened a new agenda for horizontal relationships and freedom of belief. This new anthropological agenda was not alien to Christianity, but hidden, not yet manifest as a specific religious vision or practice. In the next paragraphs I will show how this other version of Christian anthropology in a Norwegian context, the much more egalitarian one, actually may be said to spring forth from Lutheran reformation principles, how it leads to very different ways of interpreting children's rights and entrance to citizenship and, therefore, how it invites intertwining ritual traditions to form.

4. The Rite of Confirmation as Composed of two Ritual Traditions

In the last hundred years, since 1905, the Norwegian church and Norwegian society have discussed what confirmation is to be, what role it has or should have when it actually no longer plays any role, when its historical mission is completed: the individual is a reality, higher education is both duty and right, and the state can manage without religion. In countries with strong Calvinist traditions, the rationale of confirmation is still a kind of examination prerequisite for membership in the church. Confirmation is still church school, and its leaving diploma is still full membership, not in civil society but in a parallel society, namely, in the society of the faithful. As such it maintains the profound idea of the existence of a society within society and the necessity of schooling, formation and training in order to be reckoned with, in order to be able to enter the inner circle of adults, in order to be an adult at all. While infant baptism in the Christian church has come to connote a kind of unconditional gift, an open welcome into the adoptive house of God, Calvinist confirmation connotes society's inevitable social obligation: the demand for a certain minimum formation into sameness in order to be able to enter into and live in society.

In the Lutheran tradition however, which is the *official* heritage of the State Church of Norway, confirmation can never be the foundation for membership. Full membership in the church comes completely from infant baptism and nothing else. Baptism is also ordination, which is to say that all the baptized, children or adults, at least in theory, count as priests in what Luther calls the general priesthood, and so also as priests in their own life. A baptized person is in theory in need of no priestly mediation between herself and the divine; she needs no cult, but stands in direct contact. Baptism is also imagined as a first spiritual marriage. The one who crawls out of baptism is perceived as married to Christ in an institution of marriage that does not bother with gender, sexual leaning, or creating family, but where the exchange is meant to go directly, daily, and completely unevenly between the two involved parties, and where the aim is to be absorbed or to be completely filled up with and clothed in what the other gives. Humans exchange their sin; Christ exchanges his love and perfection.

Societal initiation, priestly ordination, and a first marriage-entry that does not rule out a second and more sensual one. These concepts are fundamental in the terminology used by Luther to explain baptism. Confirmation, on the other hand, forms only a small part of what Luther calls modeling and upbringing from child to adult, which for him, and conventionally for his time, means the actualization of the above mentioned baptismal gifts and a full transfer from being enslaved to being free. The Christian child and young person are still enslaved to passions and instincts, or to others' authority and mistaken theological opinions. The

Christian adult on the other hand has the full potential of inner freedom through her paradoxical marriage with Christ. In *The Tractate on Christian Freedom*[1], Luther writes that,

> No-one can go through life without ceremonies and good deeds. On the contrary, the severe and immature age of youth needs such bonds in order to be held in check and

1 All Luther quotations are unauthorized translations from the Norwegian version 'Traktatet om den kristne frihet', in I. Lønning/T. Rasmussen (ed.), Martin Luther Verker i Utvalg II, Oslo, 232ff.

contained, and everyone must call the body to account through that kind of activity. (Luther: 1979, 232).

At the same time, he warns against giving ceremonies and traditions greater place than they should have:

Therefore ceremonies should not take any place in the Christian life other than what models take for craftsmen and artists: They are set out when something is to be built or created. They are not made out to be or remain anything of significance, but only because it is impossible to build or craft without them. When the work is done they are put away. (1979, 233).

Concerning those who bind themselves to the models and traditions and crave continuous learning, but who never reach knowledge of the truth no matter how much they learn, Luther says "They remain on the surface of God-fearing knowledge but do not come into contact with its power." (1979, 233). The alternative is to become theodidactic, which Luther defines as being willing to learn from Godself, to allow Godself to teach inner wisdom, independent of other people and social institutions.

The pietistic institution of confirmation with its project of discipline and obligatory confession, which Christian VI introduced to Denmark-Norway in 1736, was therefore in sharp contrast with Luther's more liberative theology and pragmatic view on what it means to be trained and what it means to inherit traditions. It was also in conflict with Luther's resistance to override baptism and make confirmation key to membership in the church.

Ever since the Norwegian state freed the school from the church and the church broke with its own pietistic non-Lutheran confirmation praxis, both of which happened at the threshold of the twentieth century and the dissolution of the union with Sweden, the Norwegian state church has been searching for a rationale for its own confirmation. If it doesn't yield membership – because the baptized is already a member – and blessing can, strictly speaking, be administered at whatever point in life with the laying on of hands, what does it then mean when the priest lays her hand on the head of a Norwegian teenager while she kneels at the altar? Is it still a stamp of a valid training in the faith? Is it still a sign that the youth is renewing their baptismal vows? Why do almost seventy per cent of Norwegian youth get confirmed in church and why is confirmation still a tradition that may be said to advance young people's wellbeing and citizenship?

5. Two Kinds of Families

In order to find the answer, we should look once again at the key words that Luther attached to baptism, namely societal initiation, priestly ordination and marriage-entry. They are core institutions in societal formation as such, whether it is a case of civil or religious society. In addition we should stop asking only what confirmation means for church and state and ask instead what it possibly may mean for the young person and her immediate society, what it possibly may mean for the constitution of Norwegian families.

According to the French anthropologist Claude Lévi-Strauss, there would be no society without families (Lévi-Strauss: 1996, 1–7). And equally: there would be no families if society did not already exist. For simplicity he divides conceptualizations of family and society into two, the verticals and the horizontals, and explains them like this:

Vertical conceptualizations see society as an aggregate of basic families, each formed by a man, a woman and their children. The primacy of the family rests on a proclaimed biological and psychological foundation: it is seen as a fact of nature that there are two sexes, that they are attracted to each other, that an instinct drives them to reproduce, that another instinct urges the mother to feed and raise her children, etc. In this so-called natural family, filiations and blood ties are fundamental. The relationship between parent and child, therefore, occupies first place, not the conjugal bond between husband and wife. After all, their relationship is not one of blood but of agreement. According to a vertical conceptualization, the reality of the family depends above all on its continuity over time. Filiations, therefore, form lines of descent so that linear faithfulness binds the generations. Lines of descent can be patrilineal or matrilineal, but are in either case unilineal. (1996, 1–7).

A horizontal conceptualization of the family will, on the other hand, says Lévi-Strauss, point out that each family is formed from the union, and hence also from the break-up, of two other families: in order for a new family to be established, two other families have to lose one of their members. Society allows restricted families to endure only for a limited time period, that is, until they give away their sons and daughters for marriage. Marriage then, and not lineal descent, is the organizing principle of society, fashioning networks of alliances, giving rise to all social organization. The relationship between husband and wife is primary in this model, but so is the brother and sister bond. In the horizontal model of the family, descent is reckoned through mother and father simultaneously, which gives us bilinear family systems in which only siblings are really family to each other. (1996, 1–7).

According to Lévi-Strauss, this dual perspective is inherent in the institution of the family, and in many societies they are also acknowledged. But as pointed out by Norwegian Anthropologist Signe Howell, one model may be more noisy and dominant, the other more silent or repressed (Howell: 1996, 253–269). When for example the biomedical complex of the West, the Christian Church, or the UN Convention on the Rights of the Child, take the vertical family model for granted – either because they are obsessed with the natural and with instincts or because they are obsessed with patrilineage and the relationship between father and son – they contribute to silence horizontal kinship and the interweaving of people, places and social institutions. Instead they point to universal principles or genitors of descent, making us all into one universal family obeying one universal norm: the Declaration of Human Rights, or something similar.

When Christian confirmation was brought to Norway, an implicit task of the institution was to solidify the paternal position of King Christian VI as the commoners' only Lord and Master, in a lineage right under God, and thus to strengthen patrilineage as a unifying, main principle of descent in a society that from old was organized according to horizontal, bilateral family models.

This is important. The crucial inter-generational link in patrilineage is between father and son, for which birth itself never has, never will, provide immediate, sure evidence. Biological paternity is invisible and hidden to the eye – as is the claimed role of the Judeo-Christian God as first progenitor – but may be created and proclaimed as social and visible reality through a powerful, intermediary third, usually a sacrifice or an offering. But it can also happen through the gesture of water baptism. The paternal "birth" confirmed through such an act is by necessity symbolic and proclamatory (Jay: 1985). Thus, to *proclaim* that those baptized in the name of the Father are to be considered adopted members of the family of God, is a constitutional custom that is both a Jewish and Roman heritage of the church.

On the other hand, there is the counter-tradition of the Son, the Christ, who does not behave according to the rules of patrilineal descent, but addresses God affectionately and with intimate names as if God was his mother's brother, thus invoking the setting of an endogamic sibling society, calling for gift exchanges based on love, trust and affection. Christianity, then, can either be regarded as a self-contradictory religion in terms of its kinship allegiance or, in alignment with Levi-Strauss' observations, be seen as explicitly making visible the dual perspective inherent in the institution of the family, setting it in motion.

In so far as Christianity reinforces vertical, disciplining, patrilineal and universalizing principles, it has helped Norway unify as nation and civil society. Yet, through its parallel, although weaker, reinforcement of horizontal, egalitarian, bilineal and networking principles, it has helped ordinary Norwegian families take hold of confirmation in their own manner, to contest the meaning of patrilineage as hegemonic norm, and to make room for gifts of another order than obedience and uniformity to be born. The first tradition has in Norway been reinforced by Calvinist inspired theological interpretations; the second by Lutheran.

6. The Rite of Confirmation Today

When confirmation came to Norway in 1736, it was set at the magical age of fifteen, which had from old been considered the coming of age for boys: then they could receive and trade property, and in principle get married. Very quickly, therefore, confirmation came to function as a rite of passage. Outwardly it was marked by new adult clothes, new work tasks, and by admission to the famous dance parties where romance and sexuality was in the air and potential marriage partners could be met. This civil side of the institution was consolidated when the urban upper-middle classes from the early 1800s started to hold large confirmation parties, a custom that from the twentieth century onwards spread to all classes and to all regions of the country, according to Norwegian ethnologist Birgit Hertzberg Johnson (1993).

The "family feast" is a unique tradition for Scandinavia and one of the reasons why confirmation has such a strong position in Norway today. There is therefore good reason to ask to what extent this party and its precedents make up their own ritual tradition that live in parallel with the church's, and dovetail with it, so being in no manner whatsoever "just a party". Compared for example to the USA, where confirmation is a quite personal affair without support from non-churchly social institutions such as the "family party", the support is down to less than forty per cent. Without the family party, there would neither be a reason to establish a non-religious alternative, the so-called Humanist Confirmation, which is also the case in Norway and which is supported by around ten per cent of young Norwegians.

The elementary structure of this party follows the prescription laid down by the Norwegian banquet and the Old Norse feasting tradition, which can be observed in full in the traditional Norwegian wedding. Particular to this feasting form is that the young person is slapped in the "high seat" in the symbolic place of the king and queen, between the mother figure and the father figure, whereupon she receives speeches and songs about the achievements of her short life, who she is and who she appears to be turning into, receiving plentiful good wishes and advice for the future. There is eating and drinking, toasting, and the giving of money and expensive gifts. The giving creates bonds and obligations, offers the young person a first, brief form of economical independence from her parents, and helps make relationships visible so that they actually may exist.

The intertwining of the ritual traditions of the church and of the house respectively comes to the fore on confirmation Sunday. The first part of this final rite of integration is a liturgical event and the gifts given are considered wholly spiritual. The second part is a meal or banquet and the gifts given are seen as adding to and anchoring the spiritual gifts already given in church, reinterpreting them into a useful form, making of them the ultimate gift: the carving and storing of moral and spiritual "ballast" deep inside a young person that eventually will enable him or her to keep life going and choose a "fit" vocation. They are envisioned as "boats" given ballast in order to sail firmly, and then "set" on the waters to try out their new freedom – although there is a tendency to employ a more passionate vocation language with boys than with girls.

Both sociological and historical confirmation research recognize that we are dealing with double traditions. The problem is just that these are not usually interpreted as parallel ritual traditions with their own religious and social profiles, with their own favorite family model and gendered markers, but are rather sorted under the labels "the religious" and "the social". So the church procedures represent the religious sphere and the real confirmation, while the folk customs represent the social and what is strictly speaking unnecessary. Based on such a dualistic typology, confirmation's church praxis can in addition be categorized as "holy", while the festive, with all its customs, that constitutes the tradition of the household, will have to be equivalently categorized as "profane". The same dualism will attach to the confirmed person such that questions about their own, or their family's, interpretation of life and life praxis will be measured by an ecclesiastical norm for what is true and authentic Christian faith, and what is deviation, folk belief or empty nominal Christianity.

This way of thinking the relation between religion and society, or between the customs of the church and those of the household, is thinking on the premises of pietism and sectarian religious association. To try to understand the Norwegian confirmation tradition by way of the holy-profane hierarchy will, therefore, not yield much more than a contribution to the creation of even greater divisions between the parish core's Sunday morning fellowship "inside" in the holy of holies, and the family's slap up feast and materialistic rain of gifts "outside" in profanity.

As a link in the process of re-evaluating the household's contribution both to confirmation and to the manifestation of church, we must therefore ask: what is a feast, really, and what kind of theological status may we give to feasting? In traditional cultures, parties, festivals, and festive ceremonies are one of the pillars of society. They usually have a strong function of social integration, and are therefore the favored metaphor for a number of religious utopias: when the time of festival lasts, social differences are erased, enmity has no place, no-one thirsts or goes hungry, generosity and hospitality rule, meanness is shown to the door. When the structure of the festive table is circular, everyone is included in principle. Then God can be revealed as the real host or waiter at the table. The bible is full of feasting metaphors and in the story of the prodigal son, Jesus uses party as an image of God's unreserved acceptance and as an action that *in itself* creates transformation in its participants.

If it is true that the party, if it is celebrated according to its intentions, is not only socially but also theologically important, then it is possible to say that confirmation as religious and cultural process consists of *two ritual traditions*, a newer Christian and an older, old Norwegian, and that they are dovetailed, and that such a dovetailing is no longer avoidable, but in fact is desirable.

7. Conclusions

Ritual traditions should not be underestimated as tools for learning to grow, not least in late modernity. Symbols are polysemic and open in a very different way than are dogmatic propositions. They may therefore include many realities simultaneously, for example – and as I have tried to show – both patrilineal and bilineal principles of descent, both churchly and worldly norms of belonging and being free.

Rites of passage – given that they are alive and therefore constantly reinterpreted and changing – are a gift to families and to societies. They take a lot of work, even financial resources, and demand that we focus on another person, not primarily on ourselves, for quite a long period of time - at least if the gift is to be realized. Yet, we may be surprised to hear that when young Norwegians are asked what they cherish the most from their confirmation process, it is neither hanging out with peers, nor being given money, nor the "bunad" (Norwegian national costume). It is either the "ballast" inducing speeches, the words given at the table, or the laying on of hands in front of the altar.

The horizon within which young Norwegians are invited to grow and become persons in the reinterpreted rite of Confirmation is the paradox of the interrelatedness between social dependence and existential separation. If we do also not respect this paradoxical character of the human situation in late modernity, we may end up with gifts for children and youth that do not advance their wellbeing and growth but merely increase their social and emotional isolation.

Therefore, the UN Convention on the Rights of the Child should be extended with an Obligation and Responsibilities of Adults as regards Children. For nobody can become a person without the crafting assistance from somebody who already is one, and nobody should be denied the right of initiation unless we feel confident that it is an equally important adult right to use our freedom to be stingy and cut short on gifts intended for the child.

References

Howell, S. (1996), Many Contexts, Many Meanings? Gendered Values among the Northern Lio of Flores, Indonesia, JRAI, Vol 2, Number 2, 253–269.

Jay, N. (1985), 'Sacrifice as Remedy for having been born of Woman', in C. Atkinson et al. (ed.), Immaculate & Powerful. The Female Sacred and Social Reality, Boston.

Johnson, B.H. (1993), Konfirmasjon og Erindring. Konfirmasjonen belyst i et Livsløpsperspektiv, Doctoral Thesis, University of Oslo.

Lévi-Strauss, C. (1996), A History of the Family, Vol I, Burguière, A et al. (ed.), Massachusetts.

Luther, M. (1979), 'Traktatet om den Kristne Frihet', in I. Lønning/T. Rasmussen (ed.), Martin Luther Verker i Utvalg II, Oslo.

Myerhoff, B. (1986), 'Rites of Passage: Process and Paradox', in V. Turner (ed.), Celebrations: Studies in Festivity and Ritual, Washington, 109–135.

http://www.ohchr.org/english/law/crc.htm

They Owe us Nothing

The Spirituality of Givenness and the Recognition of Children

TRYGVE WYLLER
University of Oslo

1. Another Gift – a Better Right

Religious discourse often claims children as gifts. Sometimes religions even claim it is more worthy to support the gift discourse than the discourse of rights. I think it is time to reconsider this antagonistic situation. There are good reasons to criticize the one-sided rights discourse in a time where the importance of context, practice and intersubjectivity is strongly increasing. But this should not lead us to a naïve return to the religious discourse of gift. What we need is new interpretations of what it means to be a gift. This article aims at developing some perspectives necessary for such an interpretation. It is only on the background of the givenness of life in general that a new understanding of gift can be developed. Children are part of the intersubjectivity in which we experience givenness. Therefore children's rights must be much more aware of the intersubjectivity and the practices we live in. This will be the future for children's rights and children's citizenship.

2. The Spiritual Demand

The French theologian Jean Vanier has developed and used the concept of gift as fundamental to his ethical reflection. Vanier is well-known in some contexts for the foundation of the the L'Arche movement. Here Vanier has created small communities where multi-handicapped children live together with grown-ups with no specific health problems. The growns-ups are not professionals, but people who think that life is richer when shared with persons with lives different from their own.

The L'Arche movement has grown to a global movement and has communities in many countries, all sharing the original ideas of Vanier. Vanier himself has also published many books reporting on the practical work, but also giving the reflection behind it. And one of the key words is gift. It is this combination of strong normativity with the religious language of gift in the context of multi-handicapped children, which I will discuss in this article. I disagree with Vanier, even if I am deeply moved by both his practice and his reflections. Being a gift is not an obvious thing. When it comes to the question of the possibility of a religious link to children's general rights, the notion of gift seems appropriate. But in the terminology of phenomenology, there is a difference between being a gift on the one hand and being given on the other. This difference will be addressed in the following. The thesis is that children's rights and citizenship are better founded in being given. The spirituality of being given is a better one than the spirituality of being a gift. I think the quality and the content of children's recognition and rights partly depend on the choice between these two different interpretations of spirituality. It is not enough to claim spirituality as an important contributor to the children's rights movement. We have to distinguish between different kinds of spirituality.

3. Traditional Gift Discourse

Vanier and his L'Arche community is evidently a religious founded practice. In simple words one could say that the idea is to give space to communities for the weakest among us, mentally ill children. Since the weakest are reckoned the most significant, L'Arche is a religious institution contributing to the recognition of children from a spiritual perspective. This is obviously to be seen in Vanier's own discourse.

There are two levels of spirituality in Vanier's gift-reflection. The first is gift as a basis for the whole community: "To love people is to recognise their gift and to help them use and deepen it. A community is beautiful when all its members are using their gifts." (Vanier: 1989, 263). The second level is focused on a certain hierarchy of gifts. There are many different gifts, from the very practical ones to the more intellectual ones. But most important, as far as I understand it, is the gift contributed by the "poor." One example: "In a mental hospital, it is often the patients who are the most prophetic people. They, more than anyone, can say, what is going badly and who are the good doctors." The most precious gift in community is rooted in weakness. It is when we are frail and poor that we need others, that we call them in love and use all their gifts. "At the heart of community are always the people who are insignificant, weak and poor." (Vanier: 1989, 262f).

Vanier's reflections on the gift come from a spiritual thinking which goes through most of his books. The inspiration comes from monastic sacramental mysticism in combination with modern critique of an unjust society. In this way there are obvious links between Vanier and the more explicit theology of liberation. My intention however, is to discuss the way Vanier uses the concept of gift. The gift is one of the most important bases for social practice in the L'Arche. One could say that it is not children's rights, but the gift of mentally ill children which is the basis of this social practice. And so Vanier is combining the spirituality of the gift and social work to improve the lives of mentally ill children. As mentally ill children, they contribute certain values which are to be put in the center by those who will contribute to the better lives of these children. In this way Vanier gives us an interesting point of departure for the paper: How far can one argue that this kind of spirituality contributes to a better life for children?

4. The Postmodern Gift

The case of Vanier is very interesting because it illustrates many of the dilemmas in modern ethical discourse: Is there any empirical basis for all the spiritual and ethical proclamations? What does it mean in practice when one says that the weakest are the strong and even most prophetic? Can we still stick to the essentialist conception of being "The weakest"? In other words: Can we still have a positive evaluation of Vanier's religious motivation (the religious significance of giving special attention to persons living in a difficult social and cultural context), and at the same time find better and less essentialistic interpretations of that practice?

These are questions, which bring the discussion of Vanier close to the discussion of gift and gift-giving raised by Jaques Derrida some decades ago (Derrida: 1992). Since Derrida seems to develop such a strong distinction between himself and positions like that Vanier, researchers have concluded that Derrida does not have much to contribute to the current discussion of rights and gifts. Derrida, in a way, undermines the whole discussion in such a way that he becomes more or less set aside. But I think this is a too quick response. Derrida's reflections on the gift open up for a non-essentialistic interpretation of both gift and spirituality in the context of children. The whole deconstructivist approach makes it impossible to accept Vanier's discourse. The kind of naïve essentialism in Vanier must be understood by Derrida as an effort to hide the traces of otherness. The suspicion behind every single line in Derrida's reflections is that someone wants to escape otherness.

However, Derrida's explicit critique is not developed in a confrontation with Vanier, but with the famous anthropologist Marcel Mauss. Still, the argument could easily have been turned also against Vanier, so there is good reason to look briefly into Derrida's analysis of Mauss. In the first part of the last century Mauss returned from his field work publishing *The Gift*, an essay which remains one of the classics in the study of humanities. The basic thesis of Mauss was clear and simple: The meaning of a gift in a community is not the receiving of it, but the giving of it away to some other. So the importance of gift was the giving of it, and the mentality of not keeping the gift for yourself.

For many years Mauss' thesis was reckoned as the final interpretation of what a gift was. But Jacques Derrida and his deconstructivist colleagues changed this totally. Derrida is also obsessed with the notion of gift, but not in the way it was developed by Mauss. For Derrida it was exactly the position of Mauss which was the false one. The analysis done by Mauss showed the problem at the centre of the gift concept. Mauss analysis shows that being a gift is not possible. The idea of a gift is to be given away, but by the calculation of giving away, the gift stops being a gift and turns into something less admirable and pleasant.

To be a real gift, there can be no calculation ever of giving away to whom and for what reason and with which kind of strategy. A gift can only be a gift when it is without any condition. It might be that Derrida interprets Mauss in an one-sided manner. There is more to say to Mauss's conception of gifts than the perspectives referred to by Derrida. Still, the most important thing in Derrida's Mauss-interpretation is not exegetical correctness, but the way he uses Mauss to clarify his own position. It has to do with the essentialisation of the gift. Every time one says that the gift "is", the gift is no more. Derrida aims at a philosophy where the brutality of the essences no longer exists. The problem is not the essensialism as such, the problem is that essensialism covers the other. She or he is not discovered, but disciplined and forced by the power of language to be a "something". In other words, saying that the weakest and most insignificant child is a prophetic gift, is a brutality, because it takes control of the other, knowing and proclaiming something of the child, something which does not cover all the other perspectives (traces) of otherness in that concrete child.

In this way, Derrida connects to Husserl. For Derrida the distinction between the given and the gift belongs to the bases of Husserl's phenomenology. According to Caputo and Scanlon (1999, 6) it is the difference between what Husserl called "intention" (meaning, signification) on the one hand and what he called "fulfillment" (givenness) on the other hand, which are the technical terms here. For Derrida this distinction contained the possibility of leaving out the givenness and concentrating on the meaning. But according to Derrida, Husserl escaped this possibility and concentrated on the phenomenological reduction where the link between the given and the meaning was to be studied. Phenomenology becomes then another kind of sophisticated essentialism, because it also aims at investigating how the thing "is".

Derrida's own solution in the context of the impossible gift, is to turn to friendship and hospitality. We cannot speak of gift, but we can behave with generosity and treat the other as a guest in our own house.

In the context of this article the distance to Vanier is not so great, after all. Vanier's point is that the weakest is the strongest and that is why the option for the children must locate itself in the experience of practices like the L'Arche. This is a fundamental experience in a religious context. Therefore one has to look both at this experience and the interpretation given by Vanier to catch the impact of it. Derrida, on the other hand fears any practice or any language that moves towards essentialism. When one says that something is a "gift" one tends to conceal that any linguistic expression lacks the difference between the signifier and the signified. The importance with this difference is that it keeps the otherness of the other open. Any kind of illusion that the word child and the empirical child are identical is brutal and leads to oppression. Therefore one can say that there is a deep normativity in Derrida's work. The basic interest is to keep the memory of the otherness of the other open. But since this is linguistically impossible, the most important then is to look for the traces, the traces of the others, that cannot be essentialised without bringing the whole practice into collapse. We know nothing but traces. Therefore we should not speak about gifts.

Paradoxically, Derrida then turns to practice. If we cannot speak about the gift, we can live in the traces. This is the reason why Derrida at the end of his sharp critique turns to friendship and hospitality. This practice is depicted in much the same way as Vanier does with the L'Arche: taking care of each other, caring for any guest, giving privilege to the less privileged.

Accordingly, it seems that the difference between Derrida and Vanier first of all is a difference of interpretation. The latter represents exactly the essentialistic position strongly criticised by Derrida. Even then, they both have the same esteem for the practice of hospitality and generosity. The social practice is the place where otherness happens to be recognised. Of course, it has to be empirically verified to see if this is the case. And it might obviously turn out that otherness is not respected. But even if this turned out to be the case, I still think the tendency remains: The social practice is the decisive place. The criteria and demands to see if the otherness of a child is recognised are to be found inside the social practice and not outside it.

According to the phenomenology of Merleau Ponty, this is not very surprising. The bodily sensation of the other body is the situation where recognition of the other happens, in practice. Merleau-Ponty calls this the pre-reflexive level. This is the given form which we cannot totally escape. We can act as if the given was not there, then we do\ not achieve to abolish it, the only achievement is the objectivation of the other. We saw above that Derrida rejected exactly this part of phenomenology. His critique was directed towards the linguistic naïvité, which connects the significant (the given) with the signifier (the gift). But recent phenomenological discussion establishes new development within this discussion.

5. A Gift of Phenomenology

The influential Danish philosopher Dan Zahavi has coined phenomenology as a reflection on the givenness of life. Zahavi is one of the modern phenomenologists who acknowledge the fundamental critique of Derrida and Levinas. They have posed the radical question of otherness. Both the importance Derrida gives to the trace and the epistemological priority given to the "face of the other" in Levinas, belong to this position. However, Zahavi does not follow Derrida and Levinas all the way. He does not think that phenomenology automatically leads to sameness. Working with a detailed analysis of Husserl and Merleau-Ponty, Zahavi argues that the givenness in ordinary life includes otherness. The position is that there is no way to otherness except through the recognition of the given.

Zahavi refers to an implicit discussion between Sartre and Merleau-Ponty. For Sartre, otherness is something secondary, an experience which comes after the subject has experienced him/herself as a subject. Being a subject, subjectivity is threatened by the other's gaze. In Sartre otherness is both a threat and second in range. This is turned upside down in the position of Merleau-Ponty. The fundamental and absolute primacy is givenness. Givenness is the sensory, non verbal connectedness to other bodies, other persons' other life world. Before any kind of verbal reflection you are exposed to the perception of other bodies and through these perceptions the life world is already there, given before any kind of interpretation. The interpretations are secondary, they reflect on the kind of givenness you are exposed to.

With this argument Zahavi claims that givenness and the pre-reflexivity of the body must be primary when any life world is to be interpreted. Here is the turning point in post-modern philosophy of otherness. For the consequence of this position is not that otherness does not exist, as especially Levinas claimed in part of his writings. The consequence is that otherness presupposes the pre-reflexivity and the given (Zahavi: 1999, 170).

This is the givenness which plays such an important role in the thinking of Merleau-Ponty. Compared to the notion of gift used by Vanier and Derrida, I think Merleau-Ponty is hinting at something else. Vanier is occupied with the gift character of the less privileged, especially the mentally disabled child. But he is not reflecting on givenness in the context of perception like Merleau-Ponty does. And because Vanier lacks a reflection of this kind of givenness, his position underestimates the importance of intersubjectivity and embodiment. It is the cognition of the child as gift, which is at the centre of Vanier, not embodied givenness, as it is in Merleau-Ponty's thinking. Therefore it is more important to start a reflection on how the child perceives the world through the senses of smell, sight, touching and listening. As the child is perceived by me as given, one must think that the child her/himself perceives the world as given. And this must be one of the important things to investigate further: What is the "content" in the child's perceiving of the world as given? The answers to this question would also give us important indications of how we should recognize the child as "subject".

At the same time Merleau-Ponty (in the interpretation of Zahavi) opens a position which avoids the critique of Derrida. The French deconstructivist, in the tradition of Levinas, claimed that the gift argument leads to nothing but economic instrumentality. But neither Derrida nor Vanier reflect on the givenness of perception as Merleau-Ponty did. In my opinion his critique seems to hit Vanier, but not Merleau-Ponty. The problem for Vanier is the cognitive way of reflecting, the problem for Derrida, is that he does not include a reflection on perception. As perception givenness does not lead to the "economy of gift". Givenness leads to nothing else than the awareness of the lifeworld perceived. And it is this lifeworld, which could be the normative demand. This is the kind of givenness that sould be investigated further in the discussion of what kind of gift and what kind of spirituality that could be most important to reflect on in the context of this book.

However, it is not only the difference between givenness and the economy of gift that is developed a little further in a comparison between Merleau-Ponty and Derrida. Just as important is the discussion of Otherness. Current critique of phenomenology is that it leads to sameness. Since the other comes to me through the perception of my own body, it is the Other as my conscious same which really comes forth to me.

The contribution of Zahavi is to present a position alternative to this. It is not such that phenomenology lacks the recognition of otherness. On the contrary, phenomenology presupposes otherness, and has it as the core of its reflection. Zahavi uses an argument of analogy. When I look at my left arm, I know that this left arm is something specific and different. So the arm is in this way an object, an other for me. But this otherness presupposes the givenness of my sensory perception. It is through perception, the givenness of it, that I perceive anything at all, including my left arm. So in my perception there is the intentionality of I-and-my-arm-being in the world. But in the reflection, the secondary reflection, I recognize my left arm as an other thing.

Parallel to this Zahavi thinks that the other person is an other for me. In the givenness of perception, the other is part of my being-in-the-world. But as soon as perception happens, I reflect on these perceptions and recognize that there is an other out there. There is therefore a dialectics of sameness and otherness in phenomenology. The perception of the other opens for the understanding of me and the other as part of the same perception, intentionality. So in this way it is impossible to understand the other as a thing out there, as if my perception of him/her has no impact on the way I perceive her/him.

On the other hand, this also leads to an otherness, which is not sameness. The secondary reflection opens for a new kind of "objectivation", different from the naturalistic object, because it presupposes the intentionality of being-in-the world.

6. A Re-Construction with Religious Impact

From this phenomenological position I return to the opening question: What does it mean to use a tradition of spirituality and religion to proclaim the child as gift in the tradition of Vanier? And how can we reach a new recognition for children as citizens from such a reflection?

In my view, Vanier's position illustrates the most important dilemma with talking about the child as gift. The two levels of gift-talk reflect implicitly the general discussion on gift which has been put on the international agenda by the late Jacques Derrida. The first level of Vanier is a general level. The best gift of any community is to let each individual develop her/himself according to their capacity and potentiality. The second gift-level is also in a way general, meaning that you do not need any specific faith to understand it. But you might need some more religious interest and engagement to really engage seriously with it. The weakest is the greatest gift. Therefore the child is a gift and the most valuable gift is the mentally retarded child.

My guess is that the majority suddenly decide for the second level of Vanier. The weak child as the most precious gift is convincing and formulated within the spiritual language which most of the global religions will understand and also favour. The weakest is the greatest gift among children.

In this way the case of Jean Vanier has been most useful to teach us the kind of challenge we are up against when re-introducing child as gift in late modern discourse on the spirituality of children. In my opinion the Vanier case shows the importance of not returning to traditional spirituality when re-introducing the discourse of spirituality in a contemporary context. I see nothing but normativity as the motivation when we use a spiritual vocabulary today. And therefore we have to be very careful with what we are doing. In a situation where the tendency to re-sacralizing is growing, we should avoid any kind of gift language which tempts us to treat the child as an object, and not as something given with a value in itself.

I therefore still find the tendency in the research of John Hull as more refreshing than that of Jean Vanier (Hull: 1991, 2000). I see Hull as a researcher who gives credit to religion, but does it in a way where the general contribution of religion is taken into consideration, not so much the specificity of religion. Vanier keeps to the specificity and loses the child by calling it a gift.

Hull urges us to take the general view of religion and can therefore use the gift-concept without ending up in a gift economy argument. Religion is a gift, not to be taken as part of an economy of giving (a kind of pseudo-missionary project), but as an effort to see the self-evident insights which arise from religion as gift.

My question is whether we here have a thinking which can be transformed into an argument in favour of the child as gift. Above I mentioned the two levels in Vanier's gift discourse. The second level is the level with which we have been occupied and which turned out to be a kind of instrumentalizing discourse. But the first level has been left out so far. That was the more general level, using the gift concept: "To love people is to recognise their gift and to help them use and deepen it. A community is beautiful when all its members are using their gifts." (Vanier: 1989, 263).

This is a position much more in accordance with Derrida's analysis of friendship. Talking about the child as gift can lead to the language of oppression, addressing children as persons who should be allowed to take their own gifts, resources and talents in the co-exsistence and relation with others, is not an instrumental discourse in the same way. Children do not in this context owe anything more to grown-up society than any other participant in this society. They are not special gifts which can be used to any kind of purpose outside themselves.

I find this close to the position of Hull. It is possible to re-introduce the language of spirituality into the context of late modern research. But there are limits to take care of when we use the language of spirituality today. We should do careful analysis of the kind of spiritual language expressed in the different religions and religious contexts. Do they treat children as persons with a value in themselves and do they act with children like persons which are supposed to use their gifts and talents. If the answers are yes, we can even talk about child as gift, paradoxically something which is not supposed to be given away to anyone. The non-giving gift forms a better notion of the child as gift. It is at the same point that the basis for the citizen should be found.

The basic agenda in this book is to investigate possible contributions from religions and spirituality to the development of children's citizenship. My argument is to take phenomenology as the point of departure for reflection. Phenomenology is not religion, but, as the Danish theologian and phenomenological philosopher K. E. Løgstrup once said, is close to a religious interpretation (Løgstrup: 1978). By this he addressed the same argument as I have developed in this essay, following Merleau-Ponty/Zahavi: There is a givenness of life, and any kind of argument in favour of rights, duties and demands cannot proceed as if there was no such givenness.

In the phenomenology of Merleau-Ponty and Zahavi this givenness or prereflexive level is not called religion. But I think that any kind of religion also should take this phenomenological interpretation of givenness into account. It is a question of belief whether this givenness has been given by any specific God. The name of this God and the way we worship him/her, is a matter of specific belief. But the givenness of life, the givenness, which holds us all in one common intersubjectivity, is not something we should stop reflecting on, when we talk about religion and spirituality. On the contrary, I think that the religion which are able to connect to this general perception of givenness will be able to contribute to the spirituality of post-modern persons. The religions that neglect common givenness, will not contribute in the same way.

One reason for this is the obvious interrelatedness of the given and rights. In the Kantian tradition, especially the superficial modern version of it, humans have rights because of their inner quality. This is the principle of autonomy and the basic principle behind any human rights movement. Because of the inner quality of each individual, and the autonomy following from this inner quality, human persons have rights. They are to be treated according to their inner quality and autonomy. In the last decades this principle of autonomy has also expanded into the discourse on children and children's rights. The obvious result of it was expressions like "the child as actor".

7. They do not Owe us Anything

In some parts of the movement for children's rights there is a suspicion towards religious traditions and their possible contributions to children's citizenship movement. In many parts of the world, religions and religious traditions have been the adversaries when it came to concrete conflicts in matters of children's role in the family and in society as a whole. This is a field of traditional thinking in discussion with more or less secular, impatient human rights activists. These people often meet religious traditions and meet them as the conservative and sometimes antagonistic part of the discussion. Family values are more important than specific citizenship rights for children, no matter what the family thinks about it.

The discussion between these two major groups in this field must, of course, develop further. From an empirical point of view I think there is a need for different kinds of research aiming at investigating how far, or: how little religious traditions have contributed to children's rights in a specific country. I do not think it is obvious that the answer will be that religious traditions have not contributed at all. But, on the other hand, I also think, the impact of religions on children's rights and dignity also depend strongly on the specific religion and the way the religions itself develops. It is not so that religion *an sich* is antagonistic to children's rights, but some developments inside a religion might be so, as other developments might be more positive and important.

I consider the phenomenological traditions I have hinted at in this article decisive for how far religions will be able to contribute substantially to children's rights in the years to come. The givenness of life is the basic phenomenological insight, but it is an insight that corresponds very well with religious interpretations. There are limits to how far you can construct your own life. Givenness cannot be constructed. It is there before me and constructs the way I perceive and reflect. Basically, the question whether religions and spirituality can contribute to children's rights or not, depends very much on how far religions reflect this way of conceiving life as given. It depends, in short, on an interpretation of life and the way the religions in their practical daily life live according to such an interpretation.

There is an already established intersubjectivity between any child and any grown-up or any kind of grown-up society. Since givenness is there before any cognitive reflection, any child has the right to be treated according to this givenness. Children are part of humanity and because of this partnership, they have the same rights as other partners to have life conditions in accordance with this intersubjective partnership. Life in society and culture would not have been the same if there were no children.

I think arguments like these should be developed further in the religious traditions. As mentioned above, such traditions have often opposed children's rights movement because of the explicit Kantian influence in these movements. Religious traditions empirically seem to have problems with words like autonomy and rights. But instead of therefore opposing the children's rights movements, religious traditions should focus strongly on the givenness of life as a phenomenological perception. In this position there is decisive support for the dignity and the rights of children. They are part of the givenness, therefore they have the right to be treated according to this givenness. Children are not gifts to anyone. Children are, as we are, given, and must expect to be given a dignity and a security in return. Children do not owe us anything. Grown-ups and grown-up society owe them a lot.

8. The Gift we Owe to Everyone

Summing up, I think it is rather obvious that the phenomenological interpretation of life is what is lacking in Vanier, Mauss and partly also Derrida. The discussion of gifts by these authors does not take the givennes of life into account and does not interpret gift in the perspective of givenness. This is the paradigm shift I think it wise to reflect on. Such a new paradigm is interesting in itself, but in my context it is first of all interesting because of its impact for children's rights and citizenship. A growing awareness of the importance of the givenness of life for the dignity of all humans, including children, seems to be significant for the discussion of rights and citizenship. I therefore think religions should develop their own contribution to children's rights and citizenship by taking this interpretation more into consideration. Religions should be aware of children as given like every other human is given, therefore religions should stimulate all efforts to construct life worlds, systems and societies that correspond to such an interpretation of life. Children are small humans that do not owe us anything, therefore big grown-ups should develop life worlds where the not-owing humans can have their dignity without deserving it at all.

References

CAPUTO, J. D./SCANLON, M. J. (ed.). (1999), God, the Gift, and Postmodernism, Indiana.

DERRIDA, J. (1992), Given Time: I Counterfeit Money, Chicago.

HULL, J. M. (1991), A Gift to the Child. Religious Education in the Primary School, Birmingham.

HULL, J. M. (2000), 'Religion in the Service of the Child Project: The Gift Approach to Religious Education', in M. Grimmitt (ed.), Pedagogies of Religious Education. Case Studies in the Research and Development of Good Pedagogic Practice in RE, Essex.

LØGSTRUP, K. E. (1978), Skabelse og Tilintetgørelse, Copenhagen.

MAUSS, M. (2002), The Gift: The Form and Reason for Exchange in Archaic Societies, London.

MERLEAU-PONTY, M. (2002), Phenomenology of Perception, London.

VANIER, J. (1989), Community and Growth: Our Pilgrimage Together, Mahwah, NJ.

ZAHAVI, D. (1999), Self-Awareness and Alterity. A phenomenological Investigation, Evanston.

The Child as Gift

John M. Hull
University of Birmingham

'How to give when the child is given', this is the theme for this, the final day of our gathering. In offering some reflections on this theme, I shall draw upon some of the resources of Christian faith, but much of what I shall suggest is not incompatible with Jewish and Muslim faith, and may indeed be in sympathy with other faith traditions as well. That is as it should be in such conferences.

1. The Gift in Scripture

First I would like to remind you that the ideas of giving and of gift are prominent in sacred scripture. In the Hebrew Bible, for example, when Leah, Jacob's wife, gave birth to a son, she said "God has presented me with a precious gift" (Gen 13:20). To give gifts to a brother is to give to God. When Jacob was reunited with his brother Esau, and gave gifts to him, he said "Accept this gift from me, for seeing your face is like seeing the face of God" (Gen 33:10).

In the Christian Testament, we read that Jesus said to the people, "If you, though you are evil, know how to give good gifts to your children, how much more will your father in heaven give good gifts to those who ask him?" (Matt 7:11), and in the Letter of James, we are told that "Every Good and perfect gift is from above, coming down from the Father of heavenly lights, who does not change like shifting shadows" (Jas 1:17). The apostle Peter says that husbands and wives are to treasure and respect each other as being "heirs together of the gracious gift of life" (1 Pet 3:7) and the Bible closes with an invitation to everyone to "take the free gift of the water of life" (Rev 22:17).

The Quran also teaches that children and indeed life itself are gifts of God. The angel tells Mary that he is a messenger from God "to announce to you the gift of a holy son" (Surah 19:19). The descendants of Abraham are also described as gifts of God. Speaking of God's mercy to Abraham, the text continues "and we bestowed upon him Isaac and, as an additional gift, a grandson" (Surah 21:72). All children are to be regarded as God's gifts. The Quran protests in the strongest terms against brutality towards children. "They are lost indeed who kill their children foolishly, without knowledge, and forbid what Allah has given to them" (Surah 6:14).

2. The Child as Gift

From a purely secular point of view, there seems to be no particular reason why children should be thought of as gifts. People often speak of 'wanted' and 'unwanted' children, meaning that one child is welcome and another was not intended and is not really very welcome, but this in itself does not lead us beyond satisfaction or dissatisfaction at the birth of a child. After all, if a man and a woman want a child, the method of producing one is quite well known, and although they would be pleased when conception took place and the obvious dangers of child birth were safely over, and although there would be happiness at the birth of the wanted child, there is nothing in this to indicate that the child should be regarded as a gift. Perhaps the child might be thought of as a gift of nature, but then again, why should nature be thought of as giving gifts? From a secular point of view, nature is simply there, and its processes require no understanding beyond their own characteristics. The sense of wonder that it should be there, the amazement that there should be anything at all: these emotions surely bring one to the threshold of religion. This threshold might take the form of deifying nature or the natural processes. This desire to personify the earth is one of the deepest religious emotions. The ancient Greeks called the earth Gaea or Ge, and although in the classical period her cult was expressed in the lives of the individual gods and goddesses, belief in the primordial power of the earth goddess survived. Gaea was regarded as the potency which produced children, and this is probably represented in the Roman custom of placing a new born child on the earth (Hammond/Scullard: 1970). There must be very few parents and grandparents who have not been touched by this sense of the strangeness, the frailty, the mystery of this latest visitor to the human realm. Such emotions are not only entirely natural, they are deeply human. But may we enquire about the logic of this emotion, about the sense in which it is an intelligence of the heart?

The older theism argued that if there is a design, then there must be a designer, but this is no longer convincing (Paley: 2006). Contemporary biology and in particular the study of evolution, has shown that nature need not be considered as designed. However, the relation between gift and giver is not similar to that between design and designer, for the latter is a logical argument, although generally today thought to be unconvincing, but the former is an attitude. To believe, and more significantly to feel that a child is a gift is to announce a certain attitude toward the child and not only toward the child but to what is greater than the child. It is an attitude of spontaneous joy, a sense of the gratuitous character of existence, of mystery, and a feeling that something very precious has been entrusted to one. This then inspires a sense of being the undeserving recipient of a mercy, the knowledge that although one has given birth to this little creature, already it is recognised by the human family. One does not have the right to reject it, let alone to kill it!

Such emotions were not always felt by parents in the ancient, classical world, where it was not uncommon to expose infants in order to destroy them, or to throw the infant on the common rubbish pile, and still today, infanticide is common enough and is more or less accepted in certain cultures. But for parents and grandparents, and for all adults and older brothers and sisters who become aware of the emotions of wonder which I have tried to describe, the child must be thought of as gift, and a response to the sacred from which the child has come is then demanded.

Such attitudes and responses take one beyond the sequence of cause and effect into the realm of the marvellous, and if there are such qualities of giftedness, then one intuitively searches for that which is beyond cause and effect, behind the gift the heart rises to discern the giver. As I have said, this is not an argument which follows from premise to conclusion; it springs from the emotional intelligence (Goleman : 1995) of faith, and whether that intuition is articulated in specifically religious terms or not, it touches the borders of the holy. To the extent that such emotions are common in the modern world, we may say that religion has moulded the conscience and the feelings of humanity.

3. The Emotional Intelligence of Faith

Since the intuition, the emotional intelligence that leads one from the child to the concept of gift, and from that to the giver, is not so much a rational argument as an implication of an emotion, it lies outside the realm of proof. All the experiences of emotional intelligence lie outside that realm. It is therefore impossible by argument to persuade someone to look upon a child as a gift, and by the same token it is impossible to show that the atheist or naturalist is wrong in regarding a child as a gift even when there is no recognition of a transcendent Giver. It is enough, we may say, that an attitude of respect and love toward the child is expressed. Yes, indeed, but two questions arise. First, although the logic of the atheist in regarding his or her child as a gift cannot be questioned in so far as it is logic, may not one ask whether the emotional intelligence of this attitude should be probed? And secondly, turning toward the person who already realises the basically religious character of the emotion of gift, may we not ask for a clearer idea of the value added character of the religious attitude?

We have already exposed the natural emotion to questioning, and have shown that the trend of the emotion, its phenomenology, points beyond itself.

It is not difficult now to indicate the value of the religious attitude when it has become overt.

Religious experience, it is well said, is self-authenticating. The person who has stood silent with wonder in the presence of a new-born child senses the miraculous. That means that the heart springs up in thankfulness and joy. These emotions easily pass into beliefs, and from there into ethical consequences. If the child is a gift, then something must be returned to the giver. This is why we have raised the question of how to give if the child is given. This is how dedication and a sense of vocation are formed. Moreover, if the child is a gift from the holy, then the child is sacred. This quality takes us beyond the character of mere respect, and although the realm of love can never be surpassed, when the loved one is received as a sacred trust, there is an added realisation of delight and duty.

The religious person may in some such way enter into an enriched experience, a more beautiful and tender sense that the child is actually the Christ child, or the Krishna Child, and that to injure or mistreat one such child is not only wicked and cruel but is an act of blasphemy.

> And whoever welcomes a little child like this in my name welcomes me. But if anyone causes one of these little ones who believe in me to sin, it would be better for him to have a large millstone hung around his neck and to be drowned in the depths of the sea (Matt 18:5–6).

This reflection upon the significance of the feeling that the child is a gift leads us to the view that not only the child, but everything is a gift (Hull: 1997, 56–60, 188f). This brings us to the concept of creation itself as given.

4. Creation as Gift

If the child is to be thought of as a gift, then the first step has been taken toward the idea that the universe is not self-sufficient. The whole world might not have been; it is gratuitous. The world is a gift. Abraham Joshua Heschel distinguished three attitudes toward nature. The first is the distinctively modern attitude of usefulness. The world is to be utilised; it becomes a commodity. The second attitude is that of the ancient Greeks – the world is beautiful. This is an aesthetic response and this is why the Greeks perceived nature as a cosmos, a beautiful whole. The third attitude is that of wonder which looks upon nature as sublime. This is what we find in the Hebrew Bible.

> The heavens declare the glory of God, and the skies proclaim the work of God's hands. Day by day they pour forth speech; night after night they display knowledge. (Ps 19:1–2).

The response of sublimity conceives the world of nature as impressed with the divine, and as expressing the holy (Heschel: 1955, 33–42).[1]

The English mystic, William Blake (1757–1827) said

> What, it will be questioned, when the sun rises, do you not see a round disc of fire, somewhat like a guinea? O no! I see an innumerable company of the heavenly host crying "Holy, holy, holy is the Lord God almighty! (Blake: 1988, 200).

5. Creation as Past

The first aspect of the idea of creation as a gift is to think of it in the past, as a gift that has been given. "In the beginning, God created the heavens and the earth" (Gen 1:1). This is an important aspect of the idea, because it signifies the non-self-sufficiency of the temporal sequence. Time itself is wonderful.

But if the idea of creation is thought of as being exhausted by the past tense, we may be led into a fatalistic or deterministic view of nature and our lives. If the complete idea is that God created, and then nothing more, then nature continues on its pre-created way. We are left with the divine gift but nothing more.

6. Creation as a Continually Given Gift

It is thus important to emphasise that the idea of creation also involves the present tense. God created and God still creates.

This is best expressed if we consider the gender implications of the idea of creation. If the act of creation is thought of as a single act, completed in the past, we are adopting a male view of it. This may be described as the Ker-Pow view of creation. There was one big bang, and then God went off to do something else! But if we regard creation as being in the present tense, then we take a more female view. Now creation is a process, and we may think of it as passing through a period of gestation, of slow growth and development. If the male God begets the world, then the female God conceives it (Johnson: 1992, 133ff, 179ff). To put it in different words, God creates the world not only from the outside but also from the inside. All knowledge has elements of body-knowledge (Johnson: 1987; Johnson/Lakof: 1999) and this is as true of the idea of creation as it is of expressions of art.

---

1 The first part of this paper, dealing with the feeling of giftedness, owes a great deal to Heschel's theology of the emotions, particularly as set out in the first few chapters of *God in Search of Man*.

The world is thus not finished. Paul expressed this by saying that "the whole universe groans in travail, longing for the glorious liberty of the children of God" (Rom 8:21–22). The world as gift is pregnant with meaning and with becoming. This also means that if the world was created in power, it grows and dwells in hope.

7. Implications for the Child

It is not difficult to see the implications of such beliefs for an understanding of the child. The child is given, in an act of human creation in which the male sperm and the female egg were fused, and the incredible cocktail of the genes produced something radically new, a new combination, a new child. But the genes have only done part of the job. The child is in the image of the female God as well as the male God. The child is being created internally as well as externally. The sacred processes of growth must be nurtured and brooded over with the wings of service and love.

Moreover, we can understand this more fully if we consider what it is that the Creator has created. God creates through creating creativity (Hartshorne: 1948, 29f). We also are creators, and the child is a creator. Genuine creativity is a mirror of the divine creativity. Human creativity, of course, is narrowed by the human finitude, and constrained by the inheritance of the previous creation. Nevertheless the creativity of the child possesses originality, freedom and delight. It is the same creativity appropriate to a created creativity as the supreme and unsurpassable creativity possessed by God (Hartshorne: 1948, 29f).

This means that any attempt to suppress the creativity of the child is blasphemous. I am not referring to attempts to nurture, or to guide, or to teach the child how to be creative, but I am speaking of the forces that would translate the child into a consumer, a commodity, a creature of desire rather than a creature of creative love. Fortunately, the research into the child as a consumer indicates that the creativity of the child is not easily crushed, and that in spite of the most alluring advertisement, children often remain strikingly critical and often contemptuous, seeing right through the intention to make a profit from them.[2]

2 Neil Postman drew attention to the power of media to subvert childhood (Postman: 1983) but more recent studies have revealed the interactive and constructive role played by children in their relations with media (Howard: 1998; Livingstone: 2002), and the possibilities of a pedagogy helping children to resist uncritical media influence (Kenway/Bullen: 2001).

8. Creation as Future Gift

Finally, we should consider the concept of creation as gift not only in the past tense and the present but in the future. We do not yet know what creation will become, nor what we ourselves will become. The full implications of the child, and of the world, are still in the womb of time. This was what Karl Rahner had in mind when he pointed out that according to the gospels, our childhood is still in the future. For we are to enter the Kingdom of God by repenting, and this must mean that we repent of adulthood (Matt 18:3, cf. Rahner: 1971, 33–50; Mitchell: 1975, 423–437). Childhood is not so much being as becoming.

In the light of this, we may regard the child as a symbol of the future. The child, the young child, in its playfulness, its complete reliance upon its family, in its freedom from the money culture, is indeed something of an ideal into which we seek to guide our whole society. So when we nurture the child in its creativity, we also nurture ourselves, and we move all humanity one tiny step forward.

9. How shall we Give if the Child is Given?

While the spirituality of the child is genuinely independent of religious faith, and consists in the innate relatedness of children (Hay/Nye: 1998), and in their innate creativity, I have suggested that if we consider this natural reality in the light of religious faith, it is enriched and deepened. This helps me to say something in response to the first part of the title for today. How shall we give if the child is given? How shall we give?

Jesus said "Whoever humbles himself like a little child is the greatest in the Kingdom of Heaven" (Matt 18:4) and "See that you do not look down on one of these little ones. For I tell you that their angels in heaven always see the face of my Father in heaven" (Matt 18:10).

These are strangely beautiful and compelling words. They point all of us who work with children or who are parents towards a divine vocation. This is not mere romanticism, not only poetry, although it is certainly at least that. It is an example of how ordinary tasks like being a parent or a teacher, a children's nurse or a social worker, or even an academic researcher, may become profoundly sacred tasks. This insight is not necessary in order to do a first rate professional job, and the appalling incidence of child soldiers, trafficking in children, and the occurrence of childhood poverty will certainly not be alleviated by this insight alone without the reformation of the economic and cultural conditions that make such things possible. Never the less, perhaps I am not the only one who thinks that if you not only do a first class professional job, but do it in the light of this religious vision, it will become something more than a job; it will become a divine service. If those who struggle against the abuse of children find encouragement in such ideals, they may find an additional source of strength and endurance to continue their work.

References

BLAKE, W. (1988), 'A Vision of the Last Judgement', in D. Punter (ed.), Selected Poetry and Prose, London.

GOLEMAN, D. (1995), Emotional Intelligence, London.

HAMMOND, N. G. L./SCULLARD, H. H. (²1970), The Oxford Classical Dictionary, article: Gaea, Oxford.

HARTSHOME, C. (1948), The Divine Relativity, London.

HAY, D./NYE, R. (1998), The Spirit of The Child, London.

HESCHEL, A. J (1955), God in Search of Man: A Philosophy of Judaism.

HOWARD, S. (ed.), (1998), Wired-up Young People and the Electronic Media, London.

HULL, J. (1997), On Sight and Insight: A Journey Into the World of Blindness, Oxford.

JOHNSON, E. A. (1992), She Who Is: The Mystery of God in Feminist Theological Discourse, New York.

JOHNSON, M. (1987), The Body in The Mind: The Bodily Basis of Meaning, Imagination and Reason, London.

JOHNSON, M./LAKOF, G. (1999), Philosophy in the Flesh: The Embodied Mind and its Challenge to Western Thought.

KENWAY, J./BULLEN, E. (2001), Consuming Children: Education, Entertainment, Advertising, Maidstone.

LIVINGSTONE, S. (2002), Childhood and the changing Media Environment, London.

MITCHELL, N. (1975), 'The Once and Future Child: Towards a Theology of Childhood' in Living Light, Vol. 12 No. 3, pp 423–437

PALEY, W. (2006), Natural Theology, Oxford, first published in 1802.

POSTMAN, N. (1983), Disappearance of Childhood, London.

RAHNER, K. (1971), 'Ideas for a Theology of Childhood' in Theological Investigations, Vol. 8 ch. 3, London.

Index of Names

List of Contributors

Marcia J. Bunge is Professor of Humanities and Theology at Christ College, the Honors College of Valparaiso University, and Director of the Child in Religion and Ethics Project. She edited *The Child in Christian Thought* (2001); has written several articles on children and childhood; and is co-editing a book on Children and Childhood: Biblical Perspectives (forthcoming).

Udi Mandel Butler is a research fellow at CIESPI, Rio de Janeiro and Goldsmiths College, University of London. His research interests include young people living in contexts of marginalization and young people's participation in public action (NGOs, social movements, community initiatives). He teaches Development Studies at the School of Oriental and African Studies, London.

Yolanda Corona is a Professor and researcher at the Autonomous Metropolitan University in Mexico where she directs a national education project on children rights and opportunities. Her current research focuses on rural children, young people's participation in resistance movements, and the ways in which indigenous children participate in their own communities.

Annemie Dillen works at the Faculty of Theology, K. U. Leuven where she from October 2007 will be Professor of pastoral care. In 2005 she obtained a PhD on family ethics and religious education. Among her recent publications is *Religious Participation of Children as Active Subjects. Towards an Hermeneutical-Communicative Model of Religious Education in Families with Young Children.*

Marta Maria Espeseth is a primary school teacher in Norway, working with music and for disabled children, and also with church related educational projects; she is Master of professional ethics from The University of Oslo with special interest in the phenomenological approach to children, spirituality and existential questions.

John M. Hull is Honorary Professor of Practical Theology at the Queens Foundation, Birmingham, UK. Hull is Professor emeritus in religious Education at The University of Birmingham and has been publishing a number of influential books and articles in his field, among them *A Gift to the Child.* The most recent publication is *Mission-shaped Church: A Theological Response* (2006).

Usha S. Nayar is Professor and Deputy Director of Tata Institute, Mumbai, India. Her special areas of work are: Policy, Planning, Administration, Monitoring and Evaluation of Educational, Health and other social sector projects with focus on women, children, rural and urban slum populations. She has rendered her consultative services to many UN agencies like UNESCO, UNICEF, UNFPA and UN Centre for Human Rights.

Carlos Pérez is a Professor and researcher at the Autonomous Metropolitan University in Mexico. Professor Pérez Zavala's current research focuses on social movements and political cultures. He is also author of several articles and journals issues on children in vulnerable situations, participation, and politics.

Irene Rizzini is Professor at the Pontifical Catholic University in Rio de Janeiro, Brazil and a director of the Center for Research and Policy on Childhood (CIESP). Prof. Rizzini is president of the Childwatch International and the author of several books, among them *Globalization and children; Niños, adolescentes, marginalidad y violencia en América Latina y el Caribe: relaciones indisociables*?

Jone Salomonsen is Professor at the Faculty of Theology at the University of Oslo, working with gender studies and theological interpretations of women studies. Prof Salomonsen combines gender and ritual studies. Her recent publication is *Enchanted Feminism.* One of her present projects is a study of the confirmation rite in Norway

Alfons H. Teipen is Associate Professor of Religion at Furman University, teaching courses in Islam, Religions of the World, gender issues, and Introduction to Religion. His academic interests include the study of the Life of Muhammad as portrayed in Ibn Ishaq's Sira, al-Waqidi's Maghazi, and Ibn Sa'd's Tabaqat, women and gender in Islam and in the Abrahamic religious traditions, and interreligious dialogue.

John Wall is Associate Professor of Religion, with a joint appointment in Childhood Studies, at Rutgers University in the United States. He is the author of *Moral Creativity: Paul Ricoeur and the Poetics of Possibility (*2005). He is currently completing a book titled *Childhood and the Creation of Society,* on how considering childhood should transform contemporary ethical thought.

Trygve Wyller is Professor at the Faculty of Theology at the University of Oslo working with systematic theology and the ethical and theological interpretations of Christian social practice. His present research interests aim at phenomenological interpretations of people living on the margins, a recent publication is "*Heterotopic diakonia*".

Between direct experience and analytic distance

V&R

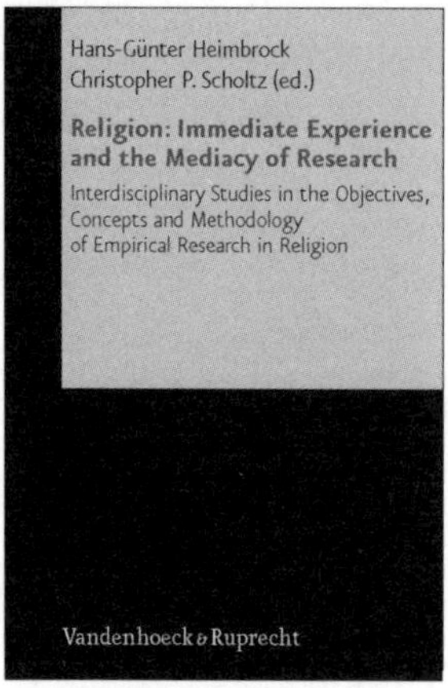

Research in Contemporary Religion, Band 1.

2007. 283 Seiten mit 5 Abbildungen, gebunden
ISBN 978-3-525-60434-2

Hans-Günter Heimbrock / Christopher P. Scholtz (ed.)

Religion: Immediate Experience and the Mediacy of Research

Interdisciplinary Studies in the Objectives, Concepts and Methodology of Empirical Research in Religion

This study focuses on the tension between the immediacy of experience and the mediacy of research, an issue that has been raised since the time of Friedrich Schleiermacher and William James. When we describe immediate religious experiences it may happen in the process of terminological reconstrucion that information is lost and sensations are not traceable, which is a serious problem for research. This volume tries to answer the question of how to solve this fundamental problem approaching the issue from the perspektives of Theology, the Philosophy of Religion, Cultural Anthropology and the Empirical Social Sciences.

Vandenhoeck & Ruprecht